Maurice Walsh grew up in Co. Tipperary and has
States, Latin America, Asia and Africa. His ess.
have appeared in *The Dublin Review*, *Granta*, the *London Review of Books*,
the *New Statesman*, the *TLS* and many other newspapers and magazines.
He is Alistair Horne Fellow at St Antony's College Oxford for 2010–11 and
teaches journalism at Kingston University.

'...admirably accessible. Walsh's analysis is sophisticated and thought-
provoking, and is supported by a wide reading of Irish, American and British newspaper history... *The News from Ireland* will be read with interest
by any scholar of those colonial wars and counter-insurgencies that have
occurred in any past or present empire.'

**Media History**

'Its scrupulous, an. ated research combines with a readable prose that will
appeal to a wider     ence than historians and journalists alone.'

**Sunday Tribune, Dublin**

'[E]xplores the     d-sets of journalists, editors and politicians with impressive insight.     al. , book has implications and insights which will be
continually     ini oth for journalism and for the conduct of public life
in an unc.     nt age.'

**John Horgan, Press Ombudsman,
Republic of Ireland,** *Journalism Practice*

'The historical detail is rich and engaging, and Walsh's analysis of the journalists' ambivalent relationship to nationalism and the political dynamics
of media management in a colonial war is very insightful. An important
contribution to journalism history.'

**Daniel Hallin, author of**
*The 'Uncensored War': The Media and Vietnam*

'The close study of the personalities involved and the intimate knowledge
of how foreign correspondents saw their role in the period after the First
World War make this an invaluable book.'

**Colm Tóibín**

'A very valuable contribution to our understanding of the factors that led to
the British decision to ... negotiate with the Dail Government.'

**Garret FitzGerald, Taoiseach of Ireland 1982–7**

'Maurice Walsh has written a fascinating and thoughtful book. His story of the relationship between journalists and government during a guerrilla war more than 80 years ago is one that few of us know and that has much relevance to understanding the parallel issues during the wars in Vietnam and Iraq.'

**Adam Hochschild, author of *King Leopold's Ghost***

'A very fine piece of work indeed – tremendously readable and very insightful.'

**John Lloyd, Director of the Reuters Institute for the Study of Journalism, Oxford University**

'[Walsh] does an excellent job of drawing from correspondents' memoirs and private papers to tell his story.'

***Journalism Studies***

# THE NEWS FROM
# IRELAND

## FOREIGN CORRESPONDENTS
## AND THE IRISH REVOLUTION

Maurice Walsh

I.B. TAURIS

LONDON · NEW YORK

New paperback edition published in 2011 by I.B. Tauris & Co Ltd
6 Salem Road, London W2 4BU
175 Fifth Avenue, New York NY 10010
www.ibtauris.com

Distributed in the United States and Canada
Exclusively by Palgrave Macmillan
175 Fifth Avenue, New York NY 10010

First published in hardback in 2008 by I.B. Tauris & Co Ltd

ISBN: 978 1 84885 673 8

A full CIP record for this book is available from the British Library
A full CIP record is available from the Library of Congress

Library of Congress Catalog Card Number: available

Typeset in Adobe Garamond Pro by Sara Millington, Editorial and
    Design Services
Printed and bound in Sweden by Scandbook AB

To Alison, Louis and Kitty.

And Mai Walsh.

# CONTENTS

# ACKNOWLEDGEMENTS

This book could not have been written without the inspiration, advice and support of many people. Ellen Hazelkorn was instrumental in turning the germ of an idea into serious research by pointing me towards James Curran at Goldsmiths. As well as being incomparably knowledgeable and an incisive reader of the early drafts of my thesis, James was the perfect supervisor; part Mr Chips, part Alex Ferguson.

I am grateful to the Arts and Humanities Research Board for a generous grant without which the research and writing would have been impossible. I wish to thank the BBC for allowing me time off to work on it. During four delightful months at the University of Michigan I was able to think through some early ideas. For this opportunity I wish to thank Charles Eisendrath, the director of the Knight Wallace Fellowship programme. At Ann Arbor I received encouragement, advice, hospitality and stimulating conversation from Jonathan Marwil who introduced me to the weekly meetings of the Military History group. John Whittier-Ferguson and George Bornstein both helped to expand my horizons. The extraordinary friendship of my fellow fellows and the accumulation of what in Milan are known as 'dead bottles' almost got in the way of any work at all but made my time there such a pleasure. I have also benefited from being able to present early versions of some chapters at seminars of the Irish Studies group in London and at Roy Foster's Irish history seminar at Hertford College in Oxford.

I owe thanks to the staffs at the following libraries: the National Library of Ireland, the National Archives of Ireland (especially Catriona Crowe), the British Library (Humanities 2), the Newspaper Library at Colindale, the National Archives at Kew, The Times Archive, the Bodleian Library, Oxford, the Library of Congress, Washington DC and Carrick-on-Suir library for access to the Hugh Ryan Collection.

Richard Bourke has been an unfailing source of support, advice and passionate argument as well as an icon of style. David Edmonds engaged with this book with far more enthusiasm and diligence than it was fair to expect and his suggestions, constant support and amendments have been invaluable. My thanks to those who read and commented on some or all of the manuscript: Brendan Barrington, Neil Belton, Paul Bew, Brian Cathcart, Michael Foley, Roy Foster, Michael Hopkinson, John Horgan, John Lloyd, Paddy Scannell, Bill Schwarz, Mark Thompson, Jeremy Treglown and Andy Whitehead. I am particularly grateful to Leo Kinlen for especially assiduous proofreading. Any errors that remain after all this generous scrutiny are entirely my responsibility.

Many other people have helped with suggestions, leads, advice and ideas including Owen Bowcott, Noel Casey, Lorna Donlon, Seamus Dooley, John Horgan, Tom Garvin, Luke Gibbons, Paul Legg, Bill McCormack, James Painter, Colm Toibin, Charles Townshend and Vincent Woods.

For hospitality and entertainment in Ireland, Britain and the USA I want to express my warm appreciation to Mike Allen and Jean College, Mark Brennock and Yetti Redmond, Seamus Dooley and Brian Cooke, Clare O'Brien, Siobhan and Deirdre Walsh, Frances Walsh, Michael and Noreen Walsh, David Welna and Kathleen Wheaton, Diana Tickell, Patricia Vasquez and Alexandre Marc, Vincent Woods and Monica Frawley.

It was the decisive intervention of Jean Seaton which brought me to Liz Friend-Smith at I.B.Tauris. Liz has been an enthusiastic, patient and gracious editor and, with Valentina Zanca, a persuasive advocate of the book's possibilities. Sara Millington was a very thorough copy editor and Ian Crane produced an impressive index at short notice. I am deeply grateful to my agent, Maggie Hanbury for her advice and encouragement at crucial moments. Most of all I have relied on my family for love and support: Alison, Louis and Kitty have endured probably a little more news from Ireland than they bargained for but they put up with having this book – in Kitty's recent coinage – 'pedollocked' on top of them with great tolerance and understanding.

# INTRODUCTION

*The news from Ireland was dull and dispiriting: an occasional attack on a lonely policeman or a raid for arms on some half-baked barracks. If one was not actually living in Ireland (as the lucky Major no longer was) how could one possibly take an interest when, for instance, at the same time Negroes and white men were fighting it out in the streets of Chicago? Now that gripped the Major's imagination much more forcibly. Unlike the Irish troubles one knew instantly which side everyone was on … And Chicago was only a fragment of the competition that Ireland had to face. What about the dire behaviour of the Bolshevists? The gruesome murders, the rapes, the humiliations of respectable ladies and gentlemen? In late 1919 hardly a day went by without an eye-witness account of such horrors being confided to the press by some returned traveller who had managed to escape with his skin.*

J.G. Farrell, *Troubles*

The Anglo-Irish War of 1919–21 finally ruptured the constitution of the United Kingdom, ending 120 years of turbulent history since the Act of Union. In the Republic of Ireland it is referred to as the War of Independence, celebrated as the heroic struggle that forged a new sovereign state. In Britain it is retrospectively regarded as the first loosened brick that presaged the crumbling of the whole edifice of imperial rule, vindicating Lord Salisbury's prediction in 1883 that if Irish separatism succeeded the Empire would disintegrate step by step.[1] Corelli Barnett has described the treaty that ended the war and established the Irish Free State as 'of the utmost significance for the future of British power'[2] and in her history of the empire Jan Morris writes that, 'it was in Ireland that the prototype of imperial revolution was launched, the precursor of all the coups, rebellions and civil wars which were to harass the British Empire from now until the end'.[3]

The new Irish state was not established by the defeat of the British forces on the battlefield. The Irish Republican Army (IRA) guerrillas and the panoply of nationalist civic organisations allied to them were merely able to endure long enough to force the British government to negotiate a new settlement. Their cause was helped enormously by the backlash provoked by the conduct of the hastily recruited gendarmerie sent to crush the rebellion, collectively known as the Black and Tans, whose lawless escapades turned even loyalists against them.  It was a moral victory, not a military triumph. In the view of the Irish historian Michael Laffan, 'Lloyd George's government changed its policy more in response to international hostility and to the shame and revulsion felt by British public opinion, than as a consequence of military weakness or defeat.[4] Corelli Barnett makes the same point from a different angle:

> [The] British decided the question of Ireland not in the light of whether or not, on drawing a balance of political and strategic factors, Ireland was worth holding, but out of humanitarian qualms as yet rare in a barbarous world. [This] was a demonstration that the British ruling classes and British public opinion after the Great War were ill-suited to the preservation of their imperial inheritance.[5]

The common theme of both these explanations is the power of public opinion to determine the strategic decisions of the British government.

What 'public opinion' means at any given moment is often elusive; what is certain is that any consideration of public opinion during the Irish revolution would have to deal with the news, analysis and opinions that appeared in the daily press, political journals and contemporary books of commentary and reportage. This book is especially concerned with the accounts and impressions of those who actually *visited* Ireland during the war which led to the signing of the Anglo-Irish treaty and the civil war that followed.

During these years events in Ireland attracted an extraordinary amount of attention from the world's press. Whether reporters tied to daily deadlines, essayists enjoying more leisure and literary licence or novelists bending their talents to the capture of contemporary history, a stream of journalists and writers arrived to record and describe Ireland's troubles. I will draw on some of this rich material to describe a crucial dimension of the Irish revolution that has sometimes been acknowledged but never fully explained.

The Irish revolution became an international media event, to some degree a forerunner of the response to the Spanish Civil War more than fifteen years later. What was happening in Ireland attracted correspondents from all over the world convinced that universal principles were at stake. At issue was the morality of the methods being used by a great power to try to suppress a movement for national independence that commanded widespread international sympathy. Thus, reports appearing in British newspapers helped to set the agenda for journalists from further afield; likewise what was appearing in French or Italian newspapers worked its way back into the assessments of British journalists and politicians.

Historians have recognised that this journalism had an important influence on the outcome of the war but have not devoted much attention to examining how it came to be written. In the first comprehensive nationalist account of the War of Independence (published in 1937 and endorsed by Eamon De Valera), Dorothy Macardle wrote of how 'great English newspapers ... were tirelessly exposing the brutal terrorist regime' in Ireland.[6] But this was a reference to reports appearing in April 1921, within a few months of the truce that preceded the treaty and after several of the worst incidents of the war. In fact, she gives credit for the original exposure of British tactics in Ireland to committees of activists both Irish and English, implying that the press correspondents joined a bandwagon near the end of its journey.[7] Sometimes she refers to British journalists collectively as 'the English Press'; at other times they are distinguished by category, either as 'sympathetic' or representatives of 'conservative opinion'.[8]

In his recent history of the Irish War of Independence, Michael Hopkinson goes much further than Macardle in giving the journalists credit for undermining the British campaign. Hopkinson argues that journalists from the London papers did more for the cause of the Irish rebels than their own formidable publicity effort:

> The eyewitness reports by muckraking correspondents were much more readable, colourful and entertaining than the propaganda sheets and came with dramatic photographs of burning buildings and the suffering and terrified populace … While it was important that a free press exposed British atrocities to world attention, events actually spoke for themselves. It is doubtful that Britain could have hidden the harsh truth from the rest of the world.[9]

Since his book spans the entire period of the war, Hopkinson doesn't have much time to explore why correspondents developed such an interest in Ireland or how Britain might have tried to conceal the atrocities committed there.

There is also a contrary view to that of Macardle and Hopkinson, an assumption that far from being relentlessly critical of coercion in Ireland the British press had connived to demonise the IRA through constant repetition of the worst assaults carried out by the guerrillas. In a book on the origins of the recent troubles in Northern Ireland, Richard Bourke argues that during the Irish revolution 'the British press had teemed with reports of unconscionable extremities … perpetrated by the Republican forces' and that this contributed to 'an air of profound suspicion' during the peace negotiations that began in London in the autumn of 1921.[10] This assertion led to Bourke being accused of believing 'that IRA atrocities existed primarily in the pages of the British press', a sign in itself of how arguments about what appears in the press are often disputes about larger issues.[11]

Which version of history is right – did the British press expose atrocities in Ireland or demonise the IRA? Did the coverage of Ireland in the British and American press help or hinder the British campaign? What drew so many writers and journalists to Ireland to observe the war and the emergence of the new state? These are questions that I hope this book will answer. At its heart is the idea that the way in which visiting correspondents wrote up the Irish revolution was crucial to its outcome, both in the sense that they affected perceptions of the war and that they connected Ireland to the world. However, it is not enough merely to accept what appeared in print as a given. Explaining why the Irish revolution came to be written up in the way it was opens up a new dimension of Anglo-Irish history and of Ireland's relationship to the rest of the world.

One reason these questions have still not been resolved is that even historians who acknowledge the influence of visiting journalists on the outcome of the Irish revolution devote little space to exploring why they wrote what they did. For all of these authors the work of journalists during the Irish revolution was but part of a much bigger mosaic. Few writers have attempted lengthier and more considered surveys of this terrain. D.G. Boyce's book, *Englishmen and Irish Troubles*, published more than thirty years ago, is still the main account of the development of British mentalities during the revolution. It is especially enlightening on Ireland's place in the English conception of the British nation. But his focus is on opinion in London rather than reportage from Ireland: he sees the press as 'a forum of national debate', quoting a particular newspaper when 'it advocated certain views with a reasonable degree of consistency'.[12] Thus his book is more concerned with political argument in London than eyewitness accounts of street warfare in Dublin and, when it comes to newspapers, it pays more attention to the views of editorial writers than to the professional practice of reporters.

Other writers offer a glimpse of the press coverage of Ireland when they deal with the propaganda campaign waged by the Irish revolutionaries. In his book on the alternative government that the revolutionaries established in Ireland to undermine British rule, Arthur Mitchell devotes some attention to the venerated propaganda efforts of the revolutionaries, listing the attributes of the publicity department that contributed to its success:

> It had the advantage of representing a nation fighting for self-government; it had the attraction of the underdog confronting and sometimes besting the bigwig, the brass hat and the bully. It possessed the Irish capacity for the ready welcome, for making visiting journalists feel like accepted companions in a common venture. It skilfully revealed and proclaimed excesses

on the part of the old regime, yet was selective in the material it supplied: while almost always avoiding lies and fabrication, it said little about the IRA and its acts of violence.[13]

All this may be true but the instrumental focus on the Irish propagandists – how they did it, how good they were at it – closes off any exploration of what the journalists they sought to influence brought to this encounter or, indeed, the nature of the shared ideas that made them 'accepted companions in a common venture'. Later I will devote a chapter to the Irish propagandists, examining them not as *sui generis* wizards of persuasion but rather in relation to their British counterparts and to the journalists whom both sides desperately wanted to influence.

The evident reluctance in Irish historiography to take an interest in the work of journalists is puzzling, since historians of modern Ireland enthusiastically use the press as a source. The truth is that newspaper evidence is often cited but rarely analysed. Macardle's chronicle of the birth of the Irish Republic is a case in point here: her book is peppered with references to British and Irish newspapers. And there are many other examples, particularly in studies of the land war and home rule movement, where historians have made use of the extensive coverage devoted to Ireland in the British press.[14]

One explanation for the reluctance of historians to explore the nature of the press coverage might be that they have a schizoid view of what appears in the newspapers, trusting the record of cold print while holding in low esteem those who produce it. For instance, David Fitzpatrick relies heavily on newspapers for his intensive study of the War of Independence in County Clare but elsewhere reveals a disdain for the competence of even the most celebrated reporters.[15] In his biography of the Irish revolutionary Harry Boland he notes how Henry Wood Nevinson, the distinguished British correspondent, misidentified Boland and a colleague in his report of speeches they delivered in Washington. 'Like many journalists', Fitzpatrick comments acerbically in an accompanying footnote, 'Nevinson was evidently at his sharpest on the morning after.'[16] This waspishness resonates with a more general scorn for journalistic writings among certain critics. The Italian political philosopher Benedetto Croce dismissed journalism as 'writings without any originality or profundity [crafted by] men with few mental scruples and almost no aesthetic sensibility'.[17]

One literary historian has summarised a widespread view in the academy of the failings of journalism, that it is 'a factual, conventional, heavy-handed commercial practice, the antithesis of literature's integrity and creativity'.[18] A more astute assessment of journalism's value was offered by J.A. Hobson, the celebrated theorist of imperialism. Hobson published much of his most serious intellectual work in newspapers and magazines and reported on the Boer War for the *Manchester Guardian*. In his autobiography he noted how 'In certain high intellectual quarters journalism has always been treated as the lowest of printed matter, as vulgar necessity … degrading in its thought and literary form…'. He protested that this attitude revealed a failure to discriminate between hackneyed copy and ambitious writing. He acknowledged that 'the hasty unchecked publication of news and opinions which strict "journalism" implies has obvious dangers to truth and literary style' but he argued that

> in its best form, in the current commentary upon important events, it has virtues of its own to set against and qualify the defects of its hasty production. Not only has it a vitality and bite of thought, feeling and expression, caught from the immediacy of the happenings it handles, but its very fragmentation evades some of the dangers that beset the longer, formal, more scientific, and philosophical expositions which claim the seats of intellectual authority.[19]

Much of the journalistic writing I will be examining in the following pages possesses the virtues that Hobson identifies, combining observation and commentary which, though written to deadline, captures the immediacy of the war in Ireland and often a vivid sense of accelerated change. Perhaps more importantly it offers a new optic through which to see the revolution, tracing how perceptions were formed on the run and how the confused events of a defining period were crystallised in print.

If historians have taken the media for granted, media scholars have treated history with a disdain almost worthy of Henry Ford. For many of the canonical books about journalism published over the last thirty years, history is at best incidental. Herbert Gans' study of American magazines and television networks, Gaye Tuchman's work on news production and Jeremy Tunstall's account of the working lives of British journalists are still cited for their insights into the modern media, although their work is very much grounded in the present (or the present of the 1970s). [20] James Curran has written of this pioneering work that its 'main limitation ... is that it is sociology. Its conclusions become potentially misleading if they are viewed as generalizations that apply outside their specific setting.'[21] Some of this work also tends to abstract the media from its historical setting, flattening out perspective and producing an atrophied account of institutions devoid of the nuances of politics, circumstances and time.

When media scholars do get around to writing history they are curiously neglectful of individual journalists. Some of the best examples of media history tend to focus on broad themes across long time spans: Michael Schudson on the emergence of objectivity as a professional totem in the USA; Jean Chalaby on the development of the modern press in Britain; and Mark Hampton on changing ideas of the place of the press in British democracy.[22] Phillip Knightley's much cited book about war correspondents from the Crimean War to Vietnam does sketch individual histories but its ambitious chronology never allows him to dwell too long on any one conflict.[23]

The scarcity of serious work looking at how specific journalists wrote about specific historical events cannot be explained by a bias against writing about individuals *per se*. The media history for the period covered in this book – from the end of the First World War to the early 1920s – is distinguished by intense interest in the British press barons. Indeed, there exists a proliferation of biographical studies of figures such as Northcliffe, Beaverbrook and Rothermere, as well as detailed accounts of the buying and selling of Fleet Street titles by a small band of plutocrats. More general accounts of the British press at this time, such as Stephen Koss's study of the relationship between newspapers and politics, are also exclusively concerned with the men at the top; editors are regarded as the only figures of consequence in newspapers and weeklies.[24] The contribution of individual reporters and writers is regarded as unworthy of detailed consideration; they remain anonymous editorial fodder whose treatment brings to mind E.P. Thompson's famous remark about 'the immense condescension of history'.

In this book I want to shift the perspective from the boardroom and the editor's desk to the correspondents on the ground. This does not mean discounting the extent to which institutions, politics and professional conventions influenced and shaped the work of correspondents who reported from Ireland. However, this approach does challenge some of the most well-known work on the early twentieth-century press in Britain and the USA in its tendency to regard what actually appeared in newspapers as merely the impoverished literary by-product of larger institutional and economic forces. Fernand Braudel once dismissed the history of events as felt and described by contemporaries on the grounds that it was concerned with 'ephemera … which pass across the stage like fireflies, hardly glimpsed before they settle back into darkness and as often as not into oblivion…'.[25] This seems to be the view some media scholars take of journalism as a whole.

Journalists should be restored to the centre of the picture because by the turn of the nineteenth century writers for the commercial press had established a degree of independence concomitant with their assertion that they were members of a profession and that their 'credibility derived in large part from a command of facts'.[26] This is often overlooked by some writers, impressed by what they see as the apparently limitless power of the press barons to dictate what appears in their news columns. Even Max Weber worried that 'the journalist worker gains less and less as the capitalist lord of the press, of the sort of "Lord" Northcliffe, for instance, gains more and more political influence'.[27]

However, by the 1920s in Britain and the USA it is clear that journalists were allowed (and would expect to enjoy) a degree of freedom to interpret events for themselves; special correspondents sent abroad and literary figures commissioned for one-off assignments enjoyed this licence. Thus, as Daniel Hallin and Paolo Mancini observed, while journalists 'have rarely asserted and almost never achieved the right to control media organizations outright … they have often been successful in achieving significant relative autonomy within those organizations'.[28] A vivid definition of that sense of entitlement to autonomy is provided by a former editor of the *Jerusalem Post* in Hallin and Mancini's book. Explaining why he resigned when his paper was taken over by an interfering Canadian proprietor, the editor said:

> Journalism is an enterprise in social judgment. The object of that judgment is the historical present, the fast flood of daily events. Journalism plucks from this infinite flow those events deemed worthy of public regard,

reporting them as honest witness … and it seeks by … interpretive judgement to help place those events in a more explicit context of narrative understanding.[29]

This sense of independence, particularly the ideal of the 'honest witness', would have been shared by special correspondents during the Irish revolution. Of course, as I have already indicated, many different influences – some professional, some institutional and some political and cultural – would have shaped their judgement of events. But in the early twentieth century the idea of journalists as interpreters of reality and not mere stenographers or hired scriveners had begun to take hold, as evidenced by the advice offered by one writer at the time to prospective recruits to the trade that 'the journalistic eye is now of far greater importance than the journalistic pen'.[30]

By the end of the First World War mass circulation newspapers dominated the political landscape. In 1913, R.A. Scott-James had noticed that newspapers had become a universal addiction:

The reading of newspapers has become a habit all over the civilized world … And now almost every man in the most modestly assured position begins his day with a perusal of the morning paper. It is with the workman when he travels by train or tram to his work, and it is replaced by the evening paper when he returns. It has insinuated itself into our culture, affording us the new material upon which to exercise such ideas as we may possess.[31]

In the first half of the twentieth century, the newspaper was the symbol of modern city life, signifying the bustle and dynamism of alert, up-to-the-minute populations. In his memoirs, Hamilton Fyfe, veteran Fleet Street foreign correspondent and editor of the *Daily Herald*, reminisced how:

You cannot take a step in a town, or even a village of any size, without having the ubiquity of the Press forced on your notice. Both early and late, newspaper contents bills, when there was plenty of paper, used to meet the eye. Vans carrying evening papers are conspicuous in the traffic. From nine o'clock in the evening until after midnight morning-paper lorries are discharging at every main-line railway terminus; special newspaper trains are leaving one after another.[32]

The effect is to conjure up a network of unavoidable stimulus. An American, writing on the eve of the First World War, may have been guilty of hyperbole in describing the extent of the influence of the press, but he came up with an arresting metaphor for his sense of how newspaper culture had infiltrated modern consciousness: 'We see it visibly affecting pretty nearly all we do and say and think, competing with the churches, superseding Parliaments, elbowing out literature, rivalling the schools and universities, furnishing the world with a new set of nerves.'[33]

This idea finds a curious resonance in Virginia Woolf's diaries where the jangling of that 'new set of nerves' creates a commotion in the real nerves of the individual conscience. In her entry for 25 October 1920, Woolf notes the funeral procession through London that day for the Lord Mayor of Cork, Terence McSwiney, who died on hunger strike in Brixton prison. This extraordinary spectacle was extensively reported in the press (and will be described in more detail later). It prompted Woolf to feel that 'life itself … for us in our generation [is] so tragic – no newspaper placard without its shriek of agony from some one'.[34] A year later the news from Ireland was still touching a nerve:

> People go on being shot & hanged in Ireland … The worst of it is the screen between our eyes & these gallows is so thick. So easily one forgets it – or I do. For instance why not set down that the Maids of Honour shop was burnt out the other night? Is it a proof of civilisation to envisage suffering at a distance…?'[35]

Joseph Conrad was struck by the same phenomenon in relation to accounts of atrocities in war: 'In this age of knowledge our sympathetic imagination … remains strangely impervious to information, however correctly and even picturesquely conveyed.'[36] Conrad seems resigned to accepting the inevitability of a degree of mass indifference towards reports of suffering, in contrast to Woolf's anxieties that any involuntary impulse to shut out the terrible news from Ireland implied a corruption of civilised values. But the mere fact that they were reflecting on this conundrum points to the ubiquity of news from distant lands and suggests the degree to which the contemporary press seemed to be demanding new levels of response to world events in the early decades of the twentieth century.

Little of the historical work on the Irish revolution has grasped this zeitgeist. In fact, an acclaimed fictional treatment of the Irish revolution has shown greater awareness of this context than the historians. In *Troubles*, the first of a trilogy charting the decline of the British Empire, J.G. Farrell writes of a crumbling Anglo-Irish seaside hotel whose inhabitants seem wilfully oblivious to the rampant decay all around them and the war going on outside. Their plight is symbolic of the inexorable marginalisation of the Irish ascendancy. The text is regularly interrupted with passages of Irish and world news extracted from contemporary newspapers that shape the views of the central character, Major Brendan Archer, a shell-shocked veteran of the trenches who has a more lucid appreciation of unfolding events than most of the guests at the hotel. It is the newspaper which gives the Major his bearings, even when he himself becomes a witness to history.

On a visit to Dublin, the Major finds himself walking along a street where an IRA ambush occurs: a retired army officer working as an intelligence agent in Dublin Castle is assassinated in front of his eyes. Although the Major saw 'bright blood scattered on the pavement' it was only by reading the newspaper the next day that he was able to make sense of his terrifying experience: 'It was the newspaper which had explained to him what he had seen.'[37] Just as for Woolf and Conrad, reading the news draws the Major outside the realm of his personal feelings of confusion and trauma and into the flow of world events. Reflecting on the experience of reading about what he himself had witnessed, the Major decides that the purpose of the newspaper is to reconcile readers to the inevitability of history. He imagined the daily accounts of the war in Ireland as

> poultices placed on sudden inflammations of violence. In a day or two all the poison had been drawn out of them. They became random events of the year 1919, inevitable, without malice, part of history ... A raid on a barracks, the murder of a policeman on a lonely country road, an airship crossing the Atlantic, a speech by a man on a platform ... this was the history of the time. The rest was merely the 'being alive' that every age has to do.[38]

This was his intellectual response to reading the newspaper, but at another level his nerves were unsettled by the reawakening of memories of his experiences on the Western Front: 'He could hardly bear to open the newspaper, for it seemed that the war, which he thought he had escaped, had pursued and caught him after all.'[39] Eventually he becomes accustomed to it 'as he had once become used to the dawn barrage'.[40] What is worth noting here is the power ascribed to the newspaper reports, an impact similar to that described by Woolf and Conrad. The Major is, of course, a fictional character and J.G. Farrell is a novelist, but his book is based on an extensive survey of some newspaper accounts of the revolution.

There is another correspondence between Farrell's fiction and contemporary commentary on the press. In *Troubles* the Major has an argument with Sarah (the daughter of the local Roman Catholic bank manager with whom he falls in love) about reports of atrocities in the newspapers: a story about a woman who had pig rings inserted in her buttocks for supplying milk to the police; a donkey knifed to death for carrying turf to the Royal Irish Constabulary (RIC) barracks. Sarah denounces these stories as British inventions designed to tarnish Sinn Féin, adding with evident vehemence: 'We've no way of knowing whether the newspapers tell the truth. Everything belongs to the British in Ireland. Everything.'[41]

Several years before this exchange was supposed to have taken place, James Joyce published an article about Ireland in an Italian newspaper in which he made the same point as the fictional Sarah. Joyce cited the story of an old man on trial for murder in the west of Ireland who spoke no English, whose interpreter failed to make a case for him in the courtroom. Joyce informed his Italian audience that the old man, 'a deaf mute before the judge', was

> a symbol of the Irish nation at the bar of public opinion. Like him, Ireland cannot appeal to the modern conscience of England or abroad. The English newspapers act as interpreters between Ireland and the English electorate … So the Irish figure as criminals, with deformed faces, who roam around at night with the aim of doing away with every Unionist.[42]

Once again, Farrell in his fiction hits upon an issue that contemporary writers had raised in commentary: could English newspapers be trusted to represent Irish reality? As we shall see later, this doubt was given considerable polemical mileage by Sinn Féin propagandists, even though they were simultaneously helping British journalists to write that reality. The nationalist revolutionaries could refer to 'journalists who had come to sneer' but at the same time – *pace* Macardle – quote the British press in support of their cause.[43]

This ambiguity was not the kind of thing that Irish revolutionary leaders were prone to reflect upon and yet it is one of the most intriguing questions of the war: why would correspondents whom Sinn Féin regarded as inveterately hostile be so critical of the British campaign in Ireland? Any explanation of this puzzle must start with the shift in contemporary perceptions of the function of the press in a democratic society. In his research on the role of the press in Britain from the mid-nineteenth to the mid-twentieth century, Mark Hampton identified two broad conceptions of how the press fitted into politics. What Hampton calls the 'educational ideal' placed the press in the classic liberal tradition of public discussion:

> [The] press was regarded as a powerful agent for improving individuals … [Newspapers] could 'influence', 'inform' or 'elevate' readers … [In] the most idealized version, newspapers were seen as creating an arena for public discussion on the 'questions of the day'.[44]

This notion, Hampton argues, held sway until around the 1880s. In the second tradition, the 'representative ideal', which took full form in the early part of the twentieth century, the press did not so much influence readers as reflect their views:

> In this rendering, newspapers conveyed the opinions, wants, or needs of readers, crystallizing them into a powerful form that could bring pressure to bear on Parliament. This version of the press is most neatly conveyed in the press's label as the 'Fourth Estate': the press was the champion of the people … Rather than seeking to involve the mass readers in a discussion or seeking to persuade these readers, those who articulated the representative ideal offered to speak on their behalf.[45]

Hampton does not posit a schematic transformation from one paradigm to the other; rather he suggests that, although the representative ideal was dominant by the early 1920s, strong vestiges of the educational ideal were still invoked to explain the purpose of the press, particularly the 'elite' newspapers.[46]

Politicians in democracies accepted rather than resisted the positioning of the press as a 'Fourth Estate'. In 1908 Asquith told the Imperial Press Conference that 'the press is the daily interpreter and mouthpiece of the tastes, the interests, the ideas – one might go further and say the passions and the caprices of the electorate'.[47] In 1919 two commentators sympathetic to the Labour Party estimated that the press was 'for the purposes of democratic government, practically the sole education which the mass of the people at present has'.[48]

By the time he wrote his war memoirs in the 1930s, Lloyd George could claim that public opinion dominated the actions of British governments.[49] Allowance must be made, of course, for the fact that this point was made to trumpet the superiority of the British system over European dictatorships. Nevertheless there is plenty of evidence – some of which we shall examine later with reference to Ireland – that Lloyd George was profoundly convinced of the centrality of the press to politics.[50] This was not just a politician's folly: a contemporary political scientist estimated that there were only two ways for public opinion to find expression in democracies: 'One is the vote at elections, the other is journalism.'[51] And even where 'elections were pro forma rubber stamps for the state, tsar and kaiser needed to manipulate and control the thing represented as "public opinion" in a way that their ancestors did not'.[52]

The emergence of the press as the 'Fourth Estate' paralleled the enlargement of the British electorate. In the general election of 1918, when Sinn Féin scored its dramatic breakthrough in Ireland, all men over twenty-one years old and all women over thirty were allowed to vote for the first time. The overlapping of the newspaper audience and the emergent electorate made press and politics evermore interlinked.

It was not only the newly expanded electorate that shaped the relationship of the press to politics. The First World War had been a 'total' war, a conflict where the whole population was mobilised in an enormous collective effort to fight and sustain the fight. For the first time the press had been deployed as 'a weapon of warfare'.[53] In the politician's eyes public opinion was now synonymous with morale, and 'propaganda began to emerge as the principal instrument of control … and an essential weapon in the national arsenal'.[54] Lloyd George acknowledged to C.P. Scott over breakfast at Downing Street in December 1917 how a combination of co-option and censorship had kept the true horror of the war hidden from the public. 'If people really knew [what was going on in the trenches] the war would be stopped tomorrow,' Lloyd George admitted. 'But of course they don't and can't know. The correspondents don't write and the censorship would not pass the truth.'[55]

After the war there were second thoughts about the success of the propaganda effort. By becoming 'the self-appointed script writer to the national morale' the press had undermined trust in the veracity of its news.[56] Norman Angell argued that the newspapers had been corrupted:

> Those who cared to exercise a little vigilance could see in every other column of their newspaper the trail of propaganda. What the reader not 'in the know' often took for unalloyed 'news' was, as a matter of fact, often a partial statement concocted for military or political purposes in the 'Information Department' of some interested Foreign (or Home) Government.[57]

Another contemporary commentator, Walter Raleigh, acknowledged that the press had helped to hold the nation together. But in doing so, Raleigh asserted, it had failed to fulfil a basic need of the British people which made their patriotism superior to that of Germans: their desire to be allowed to regularly exercise reason and imagination. Instead of presenting facts the newspapers had dealt in 'flattery and flight': they had been timid in admitting to reverses and never conceded the humanity of the enemy.[58] 'If I had my way,' Raleigh concluded, 'I would staff the newspaper offices, as far as possible, with wounded soldiers, and I would give some of the present staff a holiday as stretcher bearers. Then we should hear more of the truth.'[59]

Raleigh might have been surprised to find that newspaper staff themselves were not immune to second thoughts about the collusion between the government and the press during the war. When Desmond FitzGerald (head of the Irish revolutionaries' publicity department) visited London to see correspondents from foreign newspapers he noted that their wartime experience made them wary of anything they construed as propaganda.[60] In considering the reporting of the British campaign in Ireland it is essential to bear in mind the context of these post-war criticisms of the British press. This is also why judging the press coverage only through the publicity work of the revolutionaries – as is often done – is inadequate because it ignores the fact that the war in Ireland coincided with a vigorous and intense discussion in political and cultural circles in Britain and the USA about the nature of the press, public opinion and propaganda.

Influential commentators like Angell argued that the deceptions of war had spilled over into peacetime; he believed it was more profitable for the press to peddle familiar falsehoods rather than confront 'unpleasant truth'.[61] He concluded that the press had become 'perhaps the worst of all the menaces to modern democracy'[62] and 'the main instrument by which any real movement towards a new social order is resisted'.[63] This climate of liberal mistrust of the press is essential for understanding the attitude of the correspondents sent to Ireland. Covering the British campaign offered an opportunity to journalists and editors to prove their critics wrong.

By the time of the Irish revolution the press had begun to articulate a vision of itself as a vigilant defender of the interests of the public. In January 1918 the *Spectator* declared: 'The function of the Press – and it may be a public service of untold good – is to act as critic and watchman, to be perpetually warning the country of the dangers that beset the State.'[64] At the end of that year the *Daily Telegraph* was also stepping up to the watchdog role. Noting the lack of publicity about the Allied intervention in the civil war in Russia ('a war … such as would have filled the newspapers at any normal time') the *Telegraph* put itself forward as proxy for the electorate demanding that 'the nation is entitled to know how the war is going, and what end to it is contemplated by the Government'.[65] As we shall see later, these justifications came to the fore during the war in Ireland: British newspapers came into conflict with the government over their coverage and had recourse to versions of this 'Fourth Estate' myth to defend themselves.

The whole debate about the press and propaganda was itself a symptom of the more general upheaval provoked by the most devastating war in history. Everywhere old norms were undermined, nowhere more so than on the map of Europe itself. A new international order was taking shape, with little resistance from the allied powers. Anthony Smith has remarked that, although the First World War was fought by bureaucratic states with colonial empires, it 'promoted the cause of ethnic nations across Europe'.[66] In many places the invigoration of nationalist movements was assisted by the great powers, often, as Mark Mazower argues, to the detriment of their own imperial futures: '[The] empires committed suicide during the 1914–18 war by fomenting nationalism as a form of political warfare against their opponents.'[67]

By the time of the Paris Peace Conference the challenge from nationalism to the old colonial system was also powerfully assisted by two universalist ideologies: Lenin's appeal for world revolution and Woodrow Wilson's crusade for self-determination. Forced to take sides, Wilsonian internationalism was the only choice from a British point of view, even if this meant letting go (in principle at least) some cherished notions of imperial supremacy that looked outdated to the Americans. The colonial system was also out of step with the growth of Washington's economic power: a world made up of self-determining nations would be more open to American penetration.[68]

The currency given to the notion of self-determination was a gift for Ireland's revolutionaries. All successful revolutions of the twentieth century, as John Dunn has observed, 'succeeded by establishing a government of a nation state in a world of other nation states'.[69] The post-war international order gave a new legitimacy to Ireland's historic claims. All this is important because the shifting ideas of a new international settlement would have informed the correspondents heading to Ireland to cover the revolution. When they arrived they would be exposed to local versions of these universal arguments since, as Ben Levitas has pointed out in a discussion of arguments about anti-Semitism between Irish polemicists, 'all sides of the cultural and political debate [in Ireland] fed off international currents of thought'.[70] Perhaps more than at any time before, political thinkers and activists in Ireland would, in the years after 1918, be compelled to connect the cause of Irish nationalism with world events.

Colonialists themselves could not afford to ignore the vogue for publicity and propaganda as they reluctantly adjusted to the new world order. C.A. Bayly has suggested that for the stewards of Britain's overseas possessions at this time, public relations became a kind of 'new imperialism'. However, diffusing the empire message cut both ways: as their masters began to adjust to the demands of public opinion, 'spokesmen of the colonized peoples also began to present their case more vigorously in metropolitan circles with the aid of telegrams, newspapers, and high-profile publicists'.[71]

Irish revolutionaries were aware of the need to appeal to this new international public sphere that exalted humanitarian values. In the late nineteenth century, Patrick Ford, the editor and proprietor of the most widely read newspaper among Irish-Americans, the *Irish World*, aligned the Irish cause with slave emancipation, arguing that Ireland's suffering was not singular but part of worldwide oppression of the common man.[72] Ford advocated that Irish revolutionaries must connect with similar movements around the world and especially in the British Empire: 'The concept of Indians as brown Irishmen, as discontented and as revolutionary-minded as themselves, was a basic tenet of Ford's strategy.'[73]

The reporting of the Irish revolution was in a sense a vindication of this strategy. The interest shown in the nationalist cause by the journalists who converged on Ireland to report the war, the commentary and reportage connecting Ireland to world themes and the prominence given to the Irish struggle in newspapers around the world combined to allow George Gavin Duffy, the first minister for foreign affairs in the new government of the Irish Free State, to boast in a memorandum in 1922: '[We] are still beyond question, in high favour among influential people on the continent and our Envoys will be much sought after ... Ireland is a world-race with great possibilities'.[74] Whatever about Ireland being a 'world-race', Ireland was indeed the centre of world attention during its revolution. This book is the story of how this happened.

# I
# THE EDUCATION OF THE WAR CORRESPONDENTS

*In the first few months of the war our General Staff ... treated British war correspondents as pariah dogs ... Long before the end of the war the Chiefs of Staff of our several armies received them regularly on the eve of every battle [and] every perilous secret we had was put into their keeping. [After the war] all the regular pariah dogs were offered knighthoods.*

C.E. Montague, *Disenchantment*

The early twentieth century was the heyday of mass-circulation national newspapers run by financially independent proprietors who had emerged in the Victorian era. It was an intensely competitive industry and the press barons invested huge sums in recruiting staff, producing increasingly bigger papers and then promoting them in an effort to win ever larger circulations.[1] Extensive news coverage emerged as the key to editorial advantage; editors vied with competitors to publish 'scoops', or at least ensure that their own paper carried the same stories as its rivals. Information not argument became the currency of success or failure, and reporters were sent out to discover facts that could produce commercial return. The 'reporter' thus emerged as a recognisable figure, forging a distinct form of writing called the news story.[2]

Jean Chalaby has identified the era of the press barons as the moment when news displaced opinion as the main content of newspapers and 'information became the prime element ... and the main commodity in the trade ... Press-owners and editors devoted increasingly important resources to collect information from local, national and international sources.'[3] Foreign news was particularly prized during an era of globalised trade. An outstanding performance by the right reporter possessed of flair and commitment could make a big foreign story a major money spinner for his newspaper. The circulation of the *Daily News* trebled on the strength of its coverage of the Franco-Prussian War in 1870.[4] From then until the outbreak of the First World War 'the publicity given to politics and foreign affairs was increased a thousand times. More people were informed, or misinformed, about the Empire and England's relations to her neighbours than ever before.'[5] Special correspondents emerged as powerful, authoritative and glamorous figures in the newspaper business, entrusted with keeping readers informed of battles in faraway places: 'Their deeds, their sweeping narratives, their bold assumption of policy-making authority and, above all, the swiftness of their communications gave them a status that none had attained before and few have achieved since.'[6]

What immediately distinguished special correspondents from their journalistic colleagues was their fame. The vast majority of journalists filled the columns of their newspapers anonymously in a literary endeavour barely removed from the industrial discipline of the factory. By contrast the special correspondents were known by their bylines and celebrated for their achievements. Other reporters admired and envied the 'specials', particularly their freedom to write (more or less) as they pleased.

In his memoir of working for Lord Northcliffe, Tom Clarke, an editor at the *Daily Mail*, described how a renowned reporter called Charlie Hands, who made his name during the Boer War, was 'worshipped by the younger folk as the greatest of special correspondents of world wide experience and reputation ... [he] had won a pedestal for himself which placed him well beyond the clatter of the crowd'.[7] The 'specials' were given licence to write about their own experiences in extravagant prose, submitting selected foreign crises to 'a bombardment of vivid reporting'.[8] They lived a glamorous life, liberated from the mundane tedium of office routine, intoxicated by their proximity to dramatic moments of history. In October 1913, Hamilton Fyfe, a leading foreign correspondent for the *Daily Mail*, wrote a private letter to Lord Northcliffe from Monterrey in northern Mexico conveying the sheer thrill of covering the revolution:

> Last week we had a two-day battle here. Bullets making funny little noise all about the streets, and shells knocking holes in house-walls. I nipped about, enjoying it immensely. There were some horrible sights of course. Imagine a big square with a dead rebel hanging from every lamppost and every telegraph pole! But the interest of it all was so great that one accepted the horrors as a matter of course.[9]

Indeed, war correspondents were ranked in public estimation alongside the military heroes their reports helped to create: the press assiduously promoted the cult of the adventurous, dashing eyewitness who risked his own death to bring news of military engagements from remote corners of the empire.[10] This celebrity was deliberately cultivated to win the attention of readers. Keeping a special correspondent in the field was an enormously expensive undertaking for a newspaper and the only rationale for paying the bills was a guarantee of winning more readers and gaining prestige.[11]

Henry Wood Nevinson, the famous liberal journalist, recalled coming across Frank Scudamore of the *Daily News* and E.F. Knight of the *Morning Post* on a hillside in Greece during the Greek-Turkish War in 1897. Nevinson noted that they had set up camp with

> all the equipment with which a war correspondent ought to be provided – a large green tent, two horses that could move, besides pack-horses, servants

and messengers, cases of provisions, cooking utensils, plates and cups and forks, bedding, field-glasses, water-jars and every other contraption that the heart could desire and the desert lacks.[12]

Scudamore evidently took pleasure in being well provisioned. In his own memoirs published a quarter of a century later he boasted how he had also retained a large staff of servants, grooms and camel-men for two and a half years, to look after his horses and camels during the British campaign in Sudan. He guiltily forestalled modern readers working themselves up to indignation over such profligacy:

Lest this description may seem to savour of extravagance, I may mention that in Nile campaigning it was necessary to prepare a series of daks for the quick conveyance of dispatches to the nearest … telegraph station, sometimes fifty miles distant. Moreover, from the first I had always made it my business to be entirely independent of assistance from headquarters in all things except the use of the wires.[13]

Scudamore travelled to Sudan in the company of journalists from other newspapers who were his friends and rivals. Then as now these foreign correspondents formed a select band of adventurers who all turned up at the same events. They shared the same lore and traded interpretations of the incidents and personalities on which they were reporting. They agreed broadly about what it was to be a correspondent and they formed a sentimental attachment to the experiences they had gone through together.[14] An assessment of the status of the war correspondent written in 1913 revealingly described all correspondents – whether from the conservative *Morning Post*, the liberal *Daily News* or the mass-circulation *Daily Mail* – as 'comrades'.[15]

Each worked at the mercy of his proprietor but it would be wrong to underestimate how professional values governed their reporting and how these values and the correspondents' status won them a degree of autonomy. The exalted position that these correspondents saw themselves as occupying, and the way in which they were encouraged to cultivate this role by their editors, can be deduced from a letter from the managing director of *The Times*, C.F. Moberly Bell, to a war correspondent in 1894 advising him to adopt a position of restrained detachment towards the flow of events. Moberly Bell cautioned that 'we are historians, not history makers'.

Around the same time he instructed a newly appointed correspondent that his duties were:

> 1. The transmission of all authentic news of importance without regard to any particular view which may be entertained by the correspondent personally or any particular policy which may be advocated by the paper. 2. The transmission of your own appreciation of the situation, well founded and without any personal prejudice.[16]

Of course, there was a tension at the heart of this advice that would become a persistent complication for the professional self-image of many correspondents. On the one hand *The Times* man was being asked to keep his personal views out of his news copy. On the other, he was being encouraged to become an authority on his subject, an aspiration that would mean the correspondent's own judgement – albeit 'well founded' – would become a critical ingredient in his reporting. This tension between the idealised freedom of the newspaper correspondent to use his own judgement and the necessity of conforming to editorial direction and the industrial discipline of the newspaper is a recurring theme in the memoirs of journalists of this era.

These memoirs are often the only source we have for reconstructing the thoughts of many of these correspondents. It was rare, even for the most distinguished reporters, to consider themselves important enough to keep diaries or collect their private papers; their celebrity was ephemeral. The episodic narratives of those who did publish their reminiscences reveal how their fame was often attached to the events they covered and did not rest on the force and originality of their own interpretations. The standard format for the correspondent's memoir is a series of discrete chapters describing behind-the-scenes adventures in one campaign after another: the hero delivers the news after being subjected to tests of character both mental and physical, and he recalls the foibles of his colleagues and his encounters with eminent and often exotic figures. Rarely is there much literary ambition, philosophical reflection or political analysis.

However, some memoirs are more penetrating than others, particularly about the reality of the correspondent's life behind the glittering public image. Philip Gibbs, a *Daily Chronicle* reporter who was one of the most famous correspondents of the early twentieth century, could write sentimentally about the camaraderie he enjoyed with his colleagues, but he could also subject his profession to critical scrutiny. His memoirs paint an extraordinarily candid portrait of life on Fleet Street – especially frank for a trade and a genre given to myth-making. For Gibbs, becoming a war correspondent was 'the crown of journalistic ambition and the heart of its adventure and romance'.[17] He succeeded in rising above the common run of journalists but he recognised that such eminence was insecure and that there was a fine line between the glamour and freedom of the special cor-respondent and the 'clatter of the crowd'.

In his autobiography he describes journalism as a 'bacillus' and com-pares the lure of Fleet Street to a spell that makes the journalist addicted to the illusion that he is a privileged observer of the machinery of power: 'Away from it he feels exiled and outside the arena of life. As a journalist, and especially as a special correspondent, he sees behind the scenes of the whirligig and is one of its recorders.'[18] He begins one account of his career by warning young people that a life in journalism is not 'a primrose path' but a job little different from other kinds of industrial labour. Proprietors and editors were the arbiters of whether the journalist was published:

> It is of uncertain tenure because no man may hold on to his job if he weakens under nervous strain or quarrels on a point of honour with the proprietor who pays him or with the editor who sets his task.[19]

The young reporter, according to Gibbs, is 'the Slave of the Machine' and he sets out to disabuse his readers of any notions of idealism:

> I have known the humiliation of journalism, its insecurity, its never-end-ing tax upon the mind and heart, its squalor, its fever, its soul-destroying machinery for those who are not proof against its cruelties … The young reporter has to steel his heart against these disappointments. He must not agonize too much if, after a day and night of intense and nervous effort, he finds no line of his work in the paper, or sees his choicest prose hacked and mangled by impatient sub-editors, or his truth-telling twisted into falsity.[20]

The significant word here is 'truth-telling'. For Gibbs and his colleagues, journalism was a realist form in which they sought 'to persuade the audi-ence to believe in the realty of the images presented and the story told' and to trust that 'these convincing devices are based on scrupulous observation and human judgement'.[21] Gibbs accepts that in the newspaper business – despite pretensions to respect individual authorship – journalists could not always ensure that they published the stories they wanted to tell: they were bounded by political, commercial or editorial strictures. However, Gibbs advises the young reporter that it is not worth dwelling too long on individual defeats, that the battle with these restraints is a continuous struggle and that 'truth-telling' is still a worthy, if not always attainable, ideal. It is important to note the tenacity of this ideal in the journalists' self-image because it will come to the fore in the coverage of the Irish revolution. The pressures on correspondents that Gibbs lays bare – essentially to follow the line favoured by the proprietor or the government – increased greatly during the First World War. As we shall see, however, the war in Ireland created a new set of circumstances and offered the correspondents more opportunities to resist them.

Throughout the Victorian period the idea that it was the special correspondent's job to side with the military was unquestioned. They were expected to provide vivid accounts of battle and get their copy to the newspaper as quickly as possible: delivering the dispatch to the telegraph office, whatever the odds, was even more important than how it was written since a scoop could potentially produce huge gains in sales. Acknowledging that transmitting his words to his paper was often the true test of his worth, Archibald Forbes, a leading correspondent of the Victorian era, described himself first and foremost as 'an organizer of means for expediting news'.[22] Many of the correspondents' most treasured anecdotes were about gruelling rides across enemy terrain to reach the telegraph before their competitors.

After speed, the correspondent's reputation depended on expertise in military matters. They were expected to be knowledgeable enough about strategy and tactics to enable them to judge a general's conduct of a campaign, to gauge if troops had been given the right equipment and transport, and to assess whether there were enough medical supplies to treat the wounded.[23] In a sense the soldiers themselves were their most important and immediate audience. Archibald Forbes believed that the correspondent had to 'write so as to earn the respect of soldiers'.[24] And William Maxwell advised any correspondent that '[in] loyally serving the Army he serves best in the end the public, his newspaper and himself'.[25] Socially the correspondents identified with the educated officer class and shared their faith in British military superiority.[26] This consonance is illustrated by the ease with which the young Winston Churchill effortlessly switched roles from soldier to correspondent and back again.[27]

The first truly famous war correspondent, William Howard Russell, made his reputation exposing the inadequacy of the British campaign in the Crimea. Russell held that it was 'not good for militarism to feel itself exempt from criticism'.[28] For most correspondents, however, fault-finding was confined to strictly military matters such as preparedness and strategy; politics and policy were avoided. Roger Stearn points out that although correspondents highlighted the technical failings of the British campaign during the Boer War (incompetent generalship and tactics, inadequate intelligence, insufficient numbers of mounted troops), the exposure of the concentration camps was mainly the work of political and philanthropic activists.[29]

The unquestioned assumption that correspondents could be both critics and cheerleaders was well expressed by F. Lauriston Bullard in his book *Famous War Correspondents*, published just before the First World War. It was essential to have correspondents with the troops, Bullard argued, because '[civilization] must have an unprejudiced witness at the front in war'. However, his idea was that the witnesses must record the daily life of the soldier, 'his shaving and his eating, his whistling and his singing' because '[graphic] pictures of the life of the camp and incidents of the battle are the stuff that patriotism thrives on'.[30] What is striking about the case of the Anglo-Irish War, as we shall see, is that for most correspondents this traditional affinity with the Crown forces suddenly dissolves. Not only are there no descriptions of Black and Tans whistling and singing as they shave; there is little attempt to bring them to life at all.

Up to then, because of their close identification with the military, war correspondents were often denounced by pacifists as warmongers.[31] Especially at the height of the Victorian era, many of the correspondents were indeed unhesitating imperialists 'who believed in the beneficence of British rule and of "the white man's burden"'.[32] However, increasingly in the early twentieth century (and especially after the Boer War) there were competing ideas of imperial strategy, arguments about whether the Empire necessarily had to be coercive or whether it could become more of a voluntary association of nations united under British moral leadership. Some Liberals defined themselves against an expansionist, militaristic imperialism. They argued that the empire should be kept together by goodwill, with national and cultural diversity recognised.[33]

The journalist Henry Wood Nevinson was a case in point. His colleague Philip Gibbs described Nevinson as 'a hater of war, though a lover of liberty, passionate in his championship of the little nations and the underdogs everywhere'.[34] One little nation to which Nevinson was particularly drawn was Ireland. Through his (married) lover Nanny Dryhurst – herself an associate of one of the heroes of 1916, Countess Markievicz – he met many figures of the Irish literary revival in London in the 1890s.[35] For Nevinson, Irish self-determination was commensurate with his belief in the compatibility between empires and nationalities. In an article in the *Nation* in 1912 he cited Parnell – along with Mazzini (the promoter of Italian unification) and Kossuth (the nineteenth-century Hungarian liberal nationalist) – among the heroes of the nineteenth century; they had 'vindicated the rights of free nationality rather than extending empires'.[36]

For Nevinson, empires were worth preserving as long as they were made compatible with selected deserving claims of nationality and they conformed to an acceptable standard of behaviour. Responding to an open invitation to contribute a series of articles about anything he wished from the American magazine *Harper's*, Nevinson wrote a devastating critique of slavery on the cocoa plantations in the Portuguese island colony of Sao Tome, which provoked questions in the House of Commons and was regarded by anti-slavery campaigners as their last great battle.[37] At the same time, he could make a distinction in his memoirs between Spaniards and the 'long-haired savages' he encountered on his first visit to an African town when he crossed over from Spain.[38] Travelling with Wilfred Pollack, an old friend from the *Daily Mail* ('a random, dare-devil, pleasant and clever fellow'), Nevinson noted that Pollack easily gave offence 'to the proud and courteous people of Spain' because he had lived in India and 'acquired the frequent habit of claiming the privileges of a British "Sahib" and regarding the rest of the world as "natives"'.[39] Nevinson himself, however, discovered during the Boer War that natives could be useful for liberal British journalists. He sent out his dispatches with black volunteers willing to put their lives at risk to carry his copy through the Boer lines in return for lucrative fees. Nevinson laconically described how once: 'The Kaffir carrying my most important message was shot dead and my message was kindly given to me months afterwards in Pretoria by the Boer who shot him.'[40]

Nevinson's biographer astutely notes that while Nevinson cultivated an image as a rebel, 'his causes were borrowed ones'. He longed to identify with those he wrote about but 'although he could act as a voice of conscience in the British press ... he could not fully empathize with those whose voices he helped to publicize'.[41] Among the causes he embraced, Ireland was especially important to him because it 'formed part of his wider agenda for the self-determination of small nations'.[42] Even if Nevinson's commitment to Irish nationhood was another of his borrowed causes, his advocacy of self-determination for small nations is significant for our understanding of the wider political currents influencing newspaper correspondents at the time. It shows how the outlooks of some of the elite band of roving reporters were accommodating changes in political fashions. No longer could all the correspondents be counted on to be simple imperialists – a shift that would benefit the Irish revolutionaries.

Indeed, by the eve of the First World War there was a sense among some of the veteran special correspondents that their elite troupe was becoming too plural. In 1913 William Maxwell complained:

> Twenty years ago the company of war correspondents was small and select, and its privileges and traditions were in safe hands. To-day the number is legion, for anyone may be a war correspondent who can induce a newspaper or a syndicate of newspapers to authorise him to represent it, with or without payment.[43]

Gradually there was an idea of an old brigade and a new generation. And there was another phenomenon that had begun to change the old ways of doing business: censorship.

In all the surveys of the role of the foreign correspondent written in the early part of the twentieth century, a frequent complaint was that the invention of the telegraph killed the old autonomy of the correspondent. Frank Scudamore, writing in the 1920s, even went so far as to say that war corresponding was a dead trade because worldwide telegraphy meant strict censorship.[44] In Victorian times, by contrast, the correspondent could wait until a battle had been resolved, with plenty of time to write letters that were never published until the information would be of no use to the enemy. William Maxwell, patriotic as ever, lamented that the telegraph had turned the correspondent into 'a menace to the army which he may have every desire and interest to serve. From a chronicler of events, it has transformed him into an unconscious spy.'[45]

Gradually, armies realised that information sent ever more speedily over the telegraph wire meant that vital knowledge was disseminated much faster. Increasingly they kept the correspondent away from the front line, making him dependent on the military for his information, and insisting that his copy be checked before it was transmitted:

> Wires do not sizzle and cables do not oscillate nowadays with the stories from the 'specials at the front'. Correspondents are kept in straight-jackets, 'cabin'd, cribb'd, confin'd', hampered, limited, and circumcribed. And therefore, we are assured, the alluring profession of the war special no longer invites the newspaper man.[46]

Sometimes the temptation was too great and a correspondent, wishing to steal a march on his colleagues, would circumvent the censor by devious means. Suddenly the correspondent, who in the past had put his faith in building a relationship with the soldier, was viewed with distrust.

In 1881 an American lieutenant, Frances Vinton Greene, was already forecasting that newspaper correspondents would become important participants. He argued that they should not be banished from the front line but treated with respect so as to heighten their sense of responsibility. They should be given 'every facility for acquiring correct information of facts, facts that already transpired'.[47] Soon two sides of an argument on censorship developed. On one side was the right of the public to know how well a campaign was being fought in its name; on the other were the operational requirements of generals to keep information from the enemy. In 1899 the War Office advised the Home Office to start thinking about introducing general controls on the press during wartime. Five years later the Conservative prime minister Balfour declared himself in favour of such a regime, beginning a debate that would continue right up to the outbreak of the First World War.[48] In May 1905, General Sir George Cockerill – who would become an influential official in the wartime censorship apparatus in London – wrote an article in *The Times* expressing approval of how the Japanese had successfully censored the foreign press during the Russo-Japanese War. Cockerill veered towards the approach Lt Greene had begun advocating a quarter of a century earlier: he believed the press should be relied upon to censor itself.[49]

In 1908 newspaper proprietors declared their opposition to legally enforced censorship but offered to cooperate with the government. They got their way, and in 1912 a joint committee was established to regulate voluntary censorship.[50] Although the British government suddenly reneged on the deal when war broke out in 1914 (creating a Press Bureau that excluded the newspaper representatives), the proprietors re-established a formal link between the Cabinet and editors within a year.[51] They had persuaded the politicians that they could be trusted and that they were prepared to sacrifice journalistic integrity to help win the war.

All belligerent governments came to realise that the press was as much of a resource as the artillery gun or the tank. The mass media 'opened new avenues for reaching vast new populations'; the right message could sustain morale, the wrong signal undermine it.[52] After the war the man who had run the British government's Press Bureau, Sir Edward Cook (himself a distinguished liberal journalist), praised the loyalty of the newspapers in cooperating with voluntary censorship. Cook believed that 'the Press did all that it possibly could, and often more than from a strictly journalistic point of view might reasonably have been expected, to print everything that the Departments desired to impart to the public'.[53]

Cook regarded the press as crucial for 'reinforcing and sustaining' the national impulse towards war. He gave as an example the coverage of Lord Kitchener's call to arms and the daily newspaper accounts of local recruiting drives, which he believed had exerted a powerful suggestive influence on those who rushed to sign up. And he summed up his praise of the newspapers with a phrase intended as a compliment but which served to undermine fatally their self-proclaimed independence from government: they had been, he wrote, '*avant*-couriers of necessary policy'.[54] In Cook's conceit, the press was 'the reporter-in-chief to the nation, and in that capacity it holds up to the rest of the world a mirror of the country's activities, thought purposes and *moral*'.[55]

When the war began, the War Office refused to give official recognition to reporters to follow the action on the orders of Lord Kitchener, who had hated war correspondents since the Sudan campaign sixteen years earlier when he dismissed them as 'drunken swabs'.[56] However, a group of younger correspondents made their way to France and, at the risk of arrest and imprisonment, travelled towards the Belgian border. Philip Gibbs, reporting for the *Daily Chronicle*, went to Paris at the beginning of the war but soon decided that he had no hope of getting credentials to go to the front: 'It was, it seemed, to be a secret war, and the peoples who had given their sons and husbands were to know nothing about it, except by brief bulletins which tell them nothing or very little.'[57] Gibbs and some of the other younger reporters thus set out on their own, without permission, to find out what was happening in the north-east. He recounted how many of these impetuous correspondents

> were arrested, put into prison, caught again in forbidden places, re-arrested and expelled from France. That was after fantastic adventures in which they saw what war meant in civilized countries; where vast populations were made fugitives of fear; where millions of women and children and old people became wanderers along the roads in a tide of human misery...[58]

This rich parade of incident contrasts markedly with Sir Edward Cook's avowal that the early part of the war was characterised by tedium and that 'there was nothing to tell'.[59]

Despite procuring Red Cross credentials in an effort to stay at the front, Gibbs ended up being detained for two weeks. He was released after his editor in London used his influence with a minister at the Foreign Office. Gibbs thought this episode had ended his career as a war correspondent in France: 'The game was up I thought. I had committed every crime against War Office orders. I should be barred as a war correspondent when Kitchener made up his mind to allow them out.'[60] He was wrong, however. Early in 1915 after pressure from the Cabinet – prompted by the proprietors – the British military authorities decided to allow correspondents into the field. The intention was to increase the supply of morale-boosting 'news', not to allow a reflective or critical portrait of life and death on the battlefield.[61]

The arrangements for the correspondents on the Western Front were a dramatic advance on the creeping military censorship in evidence during the previous two decades. They offered unprecedented facilities and assistance to the correspondents in return for submission to a regime that shielded them from the realities of the fighting and virtually dictated the broad lines of their copy. Henry Wood Nevinson contrasted the life of a war correspondent at the turn of the century with the new dispensation. During the Boer War, 'a correspondent with the British army had to look after his own supplies and transport and the task, as a rule, occupied about half his working time'. In comparison, as an officially accredited correspondent in France fifteen years later:

> the Staff motor appeared at the door exactly at the appointed time; a friendly Staff officer accompanied me to whatever part of the line or advance I wished to visit ... food appeared, falling like manna from heaven without any stir; servants appeared when required, like slaves in the 'Arabian Nights'.[62]

C.E. Montague, a *Manchester Guardian* journalist who served as a conducting officer chaperoning journalists in France, captured even more vividly how the combination of pampering and insinuation had entirely co-opted the correspondents:

> They would visit the front now and then ... but it could be only as afternoon callers from one of the many mansions of G.H.Q., that heaven of security and comfort. When autumn twilight came down on the haggard trench world of which they had caught a quiet noon-day glimpse, they would be speeding west in Vauxhall cars to lighted chateaux gleaming white among scatheless woods ... feeling the presence of horrible fatigues and the nearness of multitudinous deaths chiefly as a dim, sombre background that added importance to the rousing scene, and not as things that need seriously cloud the spirit or qualify delight in a plan.[63]

Literally under the eyes of the censors the correspondents elaborated these 'rousing scenes' in prose which discarded verisimilitude. Their dispatches were stuffed with 'abstract euphemistic spiritualized words and phrases under which were buried the realities of modern mechanized warfare'.[64] W. Beach Thomas of the *Daily Mirror* described how the corpse of the British soldier appeared 'more quietly faithful, more simply steadfast, than others ... as if he had taken care when he died that there should be no ... heroics in his posture'.[65] On the first day of the Battle of the Somme, the dispatch from Philip Gibbs managed to omit mentioning that 20,000 British soldiers were killed:

> The attack which was launched today against the German lines on a twenty-mile front began satisfactorily. It is not yet a victory, for victory comes at the end of a battle, and this is only a beginning. But our troops, fighting with very splendid valour, have swept across the enemy's front trenches along a great part of the line of attack … And so, after the first day of battle, we may say with thankfulness: All goes well. It is a good day for England and France. It is a day of promise in this war, in which the blood of brave men is poured out upon the sodden fields of Europe.[66]

After his earlier skirmishes with Kitchener, Gibbs had become one of five official war correspondents who, kitted out in army uniform, were provided with a house to work in, daily transport to the front, conducting officers and on-the-spot censors.[67] Gibbs, who had been disdainful of official sanction, became a kept man of the high command. In his memoirs and autobiography published after the war, Gibbs – who was knighted for his work as an official correspondent – betrays a sense of shame about his submission to the censorship.[68] In *Realities of War*, published in 1929, he writes of an encounter between the correspondents and General Haig. The general listened to the journalists' petition to be allowed to mention the names of combat units in order to 'give honour to the troops'. Haig appeared sympathetic:

> I think I understand fairly well what you gentlemen want. You want to get hold of little stories of heroism and so-forth to write them up in a bright way to make good reading for Mary Ann in the kitchen and the man in the street.[69]

Gibbs and his colleagues took umbrage at this 'slur' on their profession:

> We took occasion to point out to him that the British Empire which had sent its men into this war yearned to know what they were doing and how they were doing and that their patience and loyalty depended upon closer knowledge of what was happening.[70]

At this, Haig relented and ordered a relaxation of rules so that men and their units could be identified more often in dispatches. This achieved, Gibbs appeared satisfied:

[In the] later stages of the war I personally had no complaint against the censorship and wrote *all that was good to write* of the actions day by day, though *I had to leave out something of the underlying horror of them all*, in spite of my continual emphasis, by temperament and by conviction, on the tragedy of all this sacrifice of youth.[71] [my emphasis]

This passage is more than a little apologetic about the accommodations necessary to continue reporting from France. In his autobiography, *The Pageant of Years*, published in 1946, the question of his cooperation with the censorship still bothered him. He explains how he was hurt by a passage in Lloyd George's war memoirs stating that, 'Gibbs lied merrily like the rest of them'. This, Gibbs writes indignantly, was 'grossly untrue' and 'very unjust'.[72] However, Lloyd George knew exactly how reticent Gibbs had been in public. In 1917 he wrote to C.P. Scott about a dinner he had attended in Gibbs's honour when the correspondent returned from France. Lloyd George described Gibbs' address to the dinner as 'the most impressive and moving description of what the war in the West really means ... Even an audience of hardened politicians and journalists was strongly affected.'[73]

Despite his protests, Gibbs was aware of what he had held back. A few pages after accusing Lloyd George of lying he writes of a conversation with his wife, Agnes, while he was home on sick leave from France in August 1918:

She hated the dispatches of war correspondents always holding out a hope which was never fulfilled, always describing the heroic valour of boys who, of course, were sentenced to death. In the end she hated mine, for the same reasons and I didn't blame her because that was the truth.[74]

Later in his autobiography Gibbs expresses a desire to put things right nearly two decades after the end of the war:

We writing men, especially we war correspondents, had something to say after our last dispatches had been written. It was to put in all that the censor or our self-imposed censorship, had omitted ... It was our bounden duty to tell the truth, however terrible.[75]

By this stage, of course, telling the terrible truth would not achieve the same impact; for a journalist, there must have been a sense of futile atonement about disclosing the true face of the war long after his last dispatches had been written. Samuel Hynes, referring to *Realities of War*, has suggested that Gibbs's avowed purpose to make 'a plain statement of realities' represented his belated rejection of the inflated prose of the war correspondents in favour of 'a soldier's style'.[76] Indeed, an anonymous officer contributing an article on the war to *The Times* in 1916 had emphasised that what he had written was 'plain fact' and not 'skilful fiction' as a way of distinguishing his own testimony from the discredited accounts of the official war correspondents.[77] However, perhaps more important is that Gibbs wished to return to the 'truth telling' he originally saw as the journalist's mission early in his career. As Hynes points out, Gibbs now believed that only 'truth telling' could persuade a public suspicious of British propaganda.[78]

The emergence of propaganda as a mobilising force during the war and the eagerness with which the press had collaborated with the censorship exposed reporters like Gibbs to vilification in the sceptical recriminations that followed. C.E. Montague, who had participated in the deception from the other side, felt the war coverage had destroyed trust in the press among the men who had fought in the trenches:

> Most of the men had, all their lives, been accepting 'what it says 'ere in the paper' as being presumptively true. They had taken the Press at its word without checking ... Now, in the biggest event of their lives, hundreds of men were able to check for themselves the truth of that workaday Bible. They fought in a battle or raid, and two days after they read, with jeers on their lips, the account of 'the show' in the papers. They felt they had found the press out.[79]

Montague believed Britain now had a press more akin to the formerly despised 'semi-offical' journalism of Germany and Russia.[80] Similarly, after the war Norman Angell described the press as 'an almost insuperable obstacle to the truth becoming known', the very opposite of the myth that journalists cherished.[81] This disillusionment was, as we have seen, shared by the correspondents themselves. Hamilton Fyfe believed that journalists had lost pride in their craft and the failures of the press during the war caused it 'to be jeered at and distrusted, created around it an atmosphere of suspicion'.[82] The Viennese satirist Karl Kraus had denounced the newspaper reporters, holding them responsible for:

[the] impoverishment of the imagination which makes it possible for us to fight a war of annihilation against ourselves ... [they] now implant in us the courage in the face of death which we need in order to rush off into battle ... [Their] abuse of language embellishes the abuse of life.[83]

Kraus' critique finds a curious echo in Gibbs's post-war estimation of the correspondent as a conduit for politicians:

It is he who brings them alive to the public and takes down the words they speak on great occasions – words of wisdom maybe or words of folly, or words of doom which pronounce a sentence of death on masses of youth who go willingly to sacrifice because of their leadership or their lies.[84]

As we shall see, the correspondents who went to Ireland declared repeatedly that their mission was to expose the government's lies about the real nature of the campaign to crush the rebellion. As Alice Goldfarb Marquis has argued, the confluence of news and propaganda during the First World War had 'permanently debased the coinage of public dialogue' but at the same time 'disillusionment also laid the foundation for a new scepticism'.[85] The practice of 'colouring news' became widely distrusted.[86] This was the context in which the special correspondents set out to report the Irish revolution.

However, a distrust of propaganda on its own might not have made a difference to how they reported Ireland. They might have been forced to submit if the pressure from the government was strong enough. They could only act on their disillusionment because of the crucial difference between the nature of the total war just ended and the guerrilla war of reprisals about to begin in Ireland. During the Great War the unity of the political elite attenuated the range of legitimate dissent: 'if a large paper went right against the national will ... it would be ruined'.[87] Ireland gave the British press an opportunity to re-vindicate its most cherished legends because this consensus lapsed. Crucially, recent history had made Irish nationalism more difficult to demonise than German militarism.

# II

# REVOLUTION IN THE MAKING

*The only news on the Rising in the* Irish Times *on Tuesday alongside reports of the races at Fairyhouse and a leader on the Spring Show:* 'SEIN *[sic]* FEIN RISING IN DUBLIN – *Yesterday morning an insurrectionary rising took place in the city of Dublin. The authorities have taken active and energetic measures to cope with the situation. These measures are proceeding favourably. (In accordance with this official statement early and prompt action is anticipated.)*'

F.A. MacKenzie, *The Irish Rebellion*

It would be hard to underestimate the degree to which Irish nationalist politics had insinuated itself into the mindset of liberal Britain by 1919. The prospect of home rule had dominated Irish politics – and by extension Westminster – for a generation. The emergence of a disciplined Irish party at Westminster in the 1880s under the leadership of the aristocratic and strategically gifted Charles Stewart Parnell put Irish issues at the centre of British politics in a way not seen since the Act of Union in 1800.

Elected on a wave of popular enthusiasm, the Irish MPs discovered they could advance their case for wholesale land reform (to break the power of the landlords and return farms to the peasantry) and self-rule by threatening to immobilise political business at Westminster. The tactic of parliamentary obstructionism – endless filibustering – guaranteed them notoriety. Before long they found themselves holding the balance of power. Both Liberal and Conservative administrations were forced into a series of concessions to the Irish party: rent control, subsidies for tenants to purchase farms from their landlords, a national university. Such was the success of constitutional Irish nationalists that they were able to '[provoke] state intervention in Irish social and economic affairs to a degree quite unparalleled in the rest of the United Kingdom'.[1]

Their pivotal coup was Gladstone's adoption of home rule as part of Liberal policy for the pacification of Ireland. From then on, as Richard English has pointed out, 'Irish nationalist argument provided the ideological framework within which English Liberals engaged with Irish politics.'[2] This alliance between Irish nationalists and English Liberals merely confirmed the power of mass mobilisation as harnessed by Parnell: he had created a party that brought together land agitators, separatists, Protestant idealists like himself and the Catholic Church in an extraordinary coalition, all intoxicated with the belief that in this moment they could take control of Ireland's political future.

To gain a full understanding of how visiting correspondents would later interpret the Irish revolution it helps to appreciate how much these nationalist movements in the late nineteenth century owed to the development of a vigorous press. Irish politics at this time bore out Benedict Anderson's insight that nationalism was invented in print language, which 'made it possible for rapidly growing numbers of people to think about themselves, and to relate themselves to others, in profoundly new ways'.[3] From the middle of the nineteenth century provincial newspapers flourished; for middle-class men of status with nationalist sympathies journalism was a more conscientious alternative to becoming a landlord or serving the government as a lawyer.[4] In 1884, John Pope-Hennessy, a Catholic landlord and MP, claimed that the newspaper audience in Ireland was 'larger than the reading public in any country in the world'.[5]

Whatever the statistical basis for this claim, newspapers certainly became the lifeblood of the spreading Land League agitation. J.F. McCarthy, a *Freeman's Journal* reporter, recalled how the newspapers brought the tenant farmers to an unprecedented level of self-awareness:

> Print had became for the first time an actuality for the Catholic peasants and part of their everyday life, speaking to them in a thrilling, palpitating language, intelligible – and there lay the marvel – yet different from anything previously known, for it enabled them to hear their friends at a distance talking to them in accents of power about the wondrous doings of the Land League.[6]

Parnell himself was entirely aware of the importance of the press to the excitement generated by his movement. And he was particularly sensitive to how much his own regal persona, which so captivated the masses, was enhanced or undermined by what was written about him. He was so concerned about his public image that when he was struck in the face by a rotten egg during a rowdy election meeting in Co. Wexford in 1880, he followed a reporter to the telegraph office to read his copy and try to persuade him (unsuccessfully) that he had been struck by an orange rather than a humiliating egg.[7]

Parnell's failure to airbrush history pre-emptively shows that he was not alone in his appreciation of the power of print. Reporters themselves had become aware of their own role in politics: in this case a nascent professional pride rested on transmitting the word 'egg' instead of 'orange'. In his memoirs, Irish journalist J.B. Hall urged his colleagues to remember that the 'entire value' of great political gatherings rested on the publicity that the reporter gave them and therefore any reporter should demand the best treatment from 'those who live, move, and have their being in the publicity which without his aid they could not secure'.[8]

Many Irish journalists at this time chose to make their careers in London with great success. A future leading light in the Irish Parliamentary Party, Tim Healy, began his career as a reporter in the House of Commons for the *Nation* newspaper, thus, 'inaugurating the journalistic revolution of Parnellism'.[9] One account of the Irish in England in the late nineteenth century concluded that

> [Irish intellect] … educates and rules in the press … There is not a newspaper in London without its one, two, three and four Irish writers and Irish reporters on its staff – indeed, Irish reporters are not alone numerous but are the best and ablest who supply the daily papers with the Court and Parliamentary records of the day.[10]

Many of them, as Fintan Cullen and R.F. Foster point out, 'were involved in marketing or publicising concerned views or interpretations of Ireland, contemporary or historical'.[11] This Irish presence at the centre of the empire established important connections between exponents of the Irish cause and British and international journalists, which helped to nourish interpretations of the war in Ireland by 1920, once it became a major worldwide story.

The diffusion of nationalist sentiment in the newspapers worried the authorities and provoked a series of arrests and seizures, although they were never enough to curb the spread of sedition. In 1887 *The Times* urged the government to take action against the Irish press:

> The whole of the so-called national movement in Ireland is nurtured by a system of what the French call *blague* … Those who have addressed themselves to the masses in Ireland have been obliged to exaggerate, to falsify, to invent, until the habit of looking for any sort of correspondence between speech and fact has been altogether lost.[12]

However, by this stage the government found it very hard to move against the press in Ireland: freedom of the press had become too embedded in British liberalism to be easily cast aside. In 1870 Gladstone introduced the Peace Preservation Bill with a clause giving the authorities in Ireland the power to seize the printing press of any newspaper thought to be propagating sedition, the first time that legislation had been introduced in the UK to deliberately control the press. Though the legislation was hardly ever used, Gladstone's government was attacked for its illiberalism.[13]

Significantly, the Irish members compared the legislation to the kind of measure dear to foreign regimes such as the Ottoman Empire, which Britain routinely condemned as despotic. Critics also pointed out that British liberalism could hardly support national movements in Italy, Hungary and Poland whilst suppressing cries of 'Ireland for the Irish'.[14] This comparative criticism, which appeared harmless at the time, was a portent of what would become a telling interpretive framework for assessing the notorious conduct of the Black and Tans. Half a century after Gladstone's heyday this notion of holding British rule in Ireland to the standards Britain proclaimed for the rest of the world would become central to coverage of the Irish revolution.

Parnellism also propagated another idea that would acquire powerful resonance by 1919: the argument that Irish nationalism was the equal of any other nationalism. Parnell sought to join the struggle against landlordism to the norms of the civilized world. In a speech in Westport, Co. Mayo, in 1879 he pointed out that in France, Russia, Belgium and Prussia landlords had been forced to sell their land or hand it over to those who occupied it.[15] He also tried to reassure his audience that their cause was the subject of intense interest abroad – 'The eyes of the world are fixed upon you' – and pointed out (no doubt for the benefit of visiting correspondents) that Ireland's aspirations were the same as those that many European nations had already achieved.[16]

Once again we can see how a concept that would shape correspondents' explanations of the Irish revolution had already been given voice in the late nineteenth century. This was the argument that Irish nationalism drew its legitimacy from a universal idea. Thus how it was portrayed and perceived elsewhere was crucial to how much nationalists felt their struggle was validated. As nationalism became increasingly recognised as the basis for a new international order, the authenticity of Ireland's claim to nationhood and the propensity for visiting journalists to accept it emerged as an important starting point for discussions of events in Ireland.

These notions would be well embedded by the time of Parnell's downfall in marital scandal and his death in 1891. For the visiting writer or journalist – often attracted to literary figures as explanatory guides – the cultural movement known as the Irish Revival would further enhance this sense of national distinctiveness. A year after Parnell's death, Douglas Hyde, a Protestant scholar, delivered a famous paper whose title – 'The necessity for de-anglicising Ireland' – constituted a pithy manifesto for a movement that drew adherents from all walks of life: sport, literature, drama and education. Restoring the declining Irish language was at the heart of their concerns and, once again, example from abroad was crucial. In 1845 John Daly, an early Celticist, asked: 'If repeal of the Union were to be carried, how was Ireland without its own language to measure up to the other nations of Europe?'[17] Hyde's answer was that Ireland would remain culturally a poor copy of modern Britain unless it cultivated its own Gaelic civilisation. The following year he founded the Gaelic League which promoted the study of the Irish language in branches that sprang up across the country.

The League served as a giant, high-minded social club as much as a cultural movement; an Irish version of Fabianism.[18] Led by 'a generation of educated, bicycling young men and women', thousands signed up for language classes and bought Irish textbooks as fast as they could be printed.[19] The League and other cultural and sporting manifestations of national consciousness such as the Gaelic Athletic Association also established branches in London attracting the exiled Irish, in addition to some curious British aficionados such as the journalist Henry Wood Nevinson and his mistress. Ostensibly the revival stretched from the efforts of Protestant literati, like those of W.B. Yeats to re-invent ancient Gaelic mythology in English, to the acerbic condemnation of any manifestation of mass British culture by the polemical journalist D.P. Moran (whose targets included music hall revues and 'smutty' Sunday newspapers). Both shared a rejection of corrupting, vulgar, urban culture – but this masked deeper arguments about the true nature of Irish identity.

As the tension between nationalism and unionism intensified, the once apolitical mission of the Gaelic League shifted to a closer alignment with militant nationalist political movements. By the time the Irish revolution began, Sinn Féin (once a small fringe party advocating a dual monarchy in London and Dublin, now the predominant mass party of Irish nationalism) was run by a generation schooled in the Gaelic League.[20]

This mobilisation of cultural and political movements served to sharpen divisions in Ireland between nationalists and unionists. Gladstone's adoption of Irish home rule as Liberal policy in 1886 also turned it into the most divisive issue in British politics. This led to Gladstone's decision to split his own Liberal party; for Conservatives his conversion amounted to, in Lord Randolph Churchill's words, 'trafficking with treason'.[21] In Ireland itself unionists – up to then a diffuse but powerful collection of individuals and groups – combined to articulate a coherent political vision that defined itself explicitly against nationalism.

At Westminster the Unionists allied themselves to the Conservatives. Every time the Liberals succeeded in passing a home rule bill they were thwarted by the Conservative majority in the House of Lords. However, in 1911 the Commons voted to remove the veto power of the Lords after it had rejected Lloyd George's 'People's Budget'. From this point, with the Irish nationalist MPs keeping the Liberals in power, the way was open for home rule. When a home rule bill was introduced in April 1912 its enactment was inevitable.

The reaction in the north-east of Ireland, where the majority of Irish unionists (almost overwhelmingly Protestant) lived, was the creation of a mass movement, the recruitment of a private army and the illegal importation of guns. Unionist leaders threatened to provoke a civil war and establish their own provisional government if they were to be forced to accept that Ireland would be run by a predominantly Catholic parliament in Dublin. They drew support from all of the leading figures of British Conservatism, who 'denied the right of the government to force the unionists to fall under the sway of a polity other than the UK parliament'.[22] For unionists, home rule for Ireland meant separation, the eventual disintegration of the UK and, in time, the unravelling of the entire British Empire.

After British officers at the Curragh barracks near Dublin said they would resign rather than fight against the Ulster Volunteer Force, the high command of the British army made it clear they were not prepared to coerce Ulster into home rule. A majority of the Cabinet appeared reluctant to even attempt to overrule the military.[23] Nationalists in the rest of Ireland took their cue from the unionists' success and recruited their own volunteer force. Thus thousands of volunteer militiamen were drilling in Ulster to oppose home rule whilst thousands had mobilised in the rest of Ireland in support of it.

By the summer of 1914 the Ulster crisis was the central drama of British politics. Suddenly, to the press, Ireland seemed to be emerging as a likely site for the kind of war usually found in Europe or the tropics. Norman Angell recalled that after a lunch with Lord Northcliffe in July 1914 the press baron invited him to his private office to show him the preparations he was making for war:

> I went up. The floor of his room was covered with photos of ambulances, artillery, nurses, Red Cross units. He gave me details of the preparations he was making for the war – in *Ulster*! ... Now, whatever else one may say of Northcliffe, he certainly had an extraordinarily keen sense of what the public were interested in. And just then, in July 1914, they were interested in Ulster; not Germany.[24]

Northcliffe organized a team of correspondents who would use a tugboat to take their copy speedily from Larne on the Antrim coast to Stranraer in Scotland where a special train was to be kept ready to rush their dispatches to London. The official historians of *The Times* revealingly described the logistical preparations as a 'safari', and the editor, Geoffrey Dawson (a committed unionist), appeared to think the whole thing had become too hysterical, writing to Northcliffe:

> Belfast, as I know from my own experience, is one of the most infectious places in the world. We want all the news. On the other hand we also want in our Correspondents the power to rise above local infection and to present an unbiased account of things, proportionate to the real importance of events.[25]

A few weeks after Dawson wrote this letter the sensational events in Belfast were dwarfed by the outbreak of war in Europe. The prevailing view was that the war in Europe would provide relief from the poisonous conflict over Ireland. In what now seems like a ludicrously misplaced sense of parochial optimism, the *Irish Times* – chief organ of Irish unionism – epitomised this mood in its editorial on 5 August 1914:

> We believe that the people of these kingdoms are today more cheerful than they have been at any time since the war cloud began to gather over Europe

... In this hour of trial the Irish nation has 'found itself' at last. Unionist and nationalist have ranged themselves together against the invader of their common liberties.[26]

Indeed, the paper's hope that the war would unify the divided factions in Ireland seemed to have some justification at the time. In a sober speech to the House of Commons the Irish Parliamentary Party leader John Redmond pledged his support for the war effort and committed his volunteers in the south to cooperating in the defence of Ireland. The war gave Redmond – 'a kind of imperialist nationalist'[27] – the opportunity to demonstrate that Ireland under home rule would be just as loyal to the King (if not even more so) as it was during the Union. At the same time this served to deflate the Ulster Unionists: threatening violence to resist home rule under the guise of allegiance to the Crown now seemed ludicrous. Catholic nationalists appeared poised to outdo their Protestant brethren in the north when it came to patriotic devotion. Even non-unionist newspapers declared it the duty of Irishmen to fight the despotic Germans. The head of the Catholic Church in Ireland, Cardinal Logue, provided doctrinal support for the war when he condemned 'the barbarity of the Germans in burning Rheims Cathedral'.[28] Redmond dreamed of thousands of his volunteers returning from a quick, victorious war for empire in France to line up proudly in Dublin for the opening of a new home rule parliament.[29]

The War Office pitched its recruitment campaign to suit the circumstances: leprechauns, shamrocks, harps and saints were the staple illustrations on recruiting posters in Ireland and frequent appeals and references were made to the Irish fighting spirit, duty, honour and the atrocities allegedly committed by the enemy.[30] In the end over 200,000 Irishmen participated in the war and some 35,000 were killed.[31] The burden of the war fell mostly on Protestants in the North, but the conflict also had cataclysmic consequences for the Ascendancy families in the South. The writer Lennox Robinson observed that 'the Big Houses were emptied of all men of a fighting age [the Great War being] the last chapter in the history of many families'.[32] By the end of the war 'in all too many Irish country houses in 1919 the Young Master was no more than a memory and a photograph in uniform on a side-table'.[33]

Throughout the worst horrors of the war the Irish gentry supported the soldiers at the front in ways 'almost indistinguishable from those followed in the quietest, loyalist village in the British Isles'.[34] Thousands of Irish Catholics not seduced by the recruiting officers crossed the Irish Sea to work in munitions factories and as seasonal labourers on farms in England.[35] In Ireland, tenant farmers who had graduated to being proprietors thanks to the government land acts benefited from increased prices, and families of serving soldiers received state allowances.[36] However, the soaring costs of food and fuel and the wage freeze imposed by the government fell heaviest on the Irish urban poor, the vast majority of whom lived on less than £1 a week.[37] As the war went on, the feeling that it was not Ireland's war gathered strength. One observer noted that behind the increasing apathy towards recruitment 'was a vague feeling that to fight for the British Empire was a form of disloyalty to Ireland'.[38]

Even so, no threat was apparent to the ambitions of the moderate nationalists of the Irish Parliamentary Party for Ireland to be both self-governing *and* an important part of the British Empire. In fact, the party's detractors in the more extreme nationalist groups appeared to be morally disarmed. Desmond FitzGerald (the future director of publicity for Dail Eireann) recalled how in 1914 he and his comrades had been in 'a very small minority, without influence, impotent'. John Redmond's exhortations that Irish people should support Britain, he wrote, had 'really represented the views of the majority of the Irish people'.[39]

FitzGerald was affiliated to the cultural revivalists dedicated to wipe out what the Catholic Bishop of Killaloe referred to, in an echo of Douglas Hyde's famous speech, as 'the leprosy of Anglicisation'.[40] Politically he and his comrades regarded the ageing satraps of the Irish Parliamentary Party with contempt. Eoin MacNeil – who had formed his own small anti-war volunteer force in opposition to Redmond – regarded the party's MPs as enfeebled and corrupt and referred derisively to their conduct at Westminster where they 'had wheedled, fawned, begged, bargained and truckled for a provincial legislature'.[41] His disdain was shared by other groups of more political militants. Some, like the Irish Republican Brotherhood, were conspiratorial revolutionaries seeking to emulate the Fenian rising of the mid-nineteenth century. Others, including Sinn Féin, had a separatist agenda without being quite sure how to achieve it.[42]

Until 1914, as FitzGerald acknowledged, these parties and movements were a threatening presence on the fringe of mainstream politics. The war created the conditions in which they came into their own. Instead of unifying the nation under the Crown, as the *Irish Times* and the Irish Parliamentary Party had hoped, the ever lengthening stalemate in the trenches helped to transform Ireland from an emerging pillar of the empire into a site of nationalist agitation of the kind that, by 1918, could be seen all over Europe.

How did this happen? For one thing the war, which seemingly held no terrors for the parliamentary nationalists, turned out to be corrosive of their hold on the public imagination. Nobody expected that the fighting would be so prolonged or so bloody. As trench warfare continued with no conclusion in sight, the prospect of achieving home rule receded into the distance. As a consequence the parliamentarians seemed more ineffective than ever. With traditional politics in abeyance there was nothing on which the party leaders could expend their campaigning energies. They even failed in their attempt to have the Irish Volunteers recognised as a separate regiment.[43]

Perhaps just as importantly, censorship prevented any public celebration of heroic deeds performed by Irishmen who were fighting around the globe in defence of the empire. A policy that in Britain was an attempt to prevent knowledge of the true meaning of total warfare from dissolving patriotism had the opposite effect in Ireland, where weakening identification with the war could only be revived by evidence that Irish soldiers were doing the nation proud.

Crucially, the Catholic bishops – once appalled by the barbarism of the Germans in Belgium – now took their cue from Pope Benedict XV's encyclical in July 1915 declaring that the war was futile and encouraging Christians to make peace. On the first anniversary of Britain's declaration of war, Bishop Edward O'Dwyer of Limerick wrote to John Redmond urging him to take heed of the Pope and proclaiming that 'the prolongation of this war for one hour beyond what is absolutely necessary is a crime against God and humanity'.[44] In parishes across the Bishop's diocese Catholics were now worried that they might be forced to take part in a war that the Pope had declared disastrous; rumours spread that the British government might introduce conscription.

By late 1915 the prospect of enforced enlistment 'was becoming an obsessional topic in rural Ireland'.[45] Instead of uniting nationalist and unionist in a common defence of empire the war emboldened those who wanted no part in Britain's crusade against Germany; rather than help Britain out of its difficulty they wanted to take advantage of Ireland's opportunity.

In November 1915 Sir Matthew Nathan, the under-secretary for Ireland, warned Redmond's deputy, John Dillon, that Sinn Féin was gaining support at the expense of the parliamentarians.[46] Little did he realise that a more secretive group than Sinn Féin had decided that the war was the moment for a dramatic strike for freedom. Around midday on Easter Monday in 1916 about 150 Irish Volunteers marched into the General Post Office (GPO) in Dublin city centre and ordered the bewildered staff to leave. Shortly afterwards Patrick Pearse walked into the street and read the Proclamation of the Irish Republic: 'Irishmen and Irishwomen: In the name of God and of the dead generations from which she receives her old tradition of nationhood, Ireland, through us, summons her children to her flag and strikes for her freedom…'

The Easter Rising had begun – to the utter astonishment of the British government and the military brass in Ireland (who were gathered at Fairyhouse racecourse outside Dublin for the Grand National).[47] The men who carried out the Rising had formed a conspiracy within a conspiracy: the anti-recruiting campaigns, pro-German sentiments and the manoeuvring of the Irish Volunteer force itself provided a cover of threatening but not apparently bellicose agitation. The conspirators' plans for a violent uprising were so closely guarded, in fact, that their intention to involve most of the Volunteer movement on Easter Sunday backfired.[48]

Famously the rebellion was carried out with scant regard for the possibility of victory. Pearse, its driving force, believed in a blood sacrifice that would revive the spirit of the Irish nation. At the end of 1915 – four months before the Rising – he exulted in the possibilities offered by the war in Europe for rousing Ireland from its lethargy:

> The last six months have been the most glorious in the history of Europe. It is good for the world that such things should be done. The old heart of the earth needed to be warmed with the red wine of the battlefields … Ireland will not find Christ's peace until she has taken Christ's sword. What peace she has known in these latter days has been the devil's peace, peace with sin, peace with dishonour…[49]

Other leaders of the rebellion also saw it as their duty to awaken the nation to the depth of that dishonour. They were joined by the socialist and Labour leader James Connolly, who – though he had disavowed Pearse's rhetoric about the purifying goodness of war, characterising anyone who thought as much as 'a blithering idiot'[50] – seized the moment as an opportunity for revolution. Connolly felt betrayed when socialist movements around Europe had abandoned internationalism to join their national war efforts. Influenced by the revolutionary rhetoric of some of the separatist leaders, he became convinced that 'Irish independence was a prerequisite for socialist success'.[51]

The Rising lasted for just six days during Easter Week of 1916 but it was still 'the most serious and sustained rebellion in Ireland for more than a century', even though the casualties – 450 killed and 2,500 wounded – bore no comparison with the slaughter in France.[52] The rebels had seized several buildings in central Dublin, besides the GPO. British forces arrived from the rest of Ireland and from England, rapidly outnumbering the rebels and, with very effective use of artillery, pounded them into surrender.

Accounts by people who were in Dublin at the time emphasise confusion, uncertainty and rumour. Some contemporaries were adamant that there was little public support for the rebellion, recording that the citizens of Dublin either looted the destroyed shops in the city centre, '[watched] the fight at the Post Office as if it were a Cinema show'[53] or, by the end, abused the defeated insurrectionists as they were led away to prison. However, the Canadian journalist F.A. MacKenzie – no partisan of the rebels – concluded from his observations that there was 'a vast amount of sympathy with the rebels' in the poor quarters of the city, 'particularly after they were defeated'.[54]

In Britain the Rising was seen as a stab in the back. The charges against the leaders arrested in Easter Week specifically accused them of 'assisting the German enemy'.[55] John Redmond – for whom the Rising was a violent affront to his authority to speak for Ireland – publicly declared that the rebellion had been engineered in Berlin.[56] Even in the confusion of the events in Dublin there was a sense of dread that some exemplary punishment was being prepared. Almost immediately after the suppression of the Rising, John Dillon wrote to Redmond: 'You should urge strongly on the government the *extreme* unwisdom of any wholesale shooting of prisoners.'[57] The wording here suggests that such a 'wholesale' response was believed to be a possibility, even at such an early stage. The *Irish Times* – which had looked forward to the harmony among Irishmen that the Great War would bring – was 'thirsting for blood'.[58]

It soon got its wish. Ninety death sentences were imposed and over a ten-day period in early May there were fifteen executions, the martyrs including Pearse and other leaders of the Rising. The effect, according to the journalists who were there, was cumulative: 'Day by day, as the Rebellion itself receded … into memory … the tale of executions was told piecemeal.'[59] Henry Wood Nevinson recalled how, recovering in the Chilterns from an illness he had developed while reporting in the Dardanelles, he learned of the execution of his Irish friends, 'in batches morning after morning, the lists being served up to the English breakfast tables with the bacon, eggs and marmalade'.[60]

In a few weeks Pearse's idea that a dramatic sacrifice would transform the consciousness of Irish people had come to pass: F.S.L. Lyons's description of the Rising as 'the point of departure … for all subsequent Irish history' is well justified.[61] Even the constitutional nationalists, who stood to lose most from the Rising and were regarded by Pearse and his comrades as traitors, were affected by the retrospective admiration now being accorded to the rebels. When the House of Commons debated the Rising on 11 May, Dillon – with the authority of someone who had been marooned in his house near the centre of Dublin throughout Easter Week – described how the civilian authorities had become powerless in the face of military government. He told of how Dublin had been gripped by rumours of secret executions at military barracks. In a passage which illustrates how the repression was transforming the perception of the rebels, Dillon told the Commons:

> [It] is not murderers who are being executed; it is insurgents who have fought a clean fight, a brave fight, however misguided, and it would have been a damned good thing for you if your soldiers were able to put up as a good a fight as did these men in Dublin…[62]

He accused the prime minister, Asquith, of 'washing out our whole life's work in a sea of blood'.[63]

His desperation had its source in an intuition that constitutional nationalism was being swept aside by the emotional reaction to the brutal suppression of the Rising. John Redmond saw the Rising as an attempt to destroy his party, and the response of the British government appeared almost calculated to help rob the parliamentarians of any remaining legitimacy. Their passionate rhetoric in the House of Commons had failed to stop the executions. In June 1916 Dillon warned Lloyd George that 'Since the executions we have a *new* Ireland to deal with – seething with discontent and rage against the government. Old historic passions have been aroused to a *terrible* extent.'[64] The promises of the parliamentary party – that home rule could be won by trusting the British government to do the decent thing – were revealed as naive; distrust of British intentions now seemed a far more astute position for Irish nationalists to take.

The suppression of the Rising brought scores of foreign reporters to Dublin. Statements by rebels were banned from Irish newspapers but not from British or American papers.[65] Officials tried to persuade the reporters that the rising had been 'a sort of street riot on an extensive scale', which prompted the question as to why it merited such a draconian response.[66] Ironically, General Sir John Maxwell, brought out of semi-retirement to oversee martial law in Ireland, blamed a distorted portrayal of his policies in the press for the public reaction to the repression.[67] A few months after the Rising, irked by the increased circulation of subversive opinions in the Irish press – some of them reprinted from mainstream American newspapers – he asked for 'a literary man or journalist' to be sent over from London to make the censorship more effective.[68] No help was forthcoming.

As we shall see later, Maxwell's sense of helplessness as he watched the reporting of the Rising presaged the attitude of the British military authorities in Ireland to the even more extensive coverage of the war that would follow the Rising. A more prescient assessment of how publicity would continue to work against military rule came from the writer George Russell (known by his *nom de plume*, Æ). In a letter to a friend in July 1916, Russell astutely observed: 'You see it is not the shooting of 50 or 1,000 people that moves public opinion, but the treatment of one person isolated and made public.'[69] As we shall see, Russell became a favoured interpreter of Ireland for correspondents who came to report the war of reprisals four years later. The significance of his insight that the appearance in the newspapers of stories of atrocities or individual suffering would touch readers and change minds would be borne out in the coverage of the guerrilla war that started in 1919.

The beneficiaries of the changed public opinion in Ireland were the revolutionaries organising under the banner of Sinn Féin. After the declaration of martial law and the executions of the leaders of the Rising they began to attract the sympathy of people who would have shunned them only a short time before. In June 1916 Dillon's colleague, Tim Healy, wrote to his brother:

> [Among] moderate Catholics who are intensely loyal I find nothing but Sinn Féin sentiment ... I heard of one man, whose son was burned alive at Suvla Bay, who said he would now rather the Germans won. The looting of the soldiers – downright robbery and ruffianism against innocent people – the shocking ill treatment of the prisoners, the insolence of the military in the streets, the foul language used to women, and the incompetence shown, all have aroused contempt and hatred for which there is no parallel in Irish history in our days.[70]

Within months of the executions requiem Masses were being held in memory of the rebels and pictures of the leaders were being circulated and displayed in houses all over Ireland. The national crusade that had been the property of the parliamentary party for the previous thirty years had been taken over by the supporters of the Rising. A police inspector in Co. Clare noticed several weeks after the Rising that the locals had become less friendly towards his constables; by December they were regarded as enemies.[71]

Understanding of the context for the Rising – it occurred during the preparations for the Battle of the Somme – is essential for explaining the British response. Trying to allay Dillon, Lloyd George excused the executions in Dublin in terms of the brutalisation caused by the war: 'People are getting accustomed to scenes of blood,' Lloyd George wrote. 'Their own sons are falling by the hundred-thousand and the nation is harder and more ruthless than it has ever been.'[72] But even Lloyd George seemed to have become aware of the impact of the executions in Ireland. When he replaced Asquith as prime minister in December 1916 the conciliation of Ireland became a priority for the Cabinet: the prisoners were released before Christmas, producing an effect in Ireland that was 'electrifying'.[73] However, on the ground, the military authorities in Ireland continued to be as repressive as ever in the year that followed.

As support for Sinn Féin and the commemoration of the Rising increased, meetings were banned, football matches and cattle fairs were disrupted by soldiers searching for suspects, and more people were arrested and imprisoned. This indiscriminate policy stoked opposition among people whose sympathies for rebellion had previously been passive or lukewarm.

This new mass movement redirected the lingering anger over the aftermath of the Rising into politics. Starting in January 1917 in North Roscommon, radical nationalist groups put up candidates under the banner of Sinn Féin against the old home rule party in a series of by-elections and won them all. It was an index of Sinn Féin's growing strength that when the British government convened a conference of Irish politicians in July 1917 to negotiate a new settlement, its leaders could boycott the convention in the knowledge that without them nothing could be achieved. By the end of that year Sinn Féin and the Irish Volunteers were publicly united under Eamon De Valera – the senior surviving commander of 1916 – in demanding independence for Ireland. The differences between the various views and factions, open and secretive, subsumed under the Sinn Féin banner seemed not to matter.

In 1918 the movement was presented with a new issue to give more impetus to the transformation of Irish politics: conscription. Compulsory enlistment had been introduced in Britain in January 1916. By October – six months after the Rising – Lord Wimborne, the lord lieutenant of Ireland, advised Lloyd George, then secretary of state for war, that extending conscription there was a non-starter: 'The fact is that it does not appear to be feasible to demand national service from any community without a general measure of consent, and of such general consent there is at present no evidence.'[74] The following months produced only a few thousand Irish recruits.

The British government appeared to accept that there was nothing it could do, until March 1918 when the Germans launched their biggest offensive on the western front. Pressure to conscript Ireland then became overwhelming. Despite the reservations of the Irish secretary, H.E. Duke ('We might almost as well recruit Germans'), the government introduced the Military Service Bill in April, which provided for conscription in Ireland.[75] Sinn Féin then absorbed proponents of violent and constitutional opposition to British rule in one campaign. Hundreds of anti-conscription meetings were held around the country. Even members of the RIC were opposed to conscription.[76] In Dublin, leaders of the trade unions, the Catholic Church and the parliamentary party joined De Valera on a platform in a united front that confirmed Sinn Féin's leadership of Irish nationalism. The declaration read out that day at the Mansion House sought to establish the principle that Ireland could not be conscripted because it was an independent nation:

> Taking our stand on Ireland's separate and distinct nationhood, and affirming the principle of liberty, that the Governments of nations derive their just powers from the consent of the governed, we deny the right of the British Government or any external authority to impose compulsory military service in Ireland against the clearly expressed will of the Irish people. The passing of the Conscription Bill by the British House of Commons must be regarded as a declaration of war on the Irish nation … It is in direct violation of the rights of small nationalities to self determination, which even the Prime Minister of England – now preparing to employ naked militarism and force his act upon Ireland – himself officially announced as an essential condition for peace at the Peace Congress.[77]

This new militancy was met with further repression. In May the government claimed it had discovered a new plot for German subversion in Ireland and seventy-three prominent Sinn Féin members were arrested and deported to England. Assemblies, processions and meetings of the Gaelic League were banned, but they continued nevertheless in open defiance of the law.[78] By June 1918 there were 100,000 troops in Ireland to keep the peace.[79] In the backlash against British militarism, the successors of Pearse and Connolly had achieved a level of popular mobilisation undreamt of by the leaders of the Rising. They commanded an armed force in the Irish Volunteers but also a broad political front ready to fight the 1918 general election on the basis that Ireland should be recognised as a separate nation. This was the prototype for the military–civilian organisation that would wage the Anglo-Irish War.

# III

# THE MORAL ACCOUNTANT:
# A JOURNALIST IN PURSUIT
# OF THE BLACK AND TANS

*I do not blame the police or soldiers for the impasse; I have seen and heard far too much of the dreadful conditions of boycott and slaughter under which they have to try to 'carry on.' But no honest man who has seen with his own eyes and heard with his own ears the fearful plight to which unhappy Ireland has been brought could fail to curse in his heart the political gamble that bred it or cease to use all the power of his pen to end it.*

Hugh Martin, *Ireland in Insurrection*

Threrasure of the Irish Parliamentary Party from the political map
was all but complete in the general election of December 1918
when Sinn Féin won seventy-three seats and the parliamentary
party just six: Sinn Féin had campaigned on securing recognition for Ireland as an independent republic and the election result signified that 'the
separatist option had … replaced the Home Rule compromise'.[1] The defining moment of this new era was the convening of Dail Eireann in Dublin
on 21 January 1919. Dail Eireann, a Gaelic term meaning 'assembly of Ireland', was the fulfilment of a dream of the separatist leader Arthur Griffith,
who argued that instead of taking their seats in Westminster, Sinn Féin
MPs should gather in Dublin to proclaim their own national parliament
and behave as if they had the power to legislate for their own nation.

The MPs who assembled in Dublin on 21 January to establish their own
Republican parliament attracted a great deal of attention from the world's
press. The *Daily News* reported that there were fifty British and foreign
journalists present in the Mansion House for the inaugural session.[2] This
meant that reporters outnumbered politicians by a ratio of two to one,
since all but twenty-seven of the seventy-three Sinn Féin MPs were interned or imprisoned. The *News* described the setting for this public act of
defiance – the Round Room of the Mansion House in Dawson Street, the
very heart of colonial Dublin – as 'a dingily ornate pavilion in the Regency
style which was built in a hurry for the entertainment of King George IV
when he visited Dublin in 1821'.[3]

The correspondent for the *Manchester Guardian* noticed a further irony
in the timing of the first session of the separatist assembly: through 'one of
those coincidences which only happen in Ireland' soldiers from the Dublin
Fusiliers, just returned from France, had been lunching in the Mansion
House just before the historic inauguration of Dail Eireann. 'As they walked
out to the tune of "God Save the King", the Republicans walked in.'[4]

The ceremonial opening of a parliament is an event that would usually
produce the kind of response from the press reserved for great symbolic
occasions. The assembly established by Sinn Féin in Dublin in 1919, however, did not provoke a familiar response among the correspondents who
arrived from London: it perplexed them. The opening of Dail Eireann may
have had the form (and even, to the extent that it was composed of elected
representatives chosen in a British general election, some of the substance)

of an event of established significance, but its legitimacy was contested: it was not the kind of ceremony that would allow the correspondents to reach for their stock phrases and pour their prose into the ready-made mould demanded by time-honoured ritual. Thus, a tone of incongruity was maintained in many of the correspondents' reports; the solemnity of the occasion was both underlined and undermined.

'On the whole it was a very interesting and notable function but one can hardly say it was impressive,' wrote the *Daily Mail* correspondent.[5] The *Manchester Guardian* was no less begrudging:

> [Dail Eireann] solemnly proclaimed Ireland's independence, appointed ambassadors to the Peace Conference, where they have not yet been bidden, passed an address to the free nations of the world and made some pretence of framing orders for its domestic procedure. Despite its importance, the session was not thrilling.[6]

*The Times* was most damning of all:

> History will probably date the definite decline of the Sinn Féin movement from the day when the National Assembly was opened in Dublin ... One may say indeed that the whole of Ireland has a new consciousness today of the utter barrenness of a policy which won nearly half a million votes at the General Election.[7]

A persistent theme was the incomprehension displayed by the MPs and the public as they were addressed from the platform in Gaelic. The *Daily Mail* correspondent noted that the Irish language was delivered by the speakers 'with varying degrees of fluency and the audience, at least those near me, understood with even wider variations of comprehension'.[8] The *Guardian* correspondent thought it wise to sketch in the anthropological background to explain the significance of the use of a foreign tongue:

> The Irish patriot suffers one galling disadvantage: that is an ignorance of his native tongue. Off the shores of the Atlantic, not one in a hundred can do more than pass the time of day in Gaelic ... But however convenient it would, of course, have gravely offended the national spirit to carry on the debates of the national assembly in the language of the Sassenach, and the result was a self-denying ordinance which kept some of the members quite silent and even reduced others to mere French.[9]

The most important statement promulgated by Dail Eireann that day was the Declaration of Independence, in which the MPs declared 'foreign government in Ireland to be an invasion of our national right which we will never tolerate' and demanded 'the evacuation of our country by the English Garrison'. This foundation text for a new Irish Republic also acknowledged the context of the First World War: 'We claim for our national independence the recognition and support of every free nation in the world, and we proclaim that independence to be a condition precedent to international peace thereafter.'[10]

This attempt to link the cause of Irish nationhood with the sweeping redrawing of the map of Europe was even more overtly stated in an accompanying 'Message to the Free Nations of the World'. This laid claim to special status for Ireland in international relations:

> Internationally Ireland is the gateway of the Atlantic. Ireland is the last outpost of Europe towards the West: Ireland is the point upon which great trade routes between East and West converge: her independence is demanded by the Freedom of the Seas: her great harbours must be open to all nations, instead of being the monopoly of England.[11]

Specifically, there was an attempt to join Ireland's case to President Wilson's espousal of self-determination as an end in itself:

> Ireland to-day reasserts her historic nationhood the more confidently before the new world emerging from the War, because she believes in freedom and justice as the fundamental principles of international law, because she believes in a frank co-operation between the peoples for equal rights against the vested privileges of ancient tyrannies, because the permanent peace of Europe can never be secured by perpetuating military dominion for the profit of empire but only by establishing the control of government in every land upon the basis of the free will of a free people...[12]

Such rhetorical grandeur cut little ice with the British correspondents in Dublin; the tone of many of their dispatches was sarcastic or whimsical. The general conclusion was that the whole exercise was futile. Thus the *Daily Mail* reported that the gathering in the Mansion House could easily be mistaken for 'a meeting to found a new musical society or something of that kind'.[13] This analogy was an echo of a phrase that appeared in the *Manchester Guardian*'s preview of the occasion. Officials from the Irish administration regarded Dail Eireann as a 'debating society', reported the *Manchester Guardian*. There was no question of preventing the meeting from going ahead because the assembly would be sure to turn out to be 'a tame business'.[14]

At this stage, the officials in Dublin Castle were taking the optimistic view that Sinn Féin's act of defiance was so much bluster and that the dramatic pageantry of Dail Eireann would fade into inconsequence if ignored. Shortly before the ceremony in the Mansion House, the viceroy of Ireland, Lord French, had expressed just such a view to the Cabinet in London. Lord French wrote with some assurance that 'the end of it will be that these 73 devils will very soon go bag and baggage over to Westminster'.[15] The similarity between this official view and the interpretations of the correspondents visiting Dublin strongly suggests the reporters were responding to the lead given to them by Dublin Castle. Two days after Dail Eireann's inaugural session, *The Times* correspondent in Dublin declared that 'the Irish Government's decision to tolerate the assembly is shown to have been wise'.[16]

The optimism among officials in the Castle that the new generation of Irish nationalists could be contained and controlled is reflected in another theme running through the dispatches from Dublin after Sinn Féin's landslide election victory. The correspondents stressed that Sinn Féin's success would expose its leaders to moderating influences. *The Times* reported in early January that the more pragmatic Sinn Féin leaders 'appear to be anxious to do nothing which might alienate middle-class opinion in the United States'.[17] Around the same time the *Manchester Guardian* asserted that responsibility had sobered Sinn Féin leaders and led them to revise their timetable for delivering Irish independence: 'years' could elapse before the Republic arrived and in the meantime the masses had to be educated. 'From playing the conqueror, Sinn Féin must undertake the part of missionary and not until the unity of the faith is established may we expect the fulfilment of the promises of the days of conflict.'[18] Similarly, the *Daily Mail* correspondent in Dublin reckoned that Sinn Féin leaders realised 'that having captured the great bulk of the emotional voters, it is now necessary to make a favourable impression on the substantial business class'.[19]

The emphasis in many dispatches on the possibility of Sinn Féin leaders eventually doing business with the British government was not far off how the Cabinet in London and the Irish administration in Dublin hoped that things would turn out. With the Irish question no longer overtly divisive at Westminster, 'bipartisanship, supported by military force was (it was hoped) a means of bringing nationalist Ireland to accept the reality of Home Rule as defined by the British'.[20] At a Cabinet meeting in February, the new chief secretary for Ireland, Ian Macpherson, argued in favour of releasing Irish political prisoners using precisely the same analysis of Sinn Féin as was appearing in the press. Macpherson confided to his colleagues that he had been in touch with some Sinn Féin representatives and knew that 'certain leaders, if released, would be valuable to the Government of Ireland and would prove a moderating influence' because they were 'terrified of the responsibility their colleagues were taking and were very anxious to rescind from it'.[21]

However, this apparent confidence coexisted in the official mind with an unfocused anxiety that events in Ireland might just as easily take a different course – a lurch towards revolution rather than accommodation. This strain of anxiety was also reflected in the correspondents' interpretations of developments in Ireland. When Macpherson referred to the terrifying responsibility that the elected Sinn Féiners had taken on he was identifying the possibility that a movement dedicated to overthrowing the existing constitutional order might eventually be outflanked by its violent wing, the Irish Volunteers.

The government was aware of the threat they posed, with Lord French advising the Cabinet that the Volunteers were 'a Republican secret society in the worst and most dangerous sense'.[22] However, just as Lord French could be both optimistic that Sinn Féin's star would fizzle out and at the same time fearful of a full-scale insurrection, reports in the London press betrayed a vague concern about the potential for an unpredictable turn of events. Thus, just before the first meeting of the Dail, the *Manchester Guardian's* correspondent warned that if words and resolutions did not bring an independent Republic any nearer, 'the danger will again arise that the activists who are prepared to stake all ... to realise their ideals, will again offer a sacrifice to their cause'.[23] After the Mansion House gathering the *Manchester Guardian* correspondent repeated his warning of dangers lurking in the background:

There must come a time when the National Assembly will get tired of twiddling its thumbs at the Mansion House. Unless it is to be dismissed as a mere pantomime, it will have to do something sooner or later, and, circumscribed as it is, any action would seem to imply violence.[24]

Similarly, *The Times* adverted to 'darker forces' behind the idealists of the national assembly who were 'quite prepared to sweep it out of existence when the time comes'.[25] And paradoxically, after finding much to mock in the inaugural meeting of the Dail, the *Daily Mail* worried that 'the Irishman's proverbial fear of ridicule' might provoke the separatists to more extreme measures.[26]

Most of the correspondents were unable to provide readers with any informed explanation of the relationship between the idealists in Dail Eireann and the 'darker forces' readying themselves to emerge from the shadows. However, one of the reporters who early on showed some inclination to delve deeper was Hugh Martin, a correspondent for the *Daily News*. After the Sinn Féin election victory many of the papers published articles assessing the state of Ireland but Martin was the only correspondent to distinguish between Sinn Féin and the Irish Republican Brotherhood, the conspiratorial group behind the 1916 Rising. Before Dail Eireann convened, Martin went to the west of Ireland to try to find out what was meant by those in Dublin who lamented that 'the provinces are getting out of hand'. In a dispatch on 16 January he set out to explain the history of support for political violence in rural areas. The left wing of the Sinn Féin movement, he wrote, was threatening to take charge of affairs through the violent methods used by the Fenians in the rebellion of 1867:

> Fenianism has never died out in Connaught. Down here, the physical force men, few in numbers but resolute in temper and supremely contemptuous of the main body with its 'moral force' programme, still press their secret doctrine as they have been preaching it this fifty years. They are never in the ascendant except at times of extraordinary national emotion. Such a time, it is only too plain, we are rapidly approaching now.[27]

Less than a week later, on the same day Dail Eireann met in Dublin, two police constables were shot dead in an ambush in Co. Tipperary. This incident is conventionally regarded as the beginning of the Anglo-Irish War. The policemen were transporting gelignite by horse and cart from Soloheadbeg quarry in Co. Tipperary when they were set upon in the mid-afternoon. A council employee accompanying them gave evidence that the masked men had shouted 'Hands up!' before shooting the constables and then making off with their rifles and the gelignite.[28] Generally, the British press separated their accounts of the ambush from the reports on the meeting of Dail Eireann. The *Manchester Guardian* reported on 24 January that the Sinn Féin leaders in Dublin were shocked by the murders in Tipperary:

> They do not talk freely to the English journalists but English people will misunderstand the situation entirely if they think that these casual and cold blooded murders form any part of the official Sinn Féin policy. On the contrary, they are utterly repudiated and detested in Harcourt Street [the Sinn Féin headquarters].[29]

To the *Manchester Guardian* correspondent the evidence suggested the killings in Tipperary were likely to have been 'a private act of assassination'. Still, he couldn't discount the possibility that the state of rebellion promoted by Sinn Féin might be taken as a licence for emulation, concluding that:

> with a so-called central authority which has repudiated all the laws of the realm, and which inferentially has invited nearly half a million electors who called it into being to defy the existing order by every means in their power, it might easily assume the form of an epidemic...[30]

Once again it was Hugh Martin who was able to point at a wider significance for the ruthless attack on the police constables. The day after the incident Martin described the police murders as the only clue to the possible future direction of events:

> They show what has been so clearly evident all along: that a central gathering of well meaning idealists such as the 'Dail Eireann' is utterly unable to control the physical-force men in the provinces. These men, as I wrote recently from Sligo, hold Dublin meetings of mere talkers about moral force in the utmost contempt. It is probably not too much to say that the coincidence of the murders with the opening of the assembly was no mere accident, but a message deliberately sent ... to the 'talking shop' in the capital. The secret movement in Ireland is forever working below the surface of the

open movement, striving to control it and force its hand. Dail Eireann, for-midable as its organisation of passive resistance may possibly prove, is less important than it looks. It has the appearance of power while the reality lies in the hands of men who hold, in the spirit of all past experience, that the salvation of Ireland is to be found in gelignite and revolvers.[31]

Gradually, over the next six months, Hugh Martin's view that the real power was in the hands of the gunmen gained credence in other British press reports. This force was represented as a relentless and disturbing threat to peace, though at the same time its agents remained shadowy and nameless; in most reports the origins of the violence were rarely subjected to scrutiny. The perception that order was breaking down was based on a series of incidents around the country and a sense of unease among the cor-respondents' informants in Dublin.

In early May the *Daily Mail*, in an article about the anger provoked in loyalist circles by the arrival of an Irish–American delegation, referred to 'the flood of sedition and disloyalty inundating the country'.[32] The previous day the *Morning Post* reported the discovery of 260 bombs buried beneath the kitchen floor of a house in Cork.[33] On 12 May the *Post*, the *Mail* and the *Daily News* all carried a news of a raid by seventy to eighty masked men on Ballyedmond Castle in Co. Down, the residence of a former officer in the Ulster Volunteer Force. The *Mail* reported that the raiders 'bound and gagged all belated wayfarers they met near the castle, to which they drove up in motor cars'.[34] It was 'beyond doubt', the *Morning Post* correspondent wrote from Belfast, that the raiders had come from the south, marking 'the first time Sinn Féiners outside Ulster have invaded the province for their nefarious work'.[35] The chief secretary himself told the House of Commons a little more than a week later that although Ireland was more prosper-ous than any other country in the world, revolutionary acts were growing steadily in force.[36]

The event that crystallised the notion that a revolution was under way was a daring raid by Irish Volunteers in May 1919. On 13 May four RIC officers were escorting a prisoner on a train from Thurles in Co. Tipperary to Cork jail when their carriage was boarded by a group of armed men at Knocklong station in Co. Tipperary. One of the constables was shot dead, another fatally wounded and the men made off with the prisoner, Sean Hogan, an associate of those who had carried out the Soloheadbeg attack in January. The *Daily Mail* reported that the scene at the station was 'terrifying' and the *Manchester Guardian* referred to 'a desperate struggle'. Both papers recounted that the men in the raiding party had worn false beards and were armed with revolvers.[37] The *Morning Post* reported that when the carriage reached Cork the bullet marks and blood splashes inside 'bore evidence of a terrible struggle'.[38]

The *Mail* quoted the complaints of an Irish nationalist newspaper that the English press was ignoring crime in Ireland because it was politically inconvenient. 'If Irish vanity is hurt, as would appear from this singular comment, it's not for want of opportunity to dilate on the increase of crime in Ireland', the *Mail* correspondent rejoined. The Knocklong raid and others like it had been denounced by priests, the *Mail* correspondent continued, but 'the extremists apparently disregard all conditions and consequences. They aim, it would seem, at creating a reign of terror.'[39] Macpherson, who only a few months before had been placing his faith in moderate Sinn Féin leaders, was so shaken by the incident at Knocklong that he told the Cabinet that it might presage a full-scale rebellion and only the dispatch of more forces to Ireland would prevent it. Significantly, he blamed the attack on 'Sinn Féiners', abandoning his previous distinction between moderates and extremists.[40]

The inquest into the deaths of the police constables at Knocklong was indicative of growing ambivalence among local people about the guerrilla campaign unfolding around them. According to an account in the *Manchester Guardian*, the jurors persisted in trying to force the surviving constables to reveal whether they had fired back at the men who attacked them on the train, a fact that would transform what had hitherto been presented as a brutal assault into a fair fight. The witnesses were instructed not to answer the question. The jurors found that the constables had been killed by persons unknown, noting that it was painful to all lovers of peace that such incidents should occur. But they declared that the British government should cease arresting respectable persons as such events caused 'bitter exasperation' among the people. They also called on the government to follow President Wilson's call for national self-determination and give Ireland its own government at once.[41]

It is from about this time – the summer of 1919 – that one can detect a growing impatience among the correspondents with the inertia of Irish policy and a steady drift towards a more adversarial portrayal of events. Partly this is expressed as exasperation with the frequency of violent incidents and the breakdown of order (not surprisingly, a tone particularly noticeable in the unionist *Morning Post*). However, there was also a growing sense that an opportunity for a settlement had been squandered, that the violence was a consequence of the British government not taking Ireland and Sinn Féin seriously. Consumed by the negotiations at the Paris Peace Conference, Lloyd George regarded Ireland as a low priority. Left to his own devices in Dublin, the Irish secretary, Ian Macpherson, was allowed to translate this inertia into a policy of refusing to engage with Sinn Féin.

This negative strategy increasingly became a target for criticism by the correspondents visiting Ireland. At the end of May the *Daily News* published a long article by Robert Lynd, the paper's assistant literary editor and a Belfast Presbyterian and nationalist. He had noticed that in some Dublin shops rosary beads were on sale stained in the Sinn Féin colours: orange, white and green. He met a foreign journalist who had come to Ireland 'to see the marks of the iron heel'. Lynd's own conclusion was that there was

> no denying that the military occupation of the country is more thorough and more threatening than it has ever been in history ... The huge policeman that you see walking in the streets of Dublin with a revolver in his belt is but an image of what is now being offered to Ireland as a substitute for freedom.[42]

However, Lynd reported that Sinn Féiners themselves were phlegmatic about coercion:

> They have a theory that whatever happens cannot but end in favour of Ireland. They seem to have a paradoxical belief that England cannot injure them without terribly injuring herself. They do not believe they could defeat the armed forces that might be sent against them but they believe that they could defeat the purpose of those who make use of the armed forces.[43]

One way to defeat the purpose of the British government was to subvert the normal attitudes of local communities in Ireland to violence. On Sunday 7 September a party of soldiers from the Shropshire Light Infantry regiment were on their way to a Wesleyan church in Fermoy, Co. Cork, carrying rifles without ammunition. As they approached the church they were attacked by a group of armed men who had driven up in cars. One soldier was shot dead, another seriously wounded. The assailants gathered up the soldiers' rifles and made off.[44] As they sped along the roads outside Fermoy, trees were felled by sympathetic local people to hinder pursuit by the police and military.[45] At the inquest into the death of the soldier killed in the raid the jury refused to describe his killing as murder; the foreman said it was their opinion 'that these men came for the purpose of getting rifles, and had no intention of killing anybody'.[46]

A few hours after this verdict some 200 soldiers from the Shropshire Light Infantry and the Royal Field Artillery regiments took to the streets of Fermoy, smashing shops and houses in the town square and two of its main streets. The jewellery shop owned by the foreman of the inquest jury was destroyed.[47] Led by an officer in mufti blowing a whistle they looted drapery stores and shoe shops: 'soldiers were seen marching back to barracks swinging boots and shoes in their hands'.[48] The troops were followed by a band of women who took some of the loot themselves.[49] This was the first military reprisal noted in the British press.

In an editorial the *Manchester Guardian* described the military riot as 'a very ugly incident, explained, but not at all excused, by the fact that it appears to have been begun as an act of retaliation'. It suggested that there was no reason to suppose that acts of violence such as the attack on the soldiers outside the church were approved by the leaders of Sinn Féin:

> It is bad enough that these acts of violence should be committed by ignorant and exasperated peasants but it is far worse when the forces which are there to represent law and order begin to take a hand in the game. Violence of course tends to breed violence and the whole wretched business goes to show how essential it is that wise and courageous statesmanship should step in to put an end alike to the cause and to the consequences of disaffection.[50]

The editor of *The Times*, Henry Wickham Steed, had already described the Cabinet's Irish policy as 'hopeless';[51] now the paper reacted to events at Fermoy with a combination of repulsion and anger. Although suggesting that the inquest jury had been intimidated into returning its hostile verdict, an editorial condemned the soldiers' riot, believing it would 'increase the feeling of disgust with which all classes here have read the recent news from Ireland'. *The Times* despaired of the government's policy:

> Are we never to get farther in Ireland than a state of deadlock, in which government negation of all policy is based upon existing disorder, and that disorder – growing by the day – can be used to justify inaction and to relegate policy to a future always more remote?[52]

The early months of 1920 saw a significant escalation in attacks by the Volunteers on the RIC. The strategy was to drive the police out of their isolated rural barracks, capture weapons and stretch their resources to breaking point. In the capital a special group of agents recruited by Michael Collins began systematically assassinating detectives of the Dublin Metropolitan Police whose job was to collect political intelligence. The Irish police – established in the mid-nineteenth century as a semi-militarised force to head off insurrection – were the most visible face of the Crown in Ireland but their role was ambiguous: they were at once 'a foreign importation' and, at the same time, a force made up overwhelmingly of Catholic Irishmen.[53] Thus, the humiliating epitaph of 'traitors' and a policy of cajoling neighbourly rejection of local police officers enabled the eventual military assault to be all the more effective. Over time the effort to soften up the RIC by turning it into a pariah force proved highly effective, fatally compromising its function as an intelligence service for Dublin Castle.

By the spring of 1920 the more daring and better organised of the Volunteer units, now equipped with their captured armoury, were prepared to undertake operations that struck at the heart of British authority in Ireland. During the last eight months of 1919 eighteen police officers were killed, and in the twelve months that followed 176 officers were killed and another 251 wounded.[54] The writer Darrell Figgis, himself a Sinn Féiner, recalled that wherever one travelled in Ireland after Easter 1920 one saw the roofless walls of burned-out police stations, sandbags still piled in the windows.[55] In August a military intelligence officer wrote to his superiors: 'Anyone passing a police barrack with its locked doors and seeing the constables looking out through barred windows will at once realise that no body of men could preserve its morale under such conditions.'[56]

The separatists matched their military achievements with political success, winning municipal elections and setting up their own courts to bypass
the official magistrates who dispensed local justice. They also managed to
establish harmonious coordination between the politicians in Dail Eireann,
a labour movement that was broadly sympathetic to nationalism, and the
Volunteers who held the guns. Significantly, it was in 1920 that the Irish
Volunteers adopted the title of the Irish Republican Army.[57]

Yet however much the rebels defined the intensifying campaign as a war,
the British government refused to do so. At a meeting with his Irish officials
in Downing Street at the end of April 1920, Lloyd George ordered that the
rebellion in Ireland be crushed whatever the cost – but without acknowledging that the government was engaged in a war. 'If there were a truce,'
he said, 'it would be an admission that we were beaten and it might lead to
our having to give up Ireland.' The viceroy, Lord French, asked the prime
minister if he would go so far as to declare war. Lloyd George replied: 'You
do not declare war against rebels.'[58] Practically, this meant the government
relied on the increasingly demoralised police force to fight the guerrillas.

Some of the support offered from London hardly inspired confidence:
the Treasury sanctioned the bulk-buying of coffins for the RIC from whole-
salers to secure a price reduction for quantity.[59] When more and more policemen buckled under the strain and resigned, the government came up
with the idea of reinforcing the RIC by recruiting an 'emergency gendarmerie' in Britain that would become a branch of the RIC.[60] The first set of
recruits immediately became known in Ireland as the Black and Tans (after
a well-known hunt in Co. Limerick) because a lack of police uniforms
forced the new recruits to combine the black RIC jackets with khaki. In
1920 a second set of former soldiers – mostly ex-officers – were recruited
as the 'Auxiliary Division' of the RIC. Though they had their own uniform
and were referred to as the 'Auxies', all recruits were most often referred to
collectively as the 'Black and Tans'.[61]

Part of the rationale for introducing English recruits with hardly any
experience of Ireland was to supersede the vulnerability of the Catholic
and Irish constables to pressure from their neighbours. Outsiders would
also be expected to have fewer constraints about being ruthless. The Black
and Tans represented 'a "stiffening" element, which implied that the reliability of the main body of the force was on a par with other colonial police

forces'.[62] Winston Churchill tried to suggest that the new recruits were an elite, declaring that they had been chosen 'from a great press of applicants on account of their intelligence, their character, and their records in the war'.[63] But F.S.L. Lyons has more dispassionately described them as

> for the most part young men who found it hard to settle down after the war, who had become used to a career of adventure and bloodshed, and who were prepared to try their luck in a new sphere for ten shillings a day all found.[64]

By the time these recruits arrived in numbers by the middle of 1920, British rule had ceased to matter in all but name in many parts of Ireland: republican guerrillas were able to do as they wished and revolutionary courts and county councils had largely succeeded in establishing a parallel government. Wresting back any semblance of control would inevitably mean using force. With the British government reluctant to accept that a state of war existed and declare martial law across Ireland, it was left to the RIC and the new gendarmerie to respond to the furtive, unexpected attacks by the guerrillas with their own brand of terror.

Despite all the signs of declining morale, the RIC maintained its discipline during the early stages of the guerrilla campaign. Robert Kee points out that, despite the significant numbers of policemen killed in this period, there was no retaliation by officers who, given an intense professional solidarity made all the more powerful by being subject to a widespread social boycott, were painfully aware of the sufferings of their colleagues.[65] Despite one isolated riot by police after the shooting of a constable in Thurles, Co. Tipperary, the telling symptoms of the corrosive effect of attacks and intimidation were increased resignations and a growing difficulty in finding new recruits.[66]

The Thurles riot might have remained an isolated case but for the arrival of the ex-servicemen from England. Contrary to Winston Churchill's rosy appraisal of their competence, the former veterans had little training and many of them had been unemployed since the end of the First World War. They had no experience of Ireland or the day-to-day routine of a rural barracks. Whatever diminishing hope an RIC constable had of drawing on his links with the local community, the newly arrived Black and Tan had none. He only confronted a hostile population and could never be sure which villager or farmer might turn out to be the gunman he would meet on a dark road. His only solace was drink. Within months the higher ranks of the RIC were despairing of the effect the new recruits were having on discipline; one officer tactfully reported that 'the character of the force is changing a good deal' under the influence of the ex-servicemen. And long after the war other RIC veterans recalled the Black and Tans as 'all English and Scotch people … very rough, f-ing and blinding and boozing and all'.[67]

There is some evidence that the Black and Tans were equally at odds with the civilian unionist population they were meant to defend from Sinn Féin. The writer Brian Inglis, in his memoir of a Protestant upbringing, described how his grandmother's distrust of the Black and Tans was greater than her distaste for Sinn Féin:

> This dislike had been shared by many of her unionist apolitical friends. At least with the rebels, their argument ran, you had known where you stood, whereas the Black and Tans, recruited by dubious methods – the riff raff of demobilised regiments, the sweepings of British jails – did not know a Unionist from a Republican and hardly bothered to make the distinction.[68]

The conflict in Ireland developed in 1920 into a pattern of tit-for-tat violence between the newly assertive volunteers and the more fiercely combative and militaristic police force. Through the work of the correspondents of the main London papers this vicious cycle of violence did not escape the notice of the British public. Coverage of this unacknowledged war of reprisals was marked by a profound shift in how the story of the troubles was construed by the British correspondents. The main threads of explanation up to then – despair over disorder, optimism about the possibility that some compromise could be reached by reasonable men on both sides and a desire for the reform of the Irish administration – were all distilled to a question of the legitimacy of the British government's methods in Ireland.

Some historians who have acknowledged this critical coverage believe it only began in response to particularly egregious acts of reprisal or after a prolonged series of incidents. Thus Jon Lawrence, writing about Ireland in the context of general perceptions of brutalisation after the Great War, asserts: 'The war in Ireland made little impact on the British public until September 1920, when a series of high profile reprisals by government forces received extensive coverage in the British press.'[69] And Peter Clarke devotes much attention to J.L. Hammond's work for the *Nation* in 1921, referring to 'his passionate exposure of British police'.[70] However, the evidence shows steadily growing disillusionment in British press coverage of Ireland that predated the arrival of the Black and Tans and was not confined to just a few reporters. It is true that, as Laurence points out, coverage of the reprisals started to make a greater impact in the autumn of 1920 but, as we have seen, British correspondents were writing about the behaviour of the security forces well before then.[71]

A useful starting point for tracing this process is the work of Hugh Martin of the *Daily News*. Well disposed towards Sinn Féin in 1919, he was convinced that there was 'every reason to believe that [they] would jump at the chance of helping to work a sound measure of Home Rule within the Empire'.[72] By late 1920 he had begun to see the Black and Tans as the enemies of any hope of accommodation. He travelled the country to report on atrocities, filling his reports with testimonies from local people and rarely mentioning the official version of events. The Irish–American journalist Francis Hackett observed Martin in the summer of 1920 interviewing the Mayor of Limerick (who was later shot in his bed). Hackett found Martin's forensic questioning 'rather trying' and described him as:

> a neat, precise, slender man in black and white with good small features but the severity of a moral accountant. His profession has taught him the need of cautiousness, but his cautiousness implied mistrust, a sort of high Liberal mistrust of the well meaning but impulsive natures with which he had to deal.[73]

General Sir Nevil Macready, commander-in-chief of British forces in Ireland, wrote to Martin's editor complaining that he seemed 'determined to get only one side of the story'.[74] Martin's work was influential among his colleagues and was frequently cited in the House of Commons by critics of the government's Irish policy. Arriving in Dublin for a lengthy reporting tour, Martin often took his cue from what was appearing in the Irish press and would travel to the scenes of the latest atrocities. This must have alarmed the authorities, for at the beginning of 1919 the Irish censor Lord Decies had advised his colleagues that 'practically every provincial correspondent for the Dublin newspapers is a Sinn Féiner' and that all of them were disposed to write up any incident of military discipline in the most unfavourable terms possible. 'This pollution of news sources will be a lasting trouble,' Decies warned prophetically.[75]

In October 1920 Martin went to investigate shootings in villages in Co. Tipperary, where two young members of the IRA had been shot dead after being dragged from their beds. Witnesses he interviewed corroborated each other's description of the assailants. One, who acted as an officer, had worn a cap and a khaki-coloured muffler tied around the lower part of his face. The others were dressed in long coats similar to those worn by the police, and soft hats. They wore 'white masks and handkerchiefs fastened so as to conceal every feature but the eyes'.[76]

Martin's reporting became heavily sarcastic about the official line. He challenged the government in London, and frequently addressed himself directly to the Irish secretary, Sir Hamar Greenwood. A report by Martin on a series of floggings of local people in Galway by the security forces began with an ironic prologue:

> By the usual methods of beleaguered governments, whether in Ireland or in Russia, a fairly complete and accurate list of active revolutionaries has been secured. With this as a chart, the police methodically set to work, more than a month ago, not as Sir Hamar Greenwood puts it, to prevent and detect crime and to arrest the criminal, but to strike terror with so savage a hand into the heart of the whole community as to force it to evacuate, so to speak, its 'bad men' ... Part of my time has been occupied with interviewing the young men whom the police have been whipping, kicking and otherwise instructing in the elements of British citizenship...[77]

Back in Dublin three days later Martin left his hotel to investigate a police raid in the street outside and was threatened by an Auxiliary cadet with a revolver.[78] In early November he went to Tralee in Co. Kerry where the police were terrorising the townspeople after two officers were kidnapped by the rebels. A notice pinned to the wall threatened 'reprisals of a nature not yet heard of in Ireland' if the kidnapped officers were not returned safely. When Martin and a colleague approached a group of policemen standing in the deserted main street of the town, they told him they were looking for a correspondent called Hugh Martin of the *Daily News* in order to kill him. Martin pretended to be another journalist from a different newspaper and escaped to Dublin.[79] News of the threat to Martin was carried by the other London papers and in the international press.[80]

Pursued in parliament, the new Irish secretary, Sir Hamar Greenwood, conceded an interview to the *News* in order to reassure the public that the government still believed in freedom of the press. Disingenuously, Greenwood declared that the government believed that what Ireland suffered from was a *lack* of publicity and argued that it was trying to help, not hinder, correspondents who wanted to disseminate the truth about the conflict.[81] In a reply published the following day, Martin absolved the British government of any responsibility for the threats made against him but his explanation could hardly have been the type of publicity that Greenwood desired. Martin wrote that the 'discipline among the forces of the Crown is so lax that a journalist who endeavours to report truthfully how those forces are behaving has not been able to do so lately without danger to his personal safety'.[82]

Martin had not been alone in putting reprisals at the centre of the debate about Ireland. Correspondents from the *Manchester Guardian* had accompanied him to scenes of random shootings of civilians, burnt out creameries, and streets of wrecked and looted shops in Sligo, Tipperary, Kerry and Longford. Accounts of the increasingly undisciplined behaviour of the Black and Tans and the Auxiliaries appeared in *The Times*. Henry Wood Nevinson also travelled the country in search of stories of atrocities. In his diary he describes coming to Dublin on a boat full of young Black and Tan recruits[83] and driving to Balbriggan where the Black and Tans had burnt down a factory and thirty-five houses.[84] The following month he toured Tipperary, Cork, Kerry and Limerick, noting wrecked creameries and talking to priests and local people (including a man who said his house had been burned down because he gave an affidavit to Hugh Martin).[85] In Co. Clare he met a niece of Matthew Arnold, the famous English cultural critic – 'very cultivated and intellectual' – who 'gave us a private lecture on reprisals as the only means of avenging murders since law will not work'.[86]

Collectively, the correspondents resisted attempts by the government to portray them as dupes of Sinn Féin propaganda. A *Manchester Guardian* editorial celebrated the British correspondents in Ireland as the sole purveyors of truth:

The correspondents of the English newspapers are neither terrorised nor misled nor corrupted. They have furnished the most trustworthy and the only trustworthy account of the horrible condition into which the Government has allowed Ireland to sink. With Sinn Féin issuing propaganda on the one hand and Dublin Castle on the other, they are the only means of enlightenment that the public have and the only means by which, if at all, the Government can be forced to do its duty.[87]

The editor of the *Guardian*, C.P. Scott, had long stood for a form of patriotism that embraced a willingness to criticise the state or the government of the day. During the Boer War, Scott was as much perturbed by the threat posed to free speech by jingoism as by the conduct of the campaign against the Boers.[88] This position made Scott and his colleagues even more scrupulous about giving an honest, factual portrayal of events:

since the *Guardian*'s opposition to the war hinged as much on the threat war posed to public discussion as on the immorality of the war itself, it could not afford to compromise the 'sacred' nature of the 'facts' upon which discussion was based.[89]

Thus the editorial defending all British correspondents in Ireland can be similarly read as an attempt to assert the authority of public opinion to judge events. But it is more than that; it is a restatement of the classical liberal theory of the press, with the journalist cast as a beacon of enlightenment in a murky sea of competing claims. How different this is from Sir Edward Cook's appraisal of the press during the Great War as the ever-willing propagator of official policy and a crucial force for sustaining morale. Critical coverage of the campaign in Ireland provided an opportunity for the most prestigious organs of the British press to rally around the myth of their own tainted heroism.

As he prepared to return to London on the eve of Armistice Day, Hugh Martin reflected on how he had arrived in Ireland a few months earlier intensely sceptical about stories of reprisals coming from Irish sources:

Three months ago, the word 'reprisals' merely recalled the later stages of the Great War. Today, to the whole of the English-speaking world it means one thing and one thing only – the method by which Great Britain is waging war upon Ireland. It has been my duty to watch at close quarters the un-folding of this drama … And now as I leave the theatre for a little while to share in my own country's celebration of the victory of the idea of freedom, what else can I, as an Englishman, do except bow my head in shame?[90]

Martin's feelings of mortification arose from how the war in Ireland un-dermined his sense that Britain stood for justice and fair play. The idea that the British government was betraying its own ideals in coercing Ireland is repeatedly evoked by other journalists in reportage and commentary from this period. Mark Hampton has noted a similar theme in the *Manchester Guardian's* coverage of the Boer War: 'the desirability of fighting the war in accordance with traditional English notions of honour and decency'.[91] These ideas had acquired even greater force by the time of the Irish rebel-lion because Britain had itself defined the war against Germany as a struggle between civilisation and barbarism, morality and militarism.

The proof of this thesis for British propagandists was provided by the outrages committed by the German army during its occupation of Bel-gium. The official British report on German atrocities in Belgium, written by Lord Bryce, was translated into ten languages and thousands of copies were circulated around the world.[92] Based mostly on testimony transcribed from interviews with Belgian refugees, Bryce's report concluded that Ger-man troops had used terror as a tool of warfare against Belgian civilians. It held German soldiers responsible for using civilians as human shields in combat, raping women and – most notoriously – cutting off the heads of babies and the hands of children. Until then it had been assumed that Eu-ropean armies would never stoop to the cruelties considered unique to the methods of warfare deployed by inferior nations.[93] Revulsion at the terror-ism described in the Bryce report 'gave voice to a radical idea, that warring nations could not break the law with impunity and must pay'.[94]

At the end of the war the British attorney general, Lord Birkenhead, stressed 'the importance of using British standards to judge German war criminals'.[95] Thus, the rhetoric of universal idealism deployed to distin-guish British civility from Germany inhumanity during the First World War rebounded twice over against British policy in Ireland. First, it became a powerful touchstone for judging the British government and a ready point of ironic comparison for journalists describing the suppression of the guerrilla campaign. And it also created expectations that it was right to hold violators of the honourable norms of warfare to account and seek sanction against them in international law. As Philip Gibbs reflected, 'civil law was abolished in Ireland, at a time when English idealists were pleading for its extension to international affairs as a nobler method of argument than that of war'.[96]

Germany had justified its methods rather than concealed them: *schreck-lichkeit*, or 'frightfulness', was openly proclaimed as official policy in the parts of Belgium under the control of the Kaiser's army.[97] The word became synonymous with barbaric cruelty, and it crops up repeatedly in the reports from Ireland of the activities of the Black and Tans, accompanied by the highly charged label 'Prussian'.[98] In his book about the war in Ireland Hugh Martin describes Lloyd George's policy as 'Potsdam ruthlessness'.[99] The dangers of 'Prussianism' appearing in Britain had been raised by liberal commentators several years earlier during the First World War. In *Questions of Peace and War*, published in 1916, L.T. Hobhouse predicted that 'the self-contained, disciplined, military State is the political entity of the coming future'.[100] And the introduction of conscription in 1918 appeared to J.A. Hobson as 'the kernel of the system of Prussianism which was being established'.[101] It was Ireland that provided tangible evidence to support these auguries.

A curious feature of the reporting from Ireland was the uncertainty among the correspondents about how to view the agents of the policy they identified as a strain of Germanic 'frightfulness'. Save for hostile exchanges like those described by Hugh Martin there were few interviews with the ordinary ex-servicemen who made up the regular Black and Tans or the ex-officers of the Auxiliary Division. British ministers defended these men as the heroes of the Western Front and, at first, critics avoided questioning their characters, instead blaming the government for encouraging them to carry out reprisals.[102] Later, when their deeds had become notorious, even the house journal of the Milner imperialists, the *Round Table*, was describing them as 'soldiers of fortune … fitted for little but fighting'.[103]

Certainly the correspondents treated them with extreme wariness. For Henry Wood Nevinson, distaste was leavened with class prejudice. He recorded how he was pleased to hear from officers in the regular British army in Ireland that they refused to accept that most of the Auxiliaries had ever been officers at all and he himself concurred, offering that 'neither the accent of many among them, nor their language, nor their conduct, is such as I have been accustomed to among officers during my thirty-five years' knowledge of the British Army'.[104] But for one of the *Manchester Guardian*'s correspondents, Donald Boyd, these men were merely more damaged versions of every man who had endured the nightmare of the trenches: 'One of the wretched things was that the Auxiliaries were men like ourselves, who had just come out of the war ... They weren't strangers; they were ourselves askew.'[105]

Just as coverage of the Black and Tans peaked in the autumn of 1920, two dramatic episodes of the war were enacted in part as spectacles on the streets of London, literally bringing the conflict home to a British audience. The first of these was the death on 24 October 1920 of the Lord Mayor of Cork, Terence McSwiney, a leading republican who had been on hunger strike for seventy-four days in protest against the establishment of military courts under the Restoration of Ireland Act. McSwiney's death occurred in Brixton Prison and his funeral, which entailed his body being carried in a procession through London to Euston Station for its return to Ireland, brought the charged emotion of a distant conflict to the central streets of the metropolis. Crowds gathered on the footpaths as the procession passed. A correspondent for the *Manchester Guardian* remarked how 'the intensity of expression of the mourners struck everyone' present.[106] For many, the *Guardian* reported, it was the first time they had seen the Sinn Féin flags of green, white and orange. Nevertheless, the correspondent noted, the attitude of the crowd was one of deep respect even among those who had been condemning the dead Lord Mayor.[107] Elsewhere in the paper, in a regular, informal column called 'Our London Correspondence', a writer reflected on how the procession had caused 'a good deal of wonder' among the many foreign correspondents who had come to London to watch it:

> The circumstances were very extraordinary and it is difficult to imagine a parallel of them in any other country. The Lord Mayor of Cork was an officer of the Irish Republic, which declared itself at war with England. Here was all the assistance of the police and the city authorities to carry through a great demonstration, with rebel flags and rebel uniforms and the whole greeted with respect by the English people. [108]

Describing the procession in the *Daily News*, Robert Lynd noted that McSwiney's funeral in London had all the appearance of the funeral of a prince: 'Hawkers in the street with Cockney voices were selling mourning cards with prayers for the dead man's soul, paper handkerchiefs with a programme for the day's events, green flags with gold harps and Republican rosettes.'[109] For Lynd, Terence McSwiney's funeral was an animated history lesson that was absorbed eagerly by the crowds that lined the streets of London:

> The windows along the route were filled with work-girls, photographers, families and their friends … for the most part it was a silent crowd – a crowd a little bewildered perhaps at finding itself the spectator of a chapter of history. London, I think, learned more Irish history yesterday than it had ever learned before. Only half-learned it perhaps. But it bared its head before the tragedy of it. The funeral that London saw yesterday was no isolated or rare event. It is a funeral that is being repeated in Irish town after Irish town and in Irish village after Irish village … What London saw yesterday is an image of all Ireland.[110]

The second event that impressed the British mind with the horror of the Irish conflict concerned the deaths of young men closer to home. On 21 November 1920 the IRA carried out one of the most ruthless operations of its campaign when eleven British officers identified by the IRA Chief of Staff Michael Collins as intelligence agents were assassinated in a couple of hours on a Sunday morning in central Dublin. Some of the officers were shot as they awoke from sleep in the presence of their wives.[111] For British correspondents used to reporting the deaths of Irish policemen, the swift and brutal extension of casualties to their own countrymen was shocking. The *Daily News* described the assassinations as 'the worst massacre of British officers since the India mutiny'.[112] The *Morning Post* was driven to link the Irish rebellion with the triumph of Bolshevism in Russia, concluding in an editorial that the future of civilisation itself was threatened by the IRA and that unless the rebels were crushed their example would be copied elsewhere:

> in all parts of the Empire conspirators are watching the drama of Ireland and waiting for the sign which will definitely tell them that they can rig up the curtain with confidence and call the world's attention to their stage.[113]

The accounts of the funeral of the officers shot in Dublin betray an acute sense of perplexed horror at what the conflict in Ireland was coming to mean for Britain. The *Manchester Guardian* described the cortege in Dublin as 'the strangest of funeral processions':

> All the solemn ceremony that the army has evolved for the honouring of its dead was observed, yet the troops moved in a formation that might have been appropriate during a march through an enemy country. Before the real procession came in sight one saw first a patrol of six steel-helmeted soldiers who carried rifles at the trail, then an armoured car with machine-guns peering from its turrets ... Great crowds assembled along both banks of the river and on the bridges. They were reverent and quiet ... one failed to observe any man who did not take off his hat and stay uncovered until the gun-carriages had passed. From other sources one hears that it was not like that everywhere and that a great many hats and caps were forcibly removed from the heads of their wearers by Auxiliaries and thrown into the Liffey.[114]

The writing repeatedly points to a disconcerting untrustworthiness in the visual evidence: the 'solemn procession' turns out to be a dangerous march; loyal Ireland is revealed as 'an enemy country'; the reverent crowd is silent but pointedly disrespectful. This is a remarkable passage, describing a scene that could have been cinematically arranged to provide a snapshot of historical change.

This sense of dissonance is also present in two accounts of the same funeral procession, from when it arrived in London en route to Westminster Abbey. *The Times* reported that the massed bands of the Irish Guards occupied the centre of the procession

> but not their music nor the crepe-bound colours so sharply stirred the crowds in the street, perhaps, as did the presence in the *cortege* of a detachment of Auxiliary RIC, the 'Black and Tans'. They wore khaki uniforms with black or khaki Balmorals and all were heavily armed. Near them marched men of the RIC carrying sidearms outside their long black overcoats.[115]

In Westminster Abbey another *Times* correspondent noted that 'a stir of bewilderment passed through the congregation who saw marching upwards from the west door a body of armed men in a dark uniform strange to London':

For a moment a corner of the veil of mystery that covers Ireland was lifted: these grim-featured carbineers were not soldiers but policemen of the civil garrison which Great Britain maintains in Ireland, the Royal Irish Constabulary. These were the men whom the tragedies of the last two years have made famous, the stern instruments of justice, and the immediate victims of revenge.[116]

The *Morning Post* correspondent also noticed the impression made by the 'grim-featured carbineers' from Ireland:

Extreme interest was aroused by firing parties of the 'Black and Tans' and the Royal Irish Constabulary; for who could resist the thought that every man of them is fighting, with imminent peril by day and night, the battle in which so many gallant gentlemen fell last Sunday? … Young men and men a trifle older, wearing officers' khaki uniform, black 'Kilmarnock bonnets', armed with rifles, bandoliers round their chest, and heavy revolvers slung from the waist, they looked a determined and fearless band, very adequate for the grim work on which they are engaged.[117]

For the correspondents and the general public the appearance of these bizarre figures in London was fascinating and horrifying in equal measure. Their reaction was heavy with a foreboding that the war in Ireland would have more profound consequences for England than had yet been imagined.

# IV
# SEEING THE SUN AT NOON:
# THE CRUSADING PRESS
# RESTORED

*What need have we of witnesses? The* Daily News, *the* Manchester Guardian, The Times, *and all the anti-Coalition papers are publishing enough news of burnings and slaughterings to make Timour the Tarter turn in his grave ... But no: everybody prefers to go on screaming and clamouring for more telescopes to enable the English (entrusted as Asquith says, by Providence with the duty of governessing Ireland) to see the sun at noon.*

George Bernard Shaw in a letter to Lady Gregory,
6 November 1920[1]

The ceaseless coverage of the reprisals in the latter half of 1920 gradually put the government in London on the defensive. Lloyd George and Irish Secretary Sir Hamar Greenwood spent much of their time in the House of Commons unconvincingly deflecting inquiries from a small but persistent band of MPs about Black and Tan atrocities – questions informed by the detailed dispatches from rural Ireland in the London papers. One way of tracing how the correspondents were able to influence the political argument is to follow the debates in the House of Commons where the government was held directly accountable for its policy in Ireland.

The coalition government established by Lloyd George dominated the Commons; independent liberals – whose figurehead was the former Prime Minister, Herbert Asquith – had only twenty-six seats. And although the rest of the opposition was composed of fifty-nine Labour MPs, the Coalition was in no danger of being defeated in a vote. However, the absence of a threat to losing its majority was offset by the energy and sense of purpose with which the government's critics attacked its Irish policy. As we shall see, much of the evidence that made these questions embarrassing for the government came from the reports of the British correspondents in the London press, as well as from a knowledge of what was being published in European newspapers. This often led to explicit criticism of the journalists by government spokesmen and the widening of the debate on Irish policy to include a dispute over the veracity of the press. Beyond this, the terms in which the government's opponents expressed their critique of Irish policy echoed the interpretation of the newspaper correspondents: namely, that the tactics being used to combat the insurgency in Ireland were a significant departure from the standards of British political morality.

'Reprisals' became a major political issue in Britain in the autumn of 1920, largely because of the coverage of the activities of the Black and Tans and the Auxiliaries in the British press. The word appears for the first time in the index to Hansard in Volume 133, covering the period from August to October. Up to then there had already been several revenge attacks by British forces on civilian targets, many of them described in the pages of the British press. One incident in the town of Balbriggan, about twenty miles north of Dublin, crystallised outrage over these assaults. Following the fatal shooting of two local officers from the RIC, their comrades took revenge by killing two local Sinn Féin leaders and burning property, including a hosiery factory, which was the town's main source of local employment. An editorial in the *Manchester Guardian* likened the destruction in Balbriggan to the sacking of the Belgian town of Louvain by German forces during the First World War.[2] A month later, Herbert Asquith made the same comparison in the House of Commons.[3] This was an early example of how the interpretations of the newspaper correspondents in Ireland made their way into political debate in London (although, as the use of the term 'Prussianism' shows, this popularisation of conceits was circular). Indeed, many of the debates about the Black and Tans in parliament turn on whether the information in the public domain was trustworthy and whether the portrayal of the war in Ireland offered by the correspondents – both from Britain, the USA and Europe – could be believed.

Over a period of months criticism of the government's policy was pressed by the same handful of MPs: Asquithian Liberals, 'high-minded Tory aristocrats'[4] and the few remaining Irish nationalists in Westminster. Each group had its own motivations and interests (which sometimes overlapped) but what is striking is the extent to which these MPs relied on the reports of the newspaper correspondents in Ireland for the evidence they used to argue their case against the government. A typical exchange took place in the Commons on 25 October 1920, when Hamar Greenwood was asked by T.P. O'Connor, the Irish Nationalist MP for Liverpool

> whether in view of the statements of the English correspondents in Ireland of responsible English journals that they themselves saw convincing evidence of the wounding and flogging of men in the villages in the West of Ireland by officers of the Crown, the Right. Hon. Gentleman persists in the denial that such outrages have occurred.[5]

When Greenwood protested that there was not enough time to answer the question another Nationalist MP from Belfast, Joe Devlin, interjected: 'Did you not see it in this morning's papers? It could have been read there.'[6] After complaining about the difficulty of gathering official information, Greenwood declared that he had 'no convincing evidence of the flogging and wounding of several men in the West of Ireland' and concluded: 'I believe the world is horrified at the murders of policemen and soldiers in

Ireland and I do not believe the world accepts the malignant untruths suggested in the question.'[7] The following exchange then took place:

> *Devlin:* Does the Right Hon. Gentleman assert that the representatives of the *Manchester Guardian, The Times* and other English newspapers are enemies of the British Empire?
>
> *Greenwood:* I do not say it and I do not assert it.
>
> *Mr Devlin:* May I ask if the Right Hon. Gentleman is aware that clear, precise and specific charges of this character have been made by these English representatives of the great English journals and they have been published in this country; therefore if he states that all who make these charges are enemies of the British Empire, does he declare that these gentlemen are enemies of the British Empire?
>
> *Greenwood:* I have answered that.[8]

Throughout the debates on reprisals the press reports were cited by critics of the government as an independent source of information; by relying on what the newspapers were publishing about Ireland these critics were advertising their own lack of partisanship. Joe Devlin – the only MP representing an Irish constituency who regularly spoke in parliament – often presented himself as a neutral, speaking against the powerful state on behalf of those who found themselves caught between the two sides in the Irish conflict. He accused Greenwood of waging war on innocent men: 'You make the lives of non-combatants impossible. It is for these people that I plead and who I am here to defend.'[9] Devlin argued that having recourse to the reports in the British press further bolstered his claim to impartiality. He countered Greenwood's dismissal of his statement that the town of Templemore in County Tipperary had been wrecked, by pointing out: 'Of course, I get my information from English papers. I am not in touch with Sinn Féin.'[10]

An argument stressing the independence of the press also underpinned Asquith's contribution to the debate on 24 November 1920, to discuss the events of Bloody Sunday (three days earlier). Asquith concentrated on tracing the accumulation of evidence over the previous few months that pointed to the activities of the police in Ireland being sanctioned by an unacknowledged reprisals policy. In Asquith's terms, the detail in the charge sheet against the government was provided by the journalists' depiction of the Black and Tans. He exalted the foreign correspondents who had gone to Ireland – and not only those from Britain – as a source of untainted truth:

> We have evidence, not from Sinn Féin sources, or anybody connected with that movement but of a vast body of absolutely independent, impartial [men], representing the great organs of the Press not only of this country but of America, France and other parts of the civilised world … who, without any prepossession or prejudices were sent there (HON MEMBERS: 'Hear, hear!') … We have the evidence of these men who have been on the spot, and who are thoroughly qualified by experience, as well as by honesty and judgment, not to distort the facts.[11]

Similarly, T.P. O'Connor held up the press as the only way of penetrating the deceit of the government: 'We have one last refuge against the conspiracy of silence, of evasion with regard to these events in Ireland.'[12] He was full of praise for Hugh Martin in particular, describing him as 'one of the most admirable and able journalists we have today' and declared: 'Ireland owes to him, as to many another English journalist and English politician, a debt of gratitude which she can never adequately repay.' It was Martin who had exposed the conduct of the British forces in Ireland and the policy of reprisals that Hamar Greenwood and the British government had refused to acknowledge:

> The Chief Secretary, in that Garden of Eden innocence, in that role of young and maidenly innocence in which he poses … knows nothing about the destruction of creameries. Mr Hugh Martin tells us all about it. He knows nothing about the execution of men by the Black-and-Tans. Mr Hugh Martin tells us all about it. He is one of the men who have held up the liberty of Ireland and the honour of England and of the English Press to which he belongs.[13]

The threats against Martin described in the previous chapter were raised in the Commons by the Liberal MP, Lt Commander J.N. Kenworthy, who asked Hamar Greenwood if he would 'give immediate orders that in no circumstances are any journalists in Ireland, British or foreign, to be attacked or punished by the police except under due process of law'. Greenwood replied that he had no information about the threat Martin had reported but promised that the government would 'take every step in their [*sic*] power to prevent any attack on any journalist in Ireland', adding that 'Ireland is the freest country in the world – for journalists'.[14] When pressed by other MPs about Martin's case, Greenwood expressed surprise that any reporter in Ireland should believe himself to be in danger, noting acerbically that 'it is not an unpopular thing in Ireland to pretend to be in danger, and, therefore, become a hero'.[15] Greenwood insisted that Martin was secure in Ireland no matter how controversial his reports:

> I can assure Mr Hugh Martin that he can sleep every night in any bed he likes in Ireland. He said mean and inaccurate things of the police, but they will stand guard over him, and they will let him say what he likes about them. He is as safe in Ireland as he would be in Fleet Street, no matter what he says; and Mr Martin or any other pressman will be welcome to Ireland, whatever his own political views on the policy or views of the paper he represents.[16]

What is significant about this passage is how Greenwood tried to undermine Martin's authority by implicitly denying that anything he had published was a fact. Martin, according to Greenwood, said 'mean and inaccurate things' about the police. Thus his writings expressed *opinions*, which did not demand contestation or refutation as facts would; they might be irritating or annoying but the police 'will let him say what he likes about them'. Here Greenwood was asserting that the reporting from Ireland – far from being a reflection of reality – was merely a political *argument* advanced by those opposed to the government or by journalists whose work was, of necessity, dictated by the politics of their newspapers.

This line of attack was potentially damaging because, at this time, the provision of untainted information and the affirmation of formal independence from political parties was an essential feature of newspapers' claim to legitimacy in the political arena.[17] And indeed, as we have seen, this was the basis for the authority the government's parliamentary critics attached to the newspaper accounts of reprisals. Greenwood tried to advance his case even further by suggesting that the journalists reporting from Ireland were not just giving vent to anti-government *views* (either their own or those of their proprietors) in place of collecting *facts*: they were also prepared to have their scripts written for them by Sinn Féin.

Greenwood introduced this charge during a debate on a censure motion proposed by the Labour Party in October 1920. He asserted that a minority of British newspapers were prepared to accept the word of the Sinn Féin propagandists who said 'everything that can be said, regardless of fact, to besmirch the name of the United Kingdom and of the British Empire and to besmirch the names of loyal servants of the Crown…'.[18] Other journalists – presumably more hostile towards the rebels – had had their lives threatened and had been forced to leave Ireland (although when pressed the chief secretary could not supply the House with their names).[19]

In November Greenwood returned to this theme: '[The Sinn Féin propagandist] has a most elaborate system of dealing with pressmen. He goes so far as actually to prepare what he likes them to say, and hands it out to them.'[20] This formulation, expressed as if it were a revelation, depends for its impact on the presentation of Sinn Féin's dealings with the press as a departure from the norm, as if journalists had never been used like this before. In fact, it sought to exploit the post-war disillusion with propaganda on the principle that 'those with purposes produce propaganda; those whose only purpose is to reflect reality produce news'.[21] Later in November, responding to Asquith's encomium for the correspondents in Ireland, Greenwood combines his charge that they are merely peddling their own opinions with the accusation that the correspondents' dispatches were being elaborated with the help of Sinn Féin. The chief secretary directly challenged Asquith's assertion that the journalists were honest recorders of the facts. He argued that – especially in the case of the Americans – the reporters were the puppets of Sinn Féin:

> I do not look [favourably] upon the opinions of certain American correspondents who, enjoying the hospitality of the murder gang itself in Ireland, traversed that country and sent their newspaper matter to America to weaken the Anglo-American friendship that happily exists, and to do their best to condemn the British Empire.[22]

Accounts of reprisals in the press had only the appearance of being a narrative of facts, according to Greenwood; these dispatches were tendentious, often sent from remote areas of Ireland where the veracity of their detail was beyond scrutiny:

It is when you get a murder in the far West of Ireland, from which a correspondent can send the news that suits his paper – [HON. MEMBERS:
'No!'] Yes, that is the usual case on which a reprisal charge is founded.[23]

Yet for all his denunciation of the press, Greenwood was never able to act
on his criticisms. He could accuse Hugh Martin of being biased and untrust-
worthy and even of contriving his own notoriety by claiming that his life
was endangered. However, the chief secretary was constrained from barring
Martin from visiting Ireland or from subjecting him to the same censorship
as Irish newspapers. On the contrary, such was the contemporary esteem for
publicity among politicians that Greenwood – at the very same time as he
denounced reports of reprisals as mere fabrications – had to present himself
as a friend of the press. Thus the chief secretary protested that

I have myself gone out of my way to provide motor cars and facilities of every kind for the Press of all parts of the world to see Ireland as it is, because
I believe … the more publicity Ireland gets from people who visit it, the
stronger and more united will be the support, not only of this country but
of civilisation, behind the British Government.[24]

The disingenuousness of Greenwood's pleading that the government
welcomed honest reporting of events in Ireland was pinpointed by Lord
Robert Cecil, a Tory. 'In the minds of some Hon. Members,' Cecil argued, 'there is no such thing as a reputable newspaper unless it supports the
Government.' He noted reports in reputable papers that reprisals had been
authorised by ministers. Cecil observed that, despite the Irish secretary's
fulminations about the coverage from Ireland, there was no sign of any
challenge by the government to the facts appearing in the press; instead
'speech after speech is delivered by Ministers of the Crown and there is no
denial'.[25]

Of course, Greenwood knew that the Black and Tans were committing
reprisals but he could not stop or control the coverage of the war in Ireland
by British and international correspondents. He could only try to discredit
the reporters, a strategy undermined from the beginning by the simultane-
ous enthusiasm with which he welcomed publicity – and further weakened
by the sheer volume of articles describing reprisals. Greenwood's uncomfortable dilemma was highlighted by a question put by the Labour MP, J.R.

Clynes. If the government could prove that the reporters were distorting the facts, he asked, why did it not submit events in Ireland to an impartial inquiry by members of the political establishment?

> I marvel at the light-hearted way in which the Chief Secretary reproved the journalists of this and other countries. What purpose can these men have to serve other than that of going to Ireland and reporting the facts that they see? Is there any journalist representing a newspaper on the side of the Government who could materially dispute, or who has attempted to disprove, any of these statements made by representatives of papers which happen to be opposed to the Government? The fact that these crimes have taken place, that civilians have been killed, that property has been destroyed and burned, has attracted to Ireland correspondents from various parts of the world, and, without wishing to do any damage to our reputation or the level of our credit, these men have told the truth.[26]

The government failed to impugn the integrity of the correspondents or discredit the deployment of their dispatches in parliament to condemn its Irish policy. The sheer weight of the press interest in Ireland, not just from Britain but from the rest of the empire, the USA and Europe, created a stream of bad publicity that none of Greenwood's evasions and denunciations could counter. In February 1921, when Captain Anthony Wedgwood Benn moved a motion declaring that the government's Irish policy had failed and 'involved the officers and servants of the Crown in a competition in crime with the offenders against the law' he could cite the continuing bad publicity for British conduct just as Asquith had three months previously.[27] Wedgwood Benn surmised that American sympathy was beyond retrieval and continued:

> In France the newspapers are full of Ireland. I could quote statements of newspapers of very different opinions all condemning the Irish administration. In Italy every paper is full of news from Ireland, with pictures of the happenings there and accounts of the anarchy and disorder.[28]

The Independent Liberal, J.N. Hogge, noted that the journalists were defining how history would regard the period: 'The facts are being recorded under one headline, "The Irish Revolution".'[29]

Hamar Greenwood, as the parliamentary defender of the government's Irish policy, could affect a weary nonchalance when confronted with the supposed calumnies of the press. However, behind the scenes the Cabinet was anything but indifferent towards the correspondents' reports. In July 1920 Austen Chamberlain wrote to his sister after a Cabinet discussion on Ireland, which he found 'puzzling and most distressing'. He worried about the resolve of his colleagues: 'A sensational Press upsets their nerves & makes them impatient, first clamorous for stern measures & then screams itself into hysterics when it sees what stern measures mean in practice.'[30]

There is plenty of evidence in the Cabinet minutes of this acute sensitivity to the press coverage of Ireland. On 13 August 1920, the minutes recorded that 'support for strong measures would be required to put down ... the extremists' but worries were expressed that 'there might come a point when public opinion would desert the Government'.[31] Later that month, according to Thomas Jones, the then Irish minister, Edward Shortt made a case for releasing the Lord Mayor of Cork Terence McSwiney from Brixton Prison, partly on the grounds that 'practically the whole press' supported his release and that this represented public opinion.[32]

What is really significant is how what was appearing in the press about Ireland affected those pushing for a hard line as much as those seeking a compromise with Sinn Féin. The Chief of the Imperial General Staff, Field Marshall Sir Henry Wilson – an Irishman and intransigent Unionist – was not someone easily moved to haunting doubt by anti-militarist sentiment. He had little sympathy for civilian scruples, contemptuously referred to politicians as 'frocks' and lampooned the premise of the Versailles treaty as, 'All "Peoples" love each other, therefore have a League of Nations'.[33] However, on Ireland throughout 1920 – as the British correspondents served up stories of atrocities and outrages committed by the Crown forces – Wilson's relationship with Lloyd George became increasingly strained because of his opposition to encouraging or at least ignoring unauthorised reprisals. Wilson noted in his diary:

[the Prime Minister's] amazing theory that someone was murdering two Sinn Féiners to every loyalist the Sinn Féiners murdered ... he seemed to be satisfied that a counter-murder association was the best answer to Sinn Féin murders. A crude idea of statesmanship, he will have a rude awakening.[34]

On 29 September he wrote:

> I had one and a half hours this evening with Lloyd George and Bonar Law.
> I told them what I thought of reprisals by the 'Black and Tans' and how
> this must lead to chaos and ruin. Lloyd George danced about and was
> angry but I never budged. I pointed out that these reprisals were carried
> out without anyone being responsible; men were murdered, houses burnt,
> villages wrecked ... I said that this was due to want of discipline, and this
> *must* be stopped. It was the business of the government to govern. If these
> men ought to be murdered, then the Government ought to murder them.
> Lloyd George danced at this, said no Government could possibly take this
> responsibility.[35]

The striking feature of Wilson's opposition to reprisals is his sense that
they were futile because people in Britain were either ignorant of the strategy or opposed to it. In August, Wilson recorded in his diary that he had
had a visit from Lord Riddell, the proprietor of the *News of the World*,
who asked what message he should give to his three-and-a-half million
readers:

> I replied, 'Let the Cabinet give up whispering in 10 Downing Street and
> come into the open. Let them hoist the flag of England and rally England
> round them. With the English behind us there is nothing we can't do, and
> without England there is nothing we can do.'[36]

A month earlier he had – according to his diary – told a confidant that

> if he [Wilson] was in the House of Commons he would march down to
> Lloyd George and say: 'You have two courses open to you. One is to clear
> out of Ireland and the other is to knock Sinn Féin on the head. But before
> you do this latter you must have England on your side, and therefore you
> must go stumping the country explaining what Sinn Féin means.'[37]

In early 1921 H.A.L. Fisher warned his Cabinet colleagues that the
longer the war went on, 'the more certain does it become that great bod-
ies of opinion in this Country will swing over to the Republican side'.[38]
By May, during a discussion of a possible truce, Churchill – the original
champion of the Black and Tans – was advising that it was 'of great public
importance to get a respite in Ireland' because the news from there was

damaging 'the interests of this country all over the world; we are getting an odious reputation; poisoning our relations with the United States...'.[39] Fisher himself now estimated that the war was 'degrading to the moral life of the whole country' and even Balfour, arguing against concessions to Sinn Féin, accepted that 'naturally we should wish to end this uphill, sordid, unchivalrous, loathsome conflict – we are sick of it'.[40] Lloyd George agreed that 'the country is a little unhappy. That is because nobody is informing the country.'[41] However, as we know, the press *was* informing the country, though not in the way Lloyd George would have wished.

The concern about press coverage – both in parliament and around the Cabinet table – was not just a function of Lloyd George's well-attested obsession with publicity. Both contemporary observers and historians since have argued that the First World War, aside from placing a premium on propaganda, allowed the press at the same time to become a powerful voice in parliamentary politics because of the wartime consensus between the major parties. The press was credited with helping to engineer the down-fall of Asquith in 1915 with 'editors and leader-writers ... unusually well placed not only to catch and reflect, but indeed create, a widespread mood of dissatisfaction with the existing order of things, government above all'.[42] Some contemporaries argued that it was 'government by journalism', with the press becoming 'a substitute for parliament'.[43]

The elaboration of this argument depends on dissecting the intimate relationships between proprietors, editors and politicians in 'the concentric circles of political society'.[44] However, in the case of the Irish revolution it makes more sense to pay attention to the work of the journalists who had gone to Ireland than to the king-making manoeuvres of press barons in Westminster or the pursuit of high politics at Whitehall dinner parties. It was the reports written by these correspondents – rather than the represen-tations made by proprietors – that unsettled the politicians in London.

It was not just reporting from Ireland that was having an impact on parliament and the Cabinet. Newspaper coverage of other parts of the empire was already been carefully studied in Whitehall. In her study of how the British government tried to manage the news from India, Chan-drika Kaul found that, by the early twentieth century, the press was the primary source of knowledge about the empire for most people in Britain: 'The influence of the quality papers on the decision-making elite, as well as the popular press on more general readers, helped to create the climate of opinion within which Parliament and Government functioned.'[45] Just as Hamar Greenwood felt he must publicly encourage journalists to visit Ireland (even though he despised their critical coverage), the secretary of state for India, Edwin Montagu, identified the provision of facilities to help the press obtain news as one of his departmental priorities.

Chandrika Kaul points out that 'for Montagu, a Government, even an imperial one, could not govern without explanation and needed to promote its policies through active publicity'.[46] She characterises parliamentary and press opinion on India as 'interdependent', a diagnosis which could easily describe the relationship outlined earlier between parliament and the press coverage from Ireland.[47] With party structures weakened during the war and no strong parliamentary counterweight to Lloyd George's coalition, it was no surprise that the correspondents in Ireland were enlisted by the government's critics. At the time, the absence of a major opposition party in the House of Commons was noted by the American political scientist A.B. Lowell. He cited the government's Irish policy as an example of what he called an 'atrophied' public opinion: without an alternative governing party to oppose the government '[the] English people were in somewhat the position of a jury without counsel to present the evidence in systematic order and argue their respective sides of the case'.[48] It was the correspondents in Ireland, through their newspapers, who stepped into this role initially.[49]

On the surface, British newspaper correspondents made unlikely critics of the government coercion in Ireland. As we have seen already, the reputation of the press was low in 1918 after its willing collaboration with government propaganda during the First World War. H.G. Wells summed up a widespread view when he wrote in 1921 that 'there has been a considerable increase of deliberate lying in the British press since 1914, and a marked loss of journalistic self-respect … a considerable proportion of the [news] is rephrased and mutilated to give a misleading impression to the reader'.[50] We have seen how the government depended on the cooperation of the press during the war. This was clearly a case of where the press became collectively, in Philip Elliott's phrase, the 'self-appointed script writer to the national morale'.[51] Why was it that the press did not perform similarly in the case of Ireland?

The key difference was that, although there was no large and effective opposition in the House of Commons, the British political elite were deeply split over the future of Ireland. During the four years of the Great War there had been public agreement among the major political parties on the principle of fighting Germany. Given the symbiotic relationship between journalism and politics these different circumstances would have a profound effect on the capability of journalists to express dissent. In his study of the American media during the Vietnam War, Daniel Hallin found that journalists were acutely sensitive to the state of debate among politicians in Washington. He concluded:

> In situations where political consensus seems to prevail journalists tend to act as 'responsible' members of the political establishment, upholding the dominant political perspective and passing on more or less at face value the views of the authorities assumed to represent the nation as a whole. In situations of political conflict, they become more detached or adversarial, though they normally will stay well within the bounds of the debate going on within the political 'establishment' and will continue to grant a privileged hearing, particularly to senior officials of the executive branch.[52]

This insight is wholly applicable to the British press coverage of the Irish revolution. As we have seen, in parliament and public debate, Lloyd George's Irish policy was assailed by Tory dissenters, the Labour Party and not least Asquith, who, in Peter Clarke's phrase, spoke with 'the authority of the premiership'.[53] In the Cabinet, some ministers were even arguing that Sinn Féin had the moral support of the Irish people.[54]

Crucially, these fundamental doubts about the campaign in Ireland were also to be found among the officials at the hub of British rule in Ireland, Dublin Castle. A new group of talented civil servants was sent over from London in 1920 after Sir Warren Fisher had condemned the previous administration in an official report as 'almost woodenly stupid and quite devoid of imagination'.[55] The views of the newcomers were 'fundamentally in tune with the idea of Irish self-government within the Empire'.[56] The career in Ireland of one of them was later described by a colleague as 'a long struggle against militarism'.[57] And echoing the arguments of opponents of coercion inside the Cabinet, another of the new Castle administrators confided to his diary that the price paid in dignity for tolerating the methods of the Black and Tans was 'grievously heavy'.[58]

So not only could correspondents in Dublin set their reports in the context of the views of anti-government politicians in London but they would also be aware of the views of officials on the ground who were, to varying degrees, opposed to the policies they were meant to be implementing. Thus the correspondents in Ireland who wrote critically about the military campaign were not intervening from the margins but contributing to a sanctioned national debate that was engaging the most powerful politicians in Britain. They could also draw on a belief firmly established in British liberalism in the nineteenth century, that states allowing freedom of expression were superior to those who denied it.[59] Indeed, the belief in the innate capacity of the British public to cope with debates that would be dangerous if allowed to flourish among lesser peoples was attested to during the great Irish famine when 'Irish journalists were censored, prosecuted and transported for what they wrote' while British journalists 'probed and commented on issues that had been agonized over for generations, alternately sympathetic and irate as circumstances altered'.[60]

During the Crimean War it was *The Times* that aggressively advanced the argument that the mark of the 'self-respecting races' was a free press: 'There is only one rule for improvement and success, whether in peace or in war, and that is to be found in publicity and discussion.'[61] The post-war critique of the press sprang from this tradition of legitimate dissent. The war in Ireland was one case where it was difficult to trump this argument by appeals to the greater good of national unity – especially as the establishment of mass democracy in 1918 had introduced 'a new imperative' to seek consensus on government policies.[62] Nearly seventy-five years after forging its myth of fearless rectitude in defence of free speech and full disclosure during the Crimean War, *The Times* was able to mount the pulpit again to denounce Sir Hamar Greenwood's lies and prevarications about the conduct of the Black and Tans in Ireland:

> The country does indeed desire to know the truth in far larger measure than it has yet heard it; but it will strongly resent the idea that it is being told only what the Irish Government may consider good for it. It wants the facts, all the facts, clearly stated ... It is ... the unwelcome duty of the Press to record as best it can a situation of every-increasing gravity.[63]

This kind of editorial and its reporting from Ireland provoked a strong reaction to a newspaper still 'regarded by the governing classes as a sort of oracle'.[64] Readers wrote in to say they were transferring to the *Morning Post* and its circulation fell; the editor, Henry Wickham Steed, received threatening letters and was offered police protection (which he declined).[65] Lord Northcliffe did agree to an armed escort after a photograph of him with a bullet hole through the forehead was delivered to Printing House Square.[66] In May 1920 Northcliffe was passed a letter by his fellow proprietor, John Walter, which he had received from a friend just returned from India. 'I believe your family founded *The Times*', the letter began. 'All honour to them. They did much to build up our great Empire by their *Patriotism*. And *The Times* today is trying to destroy that Empire by its want of Patriotism.' It became clear that its coverage of Ireland had played a part in the collapse of confidence in *The Times* among the expatriate acquaintances of Walter's correspondent:

> Much Indian unrest, Egyptian unrest and Irish unrest, to say nothing of American self-satisfaction is due to the want of patriotism of your paper ... Set Patriotism ever before you Sir, and return to Empire building, not petty squabbling and fault-finding.[67]

By December 1920 Walter ceased to make his points indirectly. He wrote to Northcliffe:

> Is not the present a favourable opportunity for the paper to reconsider its attitude towards Ireland? I allude not so much to its policy as to its tone, which has been creating an impression for some time past that we are more anxious to damage Lloyd George than to achieve a settlement with the Irish. I believe that this attitude is losing the paper its authority as well as its readers.[68]

Northcliffe supported Steed, though, as *The Times* official historians put it, 'without conviction'.[69] In mid-December when the centre of Cork city was burned down, *The Times* correspondents immediately blamed British forces for another outrageous reprisal:

> Lorries drove rapidly around the principal streets, and their occupants discharged their rifles at short intervals. There was a scene of panic and people fled in all directions ... Before the curfew hour of 10 o'clock the city was

deserted by the ordinary public and incendiaries were going about burning and looting, removing valuables in portmanteaux.[70]

The lack of hesitation in publishing such a damaging report drew the condemnation of the *Morning Post*, which charged that *The Times* 'used at least to wait for evidence when something injurious to a British cause was alleged'. For the *Post*, the public buildings of Cork city were

> as dust ... compared with the loss of those dear young Englishmen slaughtered while doing their duty. And when we see English newspapers clamouring over bricks and stones while the murdered corpses of these poor lads are thrown in the shadow, we begin to be ashamed of the British Press.[71]

In March 1921, Steed had to fend off the commander of the British forces in Ireland, General Sir Nevil Macready, who wrote complaining about the 'unreliability' of *The Times* correspondents in Ireland. Steed replied with a revealing explanation of the correspondents' attitudes:

> I have sent from time to time to Ireland men who constantly risked their lives during the war as accredited correspondents in recording the deeds of the British and Allied forces in France and in other theatres of war. But though they naturally went with feelings of loyalty and admiration for the Forces of the Crown, they returned filled with loathing at the manner in which operations in Ireland are conducted on both sides.[72]

Significantly, *The Times* and the other British newspapers were able to withstand criticism of their adversarial reporting from Ireland because the intense debate at the heart of the British government meant that it was difficult to impugn the patriotism of the correspondents; as we saw in the last chapter, C.P. Scott even defined criticism itself as a patriotic act. The campaign in Ireland was a limited war in which, as with the early days of US war in Vietnam, there was 'a high premium on appearances'.[73] Reprisal was never admitted publicly as a policy or a tactic. The authority of the correspondents for filing dispatches highlighting the brutality and ill-discipline of a militarised police force fighting a covert war was underpinned by opposition to this counter-guerrilla strategy at the highest levels of the British political system. The special correspondents were able to use their status to challenge the government directly in the knowledge that, when attacked by the government's official spokesmen, they would be supported by influential public figures and further protected by the private views of senior politicians and civil servants.

Even though the influence of the reports from Ireland on political opinion in London appeared to resonate with a similar burgeoning sensitivity to the news from India, nevertheless the war in Ireland attracted far more notice than other imperial adventures. Small colonial wars may not have been as obscure to metropolitan publics as they were in the nineteenth century but they still merited little attention in major newspapers at this time, whichever empire was fighting them. Max Boot has written how in the USA – where the idea of empire still possessed novelty value – 'few Americans paid attention to what their troops were doing on the periphery of empire'.[74] When news did reach the metropolis it was hardly timely. In the first seven months of 1920, when accounts of reprisals in Ireland were prominent in the pages of the London dailies, the RAF bombed villages in the British protectorate of Mesopotamia twenty-five times to punish tribes resisting the imposition of taxes. A revolt against British rule spread across the whole country in June and two divisions of British and Indian troops were deployed to suppress it. However, the English public had little idea of operations in Mesopotamia until mid-July when questions were asked in parliament.[75]

In the case of one of the most notorious episodes of British rule in India, the massacre of at least 400 people at Amritsar in April 1919, a combination of distance and censorship meant it took eight months before anything more scandalous than the official telegrams appeared in the London press, when the findings of the Hunter Committee hearings were first published by the *Express*.[76] In general, as one study of British counterinsurgency concluded, up until the early twentieth century, '[even] when colonials were subjected to excessive force, Victorian racial attitudes ensured that there was likely to be little outcry over the brutalization of non-Europeans' so scorched-earth campaigns were regularly undertaken without debate or censure. Crucially, '[the] absence of intense media coverage removed yet another inducement to moderation'.[77] Despite the carnage in Europe, the peace-loving Victorian liberal caricatured by George Dangerfield – 'he liked his wars to be fought at a distance and, if possible, in the name of

God' – could still remain untroubled in 1920, at least in relation to colonial policing.[78]

The Irish revolution was about to intrude itself on this state of wilful ignorance. Bill Schwarz has argued that 'Ireland condensed the anxieties about Britain's imperial position as no other could…'.[79] And in the sense of holding the line against insurgencies and emerging nationalist movements this is true: in an effort to demonstrate how ludicrous was Lord Milner's recommendation in 1920 that Egypt be granted independence, Churchill suggested leaving out the word 'Egypt' and substituting the word 'Ireland', a small change that would 'make perfectly good sense and would constitute a complete acceptance of Mr De Valera's demands'.[80]

Ireland provoked anxieties beyond the obvious concerns of imperial defence, however. The intense press coverage of the campaign in Ireland exposed to public view tactics of colonial repression normally concealed by distance, ignorance or indifference. And this at a time when someone like Edwin Montagu – who prided himself on his public relations skills – was trying to repackage the empire as an association dependent on goodwill rather than coercion.[81] Derek Sayer has argued that the controversy over whether General Dyer was merely doing his duty when he ordered his riflemen to fire into the unarmed crowd at Amritsar was 'a thinly coded discussion of Ireland'. However, the reaction to the assiduous coverage of the Black and Tans by correspondents visiting Ireland suggests the reverse was equally true: their coverage made such an impact in British politics because it represented a thinly disguised discussion of the normal but usually unseen methods of colonial warfare.[82]

A common reaction to the Amritsar massacre among politicians once it became a matter of public controversy was that it was a grotesque aberration. Churchill told parliament it was 'an episode … without precedent or parallel in the modern history of the British Empire … an extraordinary event, a monstrous event, an event which stands in singular and sinister isolation'.[83] It was certainly not the British way of doing things, according to Churchill: 'Frightfulness is not a remedy known to the British pharmacopoeia,' he concluded.[84] Such rhetoric seemed appropriate because at this time the common belief was that British military missions in foreign lands were conducted to the highest standards and for the best motives. By 1914 the British soldier was seen at home as 'disciplined, regulated and orderly' and 'had come to be equated with ideals of advancement and to be perceived as a harbinger of civilization. British troops took law and order with them to the far reaches of the Empire…'.[85]

The brand of law and order brought by British ex-servicemen to Ireland jarred massively with this myth. Oswald Mosley, who left the coalition benches and joined the opposition when his speeches against reprisals were jeered, wrote that 'every rule of good soldierly conduct' was being disregarded in Ireland.[86] Another Conservative, Lord Robert Cecil – Mosley's mentor – repeatedly warned that the universal validity of British notions of justice was being undermined by the government's policy in Ireland.[87] Reprisals, Cecil argued, subverted a basic principle of British law:

> The experience of the world shows it is vital not only for conscience but for mere prudence to take care you only punish the guilty, and our law, the greatest system of law and order in the world, has shown no characteristic greater than the enormous precaution it erects around the innocent man to prevent him being brought into peril. This is lawlessness; reprisals are the very negation of law.[88]

For Cecil, Britain's worldwide prestige was being ruined by the news about atrocities in Ireland spreading around the globe: a scandalous departure from its own legal norms exposed the empire as predatory, vindictive and unheroic:

> I am confident that the British Empire stands only on the basis of justice and equity and freedom. Anything that attacks justice, equity and freedom attacks the whole basis on which the British Empire stands. That is really the issue in this matter, for it is the supremacy of the law that is the guarantee of freedom … There is nothing more valuable than the supremacy of the law, which, as this country has taught the world, is the great secret of freedom.[89]

Just as with Churchill's denunciation of the Amritsar massacre, Cecil placed the behaviour of the Black and Tans in Ireland against an otherwise irreproachable imperial record in which coercion never featured. From this viewpoint, Ireland had been turned, to appropriate T.P. O'Connor's metaphor, into a sinful corner of the Garden of Eden by a malevolent but inexplicably capricious display of official cruelty. The connection was never made between collective punishments dispensed in India – a wedding party flogged because it was judged to be an illegal gathering, men whipped in front of prostitutes for visiting a brothel during curfew – and similar medicine being dispensed in Ireland, such as the public floggings witnessed by Hugh Martin.[90] Perhaps such a connection was deliberately or, at least, subliminally avoided.[91]

No doubt the revulsion against the methods of the Black and Tans voiced by many people was genuine, but the terms in which denunciations were formulated presented these tactics as an extraordinary departure from cherished national ideals. Sometimes this idea was pressed to excess. Philip Gibbs – who, as we saw earlier, resigned from the *Daily Chronicle* because of Lloyd George's Irish policy – regarded the campaign in Ireland as terrorism. He believed Britain's global supremacy depended on its reputation for fair dealing rather than the power of its guns:

> Not deliberately, or without an immense amount of argument in self-justification, can we, as a people, accept a policy of brutality or tyranny. There is an inexhaustible store of generous feeling among English folk, amounting almost to weakness, in regard to smaller people than themselves, to all helpless and little things and to all under-dogs. That generosity can only be overwhelmed by a wave of passion, or blinded by ignorance that tyranny is at work or injustice established.[92]

Gibbs did not come up with any examples of the display of British 'weakness' towards peoples smaller than themselves, but he did attempt an intriguing explanation as to how the reprisals policy was allowed to take shape in the first place. English newspapers, he alleged, were forced into a conspiracy of silence. Until a year after the war in Ireland ended, '[only] by rumours, by tales told privately, in whispers, by seeing smoke and suspecting fire, was the average Englishman aware of any dirty work which might besmirch our honour in the world'.[93] Later in the same memoir he acknowledges the work of Hugh Martin and others in thrusting 'ugly facts … through the screen of silence'.[94] However, the contradiction is instructive: the average Englishman could only countenance repressive colonial policing in circumstances where he was unaware of it.

For politicians the most discomforting feature of events in Ireland was that tactics of imperial repression usually concealed were now being documented and described in the daily press. Explaining the scale of denunciation to which Lloyd George was subjected, Gary Peatling has written that

> British critics of government policy in Ireland were moved to a hysterical pitch of indignation because they could not reconcile visible policies of coercion in nationalist Ireland – in spite of their moderation compared to policies elsewhere in the British Empire – with their patriotic faith in Britain's uniqueness.[95]

It was the press reporting from Ireland that made these policies visible. Some clear-sighted commentators did not need recourse to the language of exceptionalism to recognise what they were seeing. In a letter to Lady Gregory in November 1920, George Bernard Shaw questioned the need for further corroboration of the stories of atrocities appearing in the press. 'What need have we of witnesses?', Shaw wrote. 'The *Daily News*, the *Manchester Guardian*, *The Times*, and all the anti-Coalition papers are publishing enough news of burnings and slaughterings to make Timour the Tarter turn in his grave…'. But even on the anti-government side, Shaw jeered, 'everybody prefers to go on screaming and clamouring for more telescopes to enable the English … to see the sun at noon'.[96]

There are some obvious reasons why a war in Ireland would receive more extensive coverage in the British press than operations in Mesopotamia – geographical proximity being one. In the next chapter we will examine why the Irish rebel cause acquired such legitimacy among the correspondents sent to Dublin. But what the war highlighted was that – however hard the government might try to co-opt the press – in certain circumstances, where dissenting voices were compelling, the press could not be relied upon to reflect the official line. Coalition ministers felt it increasingly necessary to include editors and journalists in the formulation of policy for India even though this desire was overshadowed by the ambivalence that 'the London press was a free press at the heart of an imperial system of coercion'.[97] Ireland was a warning of what could go wrong from the official point of view.

# V

# THE PROPAGANDA WAR

*Propaganda being entirely outside my province, I lost no time in draw-ing Sir Hamar Greenwood's attention to the importance of taking steps to counter the most effective arm in the hands of the rebels ... This cry I repeated constantly up to the time when hostilities ceased, but little came of it ... The Chief Secretary himself on occasions did his best to beat the propaganda drum in the House of Commons in defence of the police and soldiers, but unfortunately his superabundant energy so often carried him beyond the boundaries of fact that he soon became as one crying in the wilderness, and in no way weakened the case as put forward by Erskine Childers and other nimble and unscrupulous propagandists on the Sinn Féin side.*

General Sir Nevil Macready, *Annals of an Active Life*, vol. i

In August 1921 a correspondent for *The Times*, Maxwell H.H. Mac-Cartney, recently returned to London from a reporting trip in Ireland, wrote a chatty letter to Sinn Féin's Director of Publicity, Desmond FitzGerald: 'I was quite the blue-eyed boy when I got back to the office,' MacCartney gloated, 'and must take this opportunity of thanking you and your office for much of such success as I have apparently managed to score in the eyes of *The Times*.'[1] MacCartney was only one among many journalists whose reporting from Ireland was aided by Sinn Féin propagandists. Many journalists followed his example in finding the revolutionaries' propaganda operation more alert, more persuasive and more attuned to their needs than the efforts of the government's spokesmen in Dublin Castle.

Over time, the propaganda successes of the revolutionaries multiplied in inverse proportion to the impact of the government's attempt to define the crisis. As Sinn Féin's public relations campaign blossomed in scale and sophistication, the officials in the Castle appeared more uncertain and increasingly overawed by the pace of events. Why, in the competition to influence the correspondents, did Sinn Féin win and Dublin Castle lose? The first point to bear in mind is that for the Sinn Féin leaders the presentation of their case for nationhood to the rest of the world was not a sideshow or a distraction but a central part of their strategy to force the British government to grant Irish independence. Their efforts were focused initially on the Paris Peace Conference where national self-determination, thanks to President Woodrow Wilson's 'Fourteen Points', was exalted as a panacea to protect the world from a repeat of the carnage seen on the Western Front.

The Sinn Féin leader Arthur Griffith – one of those MPs absent from the Mansion House because he had been arrested – wrote to his followers from Gloucester Prison the day after the inaugural meeting of the Dail, urging them to 'above all concentrate on the Peace Conference...'. He warned them not to dismiss Wilson:

> It is a mistake in tactics to suggest that Wilson is not sincere. If he is not the suggestion will not help Ireland, and if he be it will dishearten him. Our attitude should be that Wilson is a sincere man striving to give effect to his programme of freedom for all nations and struggling against all the forces of tyranny, imperialism and lusty world power which are seeking to dominate the Peace Conference.[2]

A Sinn Féin delegation was sent to Paris to try to get Ireland's case onto the main agenda. They attempted to be taken seriously by the major powers drawing up the map of a new world order. In this post-war context, 'global recognition of Irish sovereignty remained the goal by which true independence would be measured'.[3] However, securing the sympathy of the delegates in Paris was only one objective of the Sinn Féin emissaries. At least as much effort was directed into cultivating favourable coverage from the newspaper correspondents. When the attempts to win official recognition floundered, persuading the press to take an interest in Ireland became all the more important.

Hundreds of journalists came to Paris for the conference and the French government established an extravagant press club in a house owned by a millionaire.[4] In March 1919 one of the Irish delegates wrote back to Dublin from Paris reporting a significant response to the circulation of a document setting out the Irish case:

> Practically every journalist who called on me during the ensuing week had the same story for me – about the excitement in diplomatic quarters … For a week or ten days after I had no time for any work outside press work. I was receiving journalists and visitors of all sorts and conditions from early morning till late at night – not leaving my room except for meals.[5]

This encouraging progress report (subtly hinting at self-sacrifice for the cause) was accompanied by a plea for more money:

> What I want is a few thousand pounds – don't be too greatly shocked by the light way I speak of it – for the purpose of smoothing a passage to the presence of the great men … and of securing the ear of the press. *You can get nothing whatsoever done otherwise.* They all expect it … and whether they are politicians or journalists or even statesmen … I must say they are very frank in letting you know their point of view in the matter.[6]

Further evidence that the press came to be seen by Sinn Féin as its main hope of a breakthrough came in May when Eamon De Valera – the president of the self-declared Republic – wrote to the delegation in Paris telling them that copies of all documents handed to delegates at the Peace Conference should also be distributed to the press. De Valera expressed himself in the language of an eager public relations agent: 'We must keep the Irish Question *continually hot* now before the public. This is the time for beginning our "big push" *everywhere*.'[7]

The reality was that the Irish delegation found the French press unsympathetic, inclined, in their estimation, to be frightened of offending the British by writing about Irish separatism. However, the mere experience of trying to cajole and persuade the correspondents to pay attention to Ireland was an education in journalistic practice. An Irish delegate wrote from Paris on 22 June:

> The only way to do effective propaganda is to get personal introductions to well-known and influential people and to get French writers interested in this way, for a paper will publish from a recognised correspondent a great deal that we would never get in otherwise … the only publicity you can count on here is what you can get through personally friendly writers and journalists…[8]

This lesson was well learned: cultivating personal relationships with journalists and writers who came to Ireland was crucial to sympathetic coverage of the national struggle. This form of ingratiation was not limited merely to political argument. When the delegation in Paris informed Dublin that an eminent French correspondent showed an interest in writing a series of articles about the Irish question, it was arranged that a copy of Yeats' poems be sent out to Paris for him.[9]

As hopes that the Irish delegation could get themselves an audience at the full conference began to fade, the attention of the Sinn Féin diplomats turned to making use of the contacts made in Paris to keep Ireland in the public eye. With money available from supporters in the USA it was suggested from Dublin 'that a small number of select American Journalists together with representatives of the French and Italian Press should be invited to visit Ireland and see for themselves the conditions obtaining here'. The headquarters staff insisted that they be vetted: 'You will realise the desirability of selecting these gentlemen carefully as it would not do to invite gentlemen here at our expense who could be got at by our friend the enemy.'[10] The work of the Irish delegation at the Paris Peace Conference was the embryo of an international publicity campaign that would flourish as the war developed. By the time of the truce in 1921 official

Irish press bureaus had been established in Berlin, Rome, Madrid, Geneva and the USA.[11]

The fact that a small independence movement was able to achieve such international reach was largely due to the leadership of two English-born men, both connected to a wider network than other Irish revolutionaries, who shaped Sinn Féin's publicity strategy throughout this period. The first effective head of the Propaganda Department of Dail Eireann was Desmond FitzGerald, an imagist poet, born in London in 1888 and brought up there.[12] Until adulthood he had only visited Ireland twice, once as a child and then again when he was twenty-one. In 1911 he married Mabel McConnell, daughter of a prominent Belfast Protestant businessman who had become an Irish nationalist. She had worked as a secretary for George Bernard Shaw and was friendly with Robert Lynd, the Belfast journalist who wrote regularly for the London press about Ireland. The couple came to live in Ireland in 1913 and it was then that FitzGerald began to work for the separatist movement in earnest. His son Garret FitzGerald (Taoiseach between 1982 and 1987) suggests that his father's attraction to Ireland can be attributed at least in part to his admiration for Yeats.[13] After Desmond FitzGerald's arrival in Ireland, however, it soon became clear that he had not come from London in search of poetry. At the end of 1914 he was expelled from Kerry by the police because of his activities in organising the Irish Volunteers; in 1915 he was sentenced to six months imprisonment for seditious speech. He had been in the General Post Office in Dublin throughout the Easter Rising in 1916. Arrested after the failed rebellion, he spent a year in prison in England.[14]

When Desmond FitzGerald took over the Propaganda Department in May 1919 he worked from 6 Harcourt Street in central Dublin, an address that was to become familiar to foreign correspondents covering Ireland. He retained the air of an upper-class bohemian. A colleague described him entering the office in a grey lounge suit, dust-coat open 'with mincing step and supercilious air ... a cigarette going and a magnificent pearl grey velours trilby ... set at a jaunty angle on his crispy light-brown hair'. She concluded that 'these affectations, however, masked an exceptionally brave character'.[15] FitzGerald's demeanour attracted other disapproving comments from his fellow (Irish) revolutionaries: one young activist recounted many years later coming across FitzGerald when they were both interned in the Curragh camp and being surprised by his 'drawling English accent' as he discussed French literature with a professor: 'I never dared to speak to FitzGerald as I quickly gathered that he was in the category of people satirised by the epigram: "My name is George Nathaniel Curzon/I am a most superior person."'[16]

However, a personality so off-putting to a rank-and-file volunteer from Dublin could win the admiration of foreign journalists and writers. After FitzGerald's death in 1947 a columnist in the *Irish Times* recalled seeing him walking into the Shelbourne Hotel to meet journalists with a yellow-backed French novel sticking out of his pocket:

> Desmond FitzGerald was an intellectual revolutionary. He always had the greatest contempt for the *sans culottes*, and, in some respects, almost might be described as a reactionary ... [But] he made quite a success of his job and his easy manner helped to convince foreigners that the *Sinn Féin* movement was something more than a mere upsurge of the Irish proletariat.[17]

An obituarist in the *Manchester Guardian* pinpointed FitzGerald's success as a propagandist: 'He had an admirable skill in directing [journalists'] movements by suggesting in such a way as to ensure without their knowing it that they would hear and see what he thought desirable and nothing else.'[18]

FitzGerald recruited another Englishman with a drawling accent to the Propaganda Department. Erskine Childers, author of a recently published and acclaimed spy novel *The Riddle of the Sands*, had already acquired a flamboyant reputation among Irish nationalists. In a famous incident before the outbreak of the Great War in 1914, he had sailed to Germany on his yacht, the *Asgard*, and returned to Ireland with a consignment of arms and ammunition. The rifles were unloaded at Howth Harbour on the north side of Dublin and the Irish Volunteers marched away with them in an open act of defiance of the authorities.

At first glance Childers had an unlikely CV for an Irish nationalist – born in London and educated at Haileybury public school (originally founded to train civil servants to govern India and whose alumni included Rudyard Kipling); a law graduate of Cambridge; a British army officer in the Boer War; and a clerk in the House of Commons. His father was professor of oriental studies at London University and a cousin of his father had been chancellor in Gladstone's government. Childers' Irish connection came from his mother's side of the family. She was from a prominent Anglo-Irish family who had owned land in Co. Wicklow since before Cromwell came to Ireland in the seventeenth century.[19] Childers appears to have become convinced of the justice of home rule for Ireland around the time when he resigned from his job in the House of Commons in 1910 to attempt to become a Liberal candidate for parliament. In a lecture in London in 1912, later published as a pamphlet, Childers set out his strategy for winning home rule for Ireland in a way that could stand as a prescription for his later work with journalists: 'England cannot be forced to accept the Irish ideal which I have ventured to place before you to-night. But she can be made to understand it, and I believe that if she understood it she would sanction it.'[20]

By 1919 Childers was offended by how the Irish nationalist cause was being represented in the international press. Ireland, he wrote, was portrayed unfairly 'as a stab-in-the-back rebellious province which didn't help in the war'.[21] When he was first brought by FitzGerald to the Propaganda Department at 6 Harcourt Street, Childers made an impression with the range of his contacts in London. One of FitzGerald's acolytes showed Childers an article from the *Daily Mail* as an example of the kind of journalism Sinn Féin was trying to counter. Childers told him he had just spoken to the editor of the *Daily News* before setting out from London and he was confident that he could get some articles favourable to Sinn Féin printed in that paper.[22] Later, the Sinn Féin leader Arthur Griffith proclaimed that Childers was a good man to have: 'He has the ear of a big section of the English people.'[23] It was clear that Sinn Féin leaders realised early on that Childers' contacts in London 'assured him access to necessary white space'.[24]

However, as with FitzGerald's intellectualism, Childers' ascendancy background, his British army career and his air of superiority also provoked resentment. There was always a lingering suspicion of him. One pro-nationalist journalist remembered the gossip that dogged Childers:

> [He] had fought for the British and written *The Riddle of the Sands* to save the British Fleet from the Germans … he was a Major and a D.S.O. And Dublin laughed at his indignant letter to the Press after a military raid on his house, and some young pup in a second lieutenant's uniform had dropped a cigarette on his best carpet. Jamey, was that all he had to vex him?[25]

In May 1919 Childers was sent to work with the delegation at the Paris Peace Conference. Like his colleagues he found it difficult to persuade journalists to write about Ireland; they were, he remarked, 'nervous as old women about offending England'.[26] He was particularly scathing about the British delegation – people of his own class, graduates (like him) of public school and Oxbridge: he complained that they 'paid court to him socially, and then poured ice-cold water on his burning ideals'.[27] This resentment provoked a rejection of his origins and the career he might have followed in favour of the risky adventure of Irish nationalism:

> I have a kind of blind fury sometimes at seeing these cultured, cold-blooded, self-satisfied people making careers out of the exploitation of humanity and crucifying the Christs with a *bon mot* or a shrug.[28]

During his few months in Paris Childers judged that he had made little headway in persuading the delegates to take the Irish cause seriously. But he was eventually persuasive in his dealings with the recalcitrant French journalists. In August 1919 *Le Temps* advocated a British withdrawal from Ireland and Childers was credited with this publicity coup.[29] He returned to London in August and by September he had moved his family to Dublin to begin work in the Sinn Féin Propaganda Department. It had not been an easy decision but the depth of commitment it entailed was revealed in a phrase used years later by his wife Molly to describe their steady conversion: 'we gradually became ready to give ourselves to Ireland'.[30]

Between 1919 and 1921 FitzGerald and Childers would between them mould Sinn Féin's Propaganda Department into the most effective operation of its kind yet seen. In early 1919 its main function was to act as a research office for the Sinn Féin leadership, providing data for speeches and statistics, and background information for the statements prepared for the Peace Conference. It also prepared articles for the Irish provincial press, election literature for the general election of 1918 and pamphlets to be distributed abroad.[31] A few months after taking over the department, FitzGerald devised a type of news sheet called the *Weekly Summary* to be distributed to the Irish and international press once a fortnight. It listed 'acts of aggression' committed by British forces in Ireland, concentrating on details of place and time.

The *Weekly Summary* was the prototype for perhaps the most successful instrument of the Sinn Féin propagandists: the *Irish Bulletin*. This was a mimeographed sheet launched on 11 November 1919, the first anniversary of the armistice. That first edition was circulated to only thirty people: the offices of the Dublin newspapers and friendly foreign correspondents staying in local hotels.[32] Within a few months the *Bulletin* was being read by political figures in London and by politicians, diplomats and journalists in Europe and the rest of the world. The *Bulletin's* success derived from the flair with which it described incidents in the unconventional war developing in Ireland. In the words of Charles Townshend, it 'excelled in portraying an exchange of shots as a battle, the sniping of a police barrack as an assault or the breaking of windows by Crown Forces as the sacking of a town'.[33] However, much of it was written in a more restrained, bureaucratic style that aimed to mimic the authority of official publications, categorizing incidents under headings such as 'Arrests', 'Armed Assaults' and 'Raids' in the same way as a police inspector might write a report to headquarters. Often, the *Bulletin's* intended effect was achieved by the absence of the hyperbole that Townshend identifies as its hallmark. For instance, the following entries appeared in the *Bulletin* under the heading 'Raids' in July 1920:

*Raids:*
The residence of Mr P. Dineen, recently elected Republican Member of Skibbereen District Council, Co. Cork was forcibly entered and searched by a British police and military raiding party.

British police and military raided the quarters of Mr P.J. Crowley, employee of the Dunmanway Union, Co. Cork.

*Murders:*
Richard Lumley, a day-labourer, aged 60 of Rearcross, Co. Tipperary was shot dead without warning by a British military and police patrol, whilst on his way home from a wake at Abbey Hotel, Rearcross on the morning of July 4th.[34]

Desmond FitzGerald's colleagues recalled how he encouraged this pared-down style. To Kathleen Napoli McKenna he was 'a stickler for unembellished truth' who would upbraid Frank Gallagher (the journalist associated with the *Bulletin*) for indulging in exaggerations.[35] Ernest Blythe recalled that FitzGerald:

resisted the pressure to which he was constantly subjected from most quarters in favour of painting outrages by British forces in a blacker hue than was justified by the facts and also the pressure in favour of accepting without investigation every report of an outrage which came in from the country.

This, for Blythe, resulted in the *Bulletin* 'having a reputation for reliability which few sheets of its kind can ever have enjoyed'.[36] When FitzGerald travelled abroad to meet journalists the *Bulletin* became his calling card and it developed into a major source for those writing about Ireland.

By 1920, as the guerrilla war intensified, the Sinn Féin Propaganda Department was regularly forced to move from one safe house to another. After curfew, armoured cars carrying Black and Tan patrols would prowl Dublin. There were several near misses, with raids on every house in the street save the one where the *Bulletin* was being produced. One house in the centre of Dublin was ransacked shortly after the propaganda office had vacated it. For a while the *Bulletin* was compiled from a flat that FitzGerald rented for his wife and newly born son.[37] In October 1920 the offices moved to the first floor of 11 Molesworth Street. A brass plate on the front door announced that the first floor was occupied by a company importing oil, a plausible business tenant in a smart neighbourhood. For Kathleen Napoli McKenna, it was a case of hiding in plain sight:

> What could be more daring, yet, at the same time more secure … than this respectable, aristocratic, snobbish Unionist street! … The Grandlodge of Freemasons, the Masonic Orphans' School, the Hibernian Church, the Molesworth Hall and the Church of Ireland Temperance Welfare Society were all neighbours of ours. In addition Messrs. James and James, the Crown Solicitors, occupied the halldoor flat, while in the flat above ours were installed two elderly, sourfaced, hoity-toity spinsters whom we surmised were engaged as librarians in Trinity College.[38]

One weekend the whole street was raided except for the first floor of number eleven. On another occasion, when a cordon was established around Molesworth Street, Frank Gallagher pushed his revolver into a stack of filed newspapers before slipping away.[39] A month later the offices were discovered during another weekend raid. All the newspaper files and printing equipment and the entire address list for recipients of the *Bulletin* were carried away by the police. The staff assembled in another under-ground office and produced a new *Bulletin* the following Tuesday. Readers were puzzled, however, to receive two copies of the *Bulletin* that week: one was a fake issued by British intelligence and produced on an Underwood typewriter confiscated in the raid.[40]

By that stage Sinn Féin spokesmen had established an extraordinary degree of trust with foreign correspondents. The correspondents would regularly come to meet FitzGerald and others in a house on Leeson Street, just south of the centre of Dublin.[41] Frank Gallagher befriended Donald Boyd of the *Manchester Guardian*, writing to his fiancée about how much he liked him. One night Boyd invited Gallagher to the Abbey Theatre and then they both returned to Gallagher's flat:

> We sipped tea and then I got Boyd to tell me his war experiences. He was exceptionally good remembering all the little things that give you a real idea of what it was like. The war and its horribleness has made him a pacifist for life and his effort is to try and make it impossible for all time. He will of course not succeed, but it is indicative of good in him to have that as his great aim.[42]

Gallagher confessed to having rowed with Boyd but reported that their differences had been resolved after the journalist 'reformed greatly'. In any case, Gallagher wrote, the argument was of no consequence because Boyd 'was always with us and was only getting fractious because he, like the rest of us, didn't understand much'.[43] The degree of trust established with some of the correspondents was shown by how, when Desmond FitzGerald was arrested in February 1921 and taken for interrogation at Dublin Castle, his wife got in touch with Boyd and Guy Moyston of the United Press news agency, 'both excellent friends of ours, most sympathetic to our Movement and fond of Desmond in a personal way due to meeting him frequent-ly…'.[44] They contacted Basil Clarke, the publicity officer at Dublin Castle and McKenna claims this saved FitzGerald some rough treatment.[45]

With FitzGerald gone, Childers took over the Propaganda Department. The move to Dublin had radicalised Childers. Initially he supported home rule and even in early 1919 – like many others in Sinn Féin – would have settled for Dominion status of Ireland within the British Empire, the same kind of autonomy enjoyed by white colonies such as New Zealand and Canada. By late 1919, when guerrilla warfare had overtaken diplomatic manoeuvring, Childers did not back away: he moved in step with the militarists. In his propaganda work he did not try to evade acknowledgment of physical force tactics and he criticised those who equivocated:

> Nothing struck me more, when I first got insight into the publicity department, than the failure of the political side to take definite responsibility for the Army and its work – a fatal failure because ... it was only by insisting that it was waging a legitimate war of defence and by basing propaganda on that principle that one could meet the torrent of defamation.[46]

Childers set about this work with diligence. His diaries are a log of meetings with foreign correspondents occasionally interspersed by the mundanity of life in the Dublin suburbs. His record of 14 May 1920 reads: 'To house with mother. To shops for wall-paper and linoleum. Weibel, Swiss journalist, spent evening.'[47] On 3 June: 'Took eleven train to Ennis. Travelled and lunched with Gregg of *New York World*. Lent him my SF Court cuttings.'[48] On 29 August: 'Twenty-one callers! including ... Editor of *Christian Science Monitor* and correspondent of *Matin*.'[49] And on 20 September: 'Coached McCarthy [Desmond] for interview with Castle official.'[50] Childers also visited London to keep in touch with British politicians. For instance, he passed material regularly to Wedgwood Benn for use in questions in the House of Commons. In October 1920 he visited London for the opening of parliament; his diary entry for 20 October illustrates the range of his contacts in the British establishment: 'On to lunch at Nat Lib Club with Hammond [J.L.] ... After saw J.A. Spender, Donald McLean. Walked with latter to House of Commons ... Saw Asquith for half an hour. Urged same points as on Simon I think in vain.'[51]

In London Childers would also see Sinn Féin's representative there, Art O'Brien, whose job was to distribute the *Bulletin* and cultivate foreign correspondents who wished to come to Ireland. The memos that passed between O'Brien in London and Childers in Dublin make clear that Sinn Féin went out of its way to facilitate journalists who travelled to Ireland. Sometimes the consequences of this enthusiasm could be comic. In a memo to Childers in March 1921, O'Brien responded to a query for a payment of £20 to an 'F. Morrell'. O'Brien explained that the name was 'Moller' not 'Morell' and that he was a correspondent for a Norwegian newspaper:

> He called upon me about mid-October saying that he was crossing to Ireland the next night, that his paper had agreed to his going but had not sent him the necessary funds. He was himself low in cash and asked if I could advance him £20 until the end of the month. I advanced the amount and advised D.F. [Desmond FitzGerald]. The end of the month came but I did not see or hear from Moller. I then wrote to him. He called after some time, said that after all he had not been able to make the journey, asked for a further delay for repayment. He has been approached again twice since then, but he makes excuses. I am afraid we shall not see the £20 again…[52]

Such rashness is indicative of O'Brien's zeal to promote the cause, an eagerness which also extended to making Childers aware of his opinions on the general thrust of propaganda. In one memo O'Brien questioned the labelling of casualties in the weekly summaries of incidents issued from Dublin:

> It seems to me that the description 'Constabulary Killed' and 'Military Killed' are misleading to the foreign reader. It would be advisable to preface the word 'English' in both cases or 'Enemy'. It is a great pity you continue to use the word 'Constabulary' and 'Police' because the foreign reader naturally comes to the conclusion that they are really 'Constabulary' and 'Police' whose only duty is to do the ordinary police duty. That is of course exactly the impression which the English Government seeks to make on the foreign reader's mind.[53]

In a sign of how he increasingly sought to polarise the conflict Childers wrote back a few weeks later in agreement: 'One of my changes was to eliminate "police" from all publicity matter. But we cannot eliminate "Constabulary" because the sections of English forces have sometimes to be distinguished.'[54] O'Brien appeared barely satisfied by this response. By return of post he challenged the use of the word 'British' to describe the Crown forces:

> What does it mean? Who is our enemy? We have no direct quarrel with Australia, S. Africa, Canada, India etc. and they are part of the British Empire. So if the word 'British' is used in that sense it is obviously misleading.

Nor have we a direct quarrel with Scotland or Wales, so that if the word 'British' is used to mean the people of Great Britain, it is equally misleading. Ireland has one enemy and one enemy in the world and that enemy is England. We should constantly make that plain to all the nations, whether they are in the British Empire or out of it. It is one of England's traps to make it appear that Ireland is the sulky naughty child in the great bright happy nursery of the British Empire.[55]

In an extraordinary remark given Childers' background, O'Brien laid the blame for wrongheaded propaganda on years of ingrained Anglicisation: 'Unfortunately even the best of our people have in some degree fallen a victim to the insidious poison of denationalising English education and we have to be constantly on the alert to guard against the effects of the poison.'[56] The contempt for British culture registered here by O'Brien is repeatedly evident among Sinn Féin leaders, and seems to have been unaffected by the sympathy displayed by British journalists and the increasingly adversarial coverage in the London newspapers of the government's campaign to crush the rebellion. It should be recalled that Childers himself believed that the Irish cause was subject to a torrent of defamation in the British press when he joined the Sinn Féin Propaganda Department in 1919. How could Sinn Féin so readily discount favourable treatment at the hands of British journalists?

One reason the notion of Ireland being incessantly defamed remained credible was its longevity: it had been a major theme of Sinn Féin propaganda in Ireland for several years. As the French historian, Marc Bloch observed about atrocity stories during the First World War, 'a false report is always born out of collective perceptions that exist before its birth'.[57] Arthur Griffith, the Sinn Féin leader who had given Childers the task of persuading English journalists that Irish aspirations were being brutally suppressed, had a very low opinion of the British press. Griffith was a tireless polemical journalist himself, described as 'extraordinarily clever' by Augustine Birrell, the chief secretary in Ireland at the time of the 1916 Rising.[58] Much of his polemical writing in the leading Sinn Féin paper, *Nationality*, was devoted to denouncing the iniquity of British proprietors such as Lord Northcliffe and Sir William Hulton.

Fleet Street proprietors occupied the attention of Sinn Féin propagandists partly because they wished to contrast the nobility of Irish life with the tawdry immorality of urban Britain. Northcliffe was reviled not only as the publisher of *The Times* and the *Daily Mail* but because he also published a stream of children's newspapers and magazines that found a ready market in Ireland. Sinn Féin writers condemned him as 'the Cromwell of journalese [sic]', an 'evil genius' seducing people with 'triviality or gross idiocy'.[59] One Sinn Féin journalist contrasted the ease with which tabloid scandal circulated in Ireland with the suppression of the separatists' wholesome advocacy of a new Irish nation: 'The grossest, most brutal, and most insane immorality may be, and has been, propagated by British newspapers and the British censor "winks the other eye".'[60]

More specifically Sinn Féin was focused on discrediting British atrocity propaganda during the war. The aim was to neutralise recruitment campaigns shaped deliberately to have an appeal in Ireland. Posters circulated by the recruiting sergeants played on Irish sympathies for Catholic Belgium; they also urged Irishmen to avenge attacks such as the sinking of the cruise ship the *Lusitania* off the southern Irish coast in May 1915 and tried to stir up fear of an invasion by the German army.[61] Arthur Griffith blamed cowardly journalists of British papers for inventing scare stories. Commenting on reports of German soldiers attacking women and children in Belgium, Griffith wrote that the 'factory for the manufacture of German atrocities' could be found in a pub in Fleet Street.[62] He came up with the idea that Britain had erected a paper wall around Ireland: 'on the inside she told Ireland what she wanted the Irish to believe about the world, and on the outside she told the world what she wanted to believe about Ireland'.[63]

The irony was that the British government could only wish to be as successful at isolating Ireland as Griffith made out. Once the Anglo-Irish War began, the paper wall – if it ever existed – was in tatters and by the end of 1919 the government appeared to have lost control of the press coverage of Ireland. Correspondents and writers from Europe, the USA and beyond portrayed Ireland as the scene of imperial atrocities. Although at first prepared to share the Irish administration's disdain for the de facto declaration of Irish independence by the Sinn Féin parliament in Dublin, British correspondents also turned to urgent questioning of Irish policy as acts of violence intensified. Writers who were in favour of self-government for Ireland condemned the use of military measures, the indecision among officials in Dublin Castle and the tendency of the government in London towards drift.

How did this happen? The root of the explanation lies in Dublin Castle. A French visitor to Ireland described the Castle as 'A world in itself, a city within a city. It is at once the palace of the viceroy, a military barrack, the seat of administration and the office of the secret police … omnipotent and omniscient.'[64] The fulcrum of British rule in Ireland had changed little since the Act of Union in 1800. It was riven with sectarian intrigue, petty careerism and antiquated procedure. In an article early in 1919 Hugh Martin had advised the new chief secretary for Ireland, Ian Macpherson, that he would find in Dublin Castle 'the most bureaucratic system in Europe' dedicated to 'a militarism more deeply entrenched than any in Whitehall'. There was, Martin wrote:

> no government machinery in good working order … no public opinion on which to play except a mass of confused resentments. In short [Macpherson] will find chaos upstairs, downstairs and in my Lady's chamber with Brute Force sitting in the drawing room.[65]

Signs of this inefficiency were especially visible in the Castle's censorship regime. Wartime censorship had been introduced in Ireland in 1914, mainly directed at the flourishing crop of Sinn Féin newspapers and magazines such as those edited by Arthur Griffith. Newspapers were shut down and presses seized, but with little lasting effect. After the Easter Rising in 1916 ad hoc measures were replaced by new, formal regulations based on the Defence of the Realm Act. The chief secretary, Augustine Birrell, told parliament it was imperative that 'news should not reach the neutral countries and particularly our friends in America, which would be calculated to give them an entirely false impression as to the importance of what has taken place, important as that is'.[66] But the new measures, for all their judicial formality, were scarcely more successful than the old piecemeal approach. Although most of the Sinn Féin propagandists were imprisoned in the months after the Rising, the 'mosquito press' – as the official censor, Lord Decies, referred to the nationalist papers – began to thrive again soon afterwards.[67]

The real problem was that the officials in Dublin Castle were unable to reconcile a policy of banning seditious speech with the reality of politics in Ireland. Lord Decies's tenure as censor in the years after 1916 is a record of bluster and uncertainty. A letter he wrote to the chief secretary in January 1917 provides a classic example of his lack of confidence. Decies gives his views on a series of nationalist publications and then comments:

> These observations lead directly to that most difficult question as to how far the discussion of the absolute independence of Ireland as a political theory, entailing, as it must, the development of anti-British feeling, is to be construed as 'likely to cause disaffection'. In dealing with this question I am most anxious to have guidance and if possible a definition.[68]

Unable to prevent the publication of nationalist propaganda, Decies's real aim was to curb criticism of the Irish administration itself. In February 1917, he stopped a telegram from an Irish stringer to the *Manchester Guardian* about the latest wave of arrests of Sinn Féiners, which concluded:

> The trust of the man in the Irish street is gone with the snows of January. He reads everything to-day as a possible move in a rather shabby game of chicane, and he is given to cynical thoughts when he reflects upon the high ideals of national liberty and free citizenship for which the Irish Divisions marched away to battle. Such is the atmosphere into which Irish affairs have drifted.[69]

Decies described the article as 'most undesirable', drawing attention to implied criticism of government policy in the last sentence by underlining it.[70]

The argument that censorship was more about self-protection for the Castle than curbing sedition was taken up repeatedly by unionist journalists. On 20 July 1917, the managing editor of the *Belfast Telegraph* wrote to Decies that

> In our view it is at the present time a great crime to mislead the British public by permitting them to form the conclusion that matters are happy and peaceful in Ireland, when some parts of the country are seething in sedition. Would it not be a more logical course for the Government to prevent the delivery of seditious speeches, and the writing of seditious articles? To withhold from the British public all knowledge of what is actually happening in this country is to mislead it ... It turns the censorship into a political instrument...[71]

In December 1918 Lord Decies submitted his final monthly report for the year and attached to it a letter of resignation. His ambiguous observations betrayed a sense of failure. In his resignation letter he advocated that censorship be ended because although 'fully justified as a war measure', in peacetime it had become 'weakened in authority and altered in character'. He had nothing but praise for the press who

> have with hardly an exception endeavoured to help rather than hinder, and have conscientiously carried out those instructions which it was my duty to issue to them … this very fact is in my judgment a strong argument for the discontinuance of censorship while yet it retains a measure of goodwill.[72]

However, the same report contains a stark admission that censorship had failed to quell subversive journalism:

> It may now be assumed that practically every provincial newspaper correspondent of the Dublin newspapers is a Sinn Féiner, and that incidents … are deliberately reported in the light most unfavourable to the authorities. This pollution of news sources will be a lasting trouble.[73]

As we have seen from the change in the tone of coverage by British correspondents in Ireland during 1919, Dublin Castle was left behind by the speed with which the press shifted its interpretation of the Irish story: increasingly in dispatches the Castle itself was being identified as part of the problem, an obstacle to a fair settlement. When a new set of more able civil servants were sent from London to rescue the Castle administration in 1920 their fresh thinking about finding a way out of the crisis extended to relations with the press. The woeful reputation of the Irish administration had enabled the special correspondents who came to Ireland for everlengthier periods during 1919 and 1920 to become more detached and oppositional.

Basil Clarke, who had been a correspondent for the *Daily Mail* during the First World War and then director of the Special Intelligence Branch at the Ministry of Reconstruction, was recruited to re-establish the authority of the Irish administration and arrived in Dublin Castle in August 1920.[74] Clarke's mission was to inculcate a spirit of professionalism in handling the press. Within less than a year, however, he too was acknowledging failure. In a series of thoughtful memos he circulated among colleagues in 1921, Clarke complained that the communiqués written at the army press office were amateurish, adding that this was no surprise since they were soldiers first and handling the press 'was as much a craft as paper-hanging or horse doctoring'.[75] Clarke lamented that he was unable to persuade the military to accept his propaganda policy; they had 'admitted quite frankly that they did not believe in that policy'.[76] In another undated memo, probably written around the same time, Clarke referred to a series of 'mishaps' in which the Castle's credibility was seriously undermined when official accounts of major incidents were subsequently discredited. These mistakes, Clarke wrote, had been 'deadly destructive of Government credit. I would say that these mishaps have in fact closed for us … a broad avenue of propaganda activities.'[77]

An example of the kind of 'mishap' Clarke may have had in mind (and of the military mentality towards the press he was trying to refine) was the futile attempt to censor news of the executions of four men in Cork on 28 April 1921. The four had been convicted of levying war against the king after being captured during and after an ambush in Co. Cork, an area where martial law had been declared. Correspondents for the Irish national papers based in Cork were ordered not to report anything about the executions beyond the bare fact that they had happened.[78] A *Daily News* correspondent who went to Cork to investigate (but took the precaution of returning to Dublin before telegraphing his dispatch to London) found that

> so haphazard is the method in which the censorship appears to be administered that … no prohibition had been put on the sending of messages … to the English papers. Several were sent away before a military officer arrived at the post office to inquire about them.[79]

The local correspondents who had filed the dispatches were ordered to appear at military headquarters the following morning where they were told by an officer that they were forbidden to send reports that reflected on the conduct of his men or encouraged the IRA. 'No charge of inaccuracy was brought against them … but they were warned against describing such matters as the execution of rebels in a way which would be considered sympathetic to the victims' and threatened with expulsion if they defied the warning.[80]

This was one of several examples where the censorship was self-defeating, where the attempt to suppress certain kinds of news ended up magnifying bad publicity for the Crown forces. The day of the executions in Cork, a party of Auxiliaries entered the offices of the *Freeman's Journal* in Dublin and ordered the staff out at gunpoint. Several foreign correspondents who were on the premises were forced into a small room; Guy Moyston of the Associated Press was singled out and told to take the next boat back to America.[81] The *Daily News* correspondent was among those subjected to rough treatment. The journalists were asked by an intimidating officer if they personally had seen anyone knocked about by Auxiliaries: 'Among those who answered "no" was a man who himself had been struck in the face with a revolver.'[82]

Such incidents must have brought on the despair to which Basil Clarke was giving vent in Dublin Castle. Within a few months even he seemed to have given up any hope that the correspondents could be influenced or persuaded. In a revealing note sent in August 1921 to a Colonel Foulkes in the small press office that General Macready had established in army head-quarters, Clarke explained how he had been trying to come up with some method of controlling the visiting correspondents. 'I cannot think of any better way of meeting this problem than that of issuing licences to all news-paper men,' Clarke wrote, 'and giving neither facilities nor information to any that are unlicensed.'[83] He went on to suggest replicating the system that had been so effective during the First World War: a group of correspon-dents should be allowed to live with the Crown forces, be given housing, transport and telegraphic facilities (all of which they would pay for) and be provided with guides who would also serve as disguised censors:

> The effect of their being in so close [sic] contact with the Crown forces would be to enable them to see problems and facts more intimately, ac-curately and probably, therefore, more sympathetically than would be the case if they were spectators from the outside.[84]

All of these observations amount to an acknowledgment that the Castle had lost the propaganda battle the previous year. The news had been de-fined by the special correspondents and the only way Clarke saw of recover-ing the initiative was to return to a system of control which, by that stage, would have been impossible to impose. The censorship already imposed by the Castle was irksome to those subject to it, but was nevertheless ineffective in preventing coverage of Sinn Féin's rebellion. As disorder spread, visiting journalists gradually switched from taking their line from government sources to holding the government responsible for the state of Ireland. Despite this, Sinn Féin propagandists still maintained that their cause was given an unfair press. The reality was that foreign correspondents were about to become adversaries of British government policy in Ireland and effective instruments in its failure.

# VI

# AN OLD WORLD FIGHT:
# AMERICAN JOURNALISTS
# IN IRELAND

*When I went to Ireland, I went not only to investigate the facts but to interpret them. I saw the situation very like the situation in Finland that we have long been familiar with; like the situation in Bohemia, the Jugo-Slav situation, the Schleswig situation, the Armenian situation, the Alsace-Lorraine situation – the situation of a people that had long been imperialized struggling to get for themselves conditions of self-development that they could not get without a new constitution – a new constitution they could only get by securing independence.*

Francis Hackett in testimony to the American Commission
on Conditions in Ireland, recounted in
*Evidence on Conditions in Ireland*

*No one doubts that the new world must be and will be different from the old, but there will be grave disagreements about the methods of reconstruction. There will be those who wish to tear down in order to rebuild and others who will seek to remake by gradual adjustment. The pendulum of history has swung from reaction to revolution, but civilization has been advanced only when the pendulum swung backward and forward evenly over the arc of Time...*

Carl Ackerman, *Trailing the Bolsheviki*

When it came to Britain's status in the post-war world the criticism of one particular spectator of the war in Ireland from outside the empire was identified as potentially devastating for Britain's future role. Among politicians and journalists, the reaction of the USA was feared to carry more practical consequences for the exercise of British power in the world than the mere loss of a liberal reputation, disabling though that was thought to be. By the end of the war the USA had come into it own as a major power. Where once it had been in debt to other nations it was now Europe's banker.[1] Its financial power was such that towards the end of 1917 Lord Northcliffe – in New York as head of the British War Mission – could send a cable to London describing the Americans as the 'complete masters'; as he put it in his favoured cabelese, 'if loan stops, war stops'.[2]

When the Germans finally surrendered, President Woodrow Wilson saw the peace settlement as a moment of opportunity for American diplomacy. Instead of retreating from the world, the USA would attempt to re-order it. Wilson defined his outlook against both the ancient European powers whose imperial rivalries were blamed for starting the war and the new revolutionary programme of Leninism: he envisaged the USA as 'the historical agent of the world's transformation from chaos and imperialism to orderly liberal rationality'.[3] The White House legal advisor explained how the ravages of the war would guarantee the triumph of Wilsonian idealism:

> Europe is bankrupt financially and its governments are bankrupt morally. The mere hint of withdrawal by America by reason of opposition to her wishes for justice, for fairness, and for peace would see the fall of every government in Europe without exception...[4]

The expansion of American trade was to be synonymous with progress, a view Wilson conveyed to a conference of salesmen in Detroit in 1916, telling them:

> [You] are Americans and are meant to carry liberty and justice and the principles of humanity wherever you go. Go out and sell goods that will make the world more comfortable and more happy, and convert them to the principles of America.[5]

A central tenet of Wilson's vision was that American power could be pro-jected without imperial conquest, that 'the United States could somehow be a great power without behaving like any previous great power'.[6] This assumption of superior moral purpose left Britain particularly vulnerable to criticism over policy in Ireland from its newly powerful ally.

Britain was chiefly concerned about the political influence of the vast Irish diaspora in the USA, particularly in Wilson's Democratic Party. Certainly, after the executions in Dublin in 1916, Irish-Americans were temporarily able to persuade a broad swathe of American opinion that the repression was a cruel overreaction to the Rising.[7] However, Americans turned out to be even more worried about German involvement with the Irish rebels.[8] By 1917, when the USA had declared war on Germany, the police were suppressing any meetings where anti-British rhetoric was heard. The new worries about fifth columnists (enemy sympathisers) were summed up by one senator, who declared in 1918 that diasporas were now under suspicion: 'The time for hyphenated Americans is over and the cowards and disloyalists in our country have got to be weeded out and held up to the execration which they deserve.'[9] Despite this change in mood, British diplomats were still wary about the power of Irish-Americans. When Britain began dismantling its wartime propaganda operation in the USA in early 1919, the embassy in Washington advised that 'there was still a need for combating the anti-British propaganda of Irish extremists'.[10]

By the time President Wilson arrived in Paris for the peace conference, Ireland was for American correspondents a newsworthy location on the troubled map of Europe. In the histories of American news agencies and the memoirs of contemporary American correspondents, deployments to Ireland are recounted as occasions for adventure, risk and professional fulfilment, fully absorbed into the romance of foreign postings. For correspondents from Associated Press, the assignment to Ireland entailed working 'under nerve-racking peril and difficulty in an atmosphere of ambushes, raids, killings and reprisals'.[11] A reporter from United Press International was driven blindfolded in a horse and carriage over bumpy roads to meet the Sinn Féin president, Eamon De Valera, and published an interview said to have enraged the British censors.[12] In his memoirs, a *Chicago Tribune* correspondent recalled his time in Ireland as 'a delight, an inspiration. Its people were wonderful, its fight against Britain was worth the sympathy of the world, its revolution was real.'[13] On one conventional reading of the relationship between Ireland and the USA this empathy is hardly surprising. American journalists would be expected to be cheerleaders for Sinn Féin, or at least susceptible to the romance of a revolution in Ireland. Such a view would be inadequate to explain the generic practice of American journalists in Ireland, however. As we shall see, an often symbiotic relationship between professional norms and political ideology could as much shape the work of American journalists in Ireland as individual romantic whimsy.

It is worth taking a closer look at two American correspondents who came to Ireland with very contrasting ideas of what journalism meant and what journalists should do. One, Francis Hackett, was Irish born, a well-known literary journalist in Washington and also a partisan Irish nationalist; the other, Carl Ackerman, was a prominent and well-travelled foreign correspondent who was an archetypal exponent of the newly established professionalism of American journalism, and who leaned heavily on British military and intelligence officials to explain Ireland to a US audience. Considered together they reveal how occupational identity, different attitudes to sources of information and political conviction could produce two very different readings of the Irish revolution.

Francis Hackett, the distinguished literary editor of the *New Republic*, was a true believer in the Irish revolution. In 1920, Hackett – who was born in Co. Kilkenny and came to the USA when he was a teenager – told the American Commission on Conditions in Ireland (a panel of politicians, clergymen and journalists assembled by the *Nation* magazine in New York) that he had always sympathised with Sinn Féin's aspirations but never believed they were practicable until 1919.[14] Hackett himself was an oddity among the staff at the *New Republic*, most of whom were graduates of Ivy League colleges and appeared to the legendary John Reed as 'aloof, calm and Olympian, removed from the world of factory and trench, picket line and caucus chamber, about which they wrote with such assurance'.[15] By contrast, Hackett had never been to university and 'could feel really at ease at a Socialist party convention or a union strike meeting'.[16] Edmund Wilson recorded how Hackett regarded monarchy as 'the most fatuous of human institutions'.[17] Among his colleagues he acquired a reputation as an

Anglophobe.[18] He clashed repeatedly with Walter Lippmann, particularly over the *New Republic*'s support for the war.[19] Hackett complained that he had never been consulted by the other editors about the decision and protested that he had backed Woodrow Wilson for the presidency because he thought he was the candidate most likely to keep the USA neutral.[20]

In the pages of the *New Republic* Hackett usually confined himself to book reviews and literary essays. His political differences with his fellow editors were mostly evident when he wrote about Ireland. After the war in Ireland began, the *New Republic*'s editors made it clear that they opposed coercion, advocating the withdrawal of British troops. Their position was that Ireland should be granted Dominion status within the British Empire, an institution that commanded their admiration:

> The existing relationship between the British Empire and its self-governing dominions is the most successful and instructive example of an essentially moral yet still effective tie among substantially independent peoples which history has to record. This is the novel ingredient of British Imperial politics and it is only by acting in the light of this admirable precedent that British statesmanship can prevent Ireland from remaining a source of weakness and demoralisation to the British Commonwealth.[21]

However, in contrast to Walter Lippmann and the other editors, Hackett held a much darker view of British imperialism. In a commentary on a statement by the British ambassador to Washington (published in the magazine as a letter, a sign of the distancing of Hackett's views from the official editorial line), he dismissed the diplomat's protestations that British policy in Ireland was essentially noble and disinterested as 'hackneyed formulae', which should not fool Americans:

> The inspiration of British policy in his time, [the ambassador] tells us, is to bring order out of chaos, to extend the boundaries of freedom, to improve the lot of the oppressed, to increase the material prosperity of the world … We know that Britain has extended the boundaries of oil territory as well as freedom, that it has inevitably been improving the lot of the oppressors as well as the oppressed.[22]

To accept the Ambassador's arguments (as his fellow editors at the *New Republic* appeared to do) would be to pervert American values, according to Hackett: '[The ambassador] has taken the line that England's role in this generation is everywhere the high moral role. This has never been true of any country and is not true of England.'[23]

At the end of July 1920 Hackett and his wife Signe Toksvig, a Danish journalist, went to Ireland and spent eight weeks travelling around the country. Their mission, according to Hackett, was 'not only to investigate the facts but to interpret them'.[24] In the months after his return he published a series of pieces in the *New Republic* describing the situation in Ireland. The question at issue, he asserted in his first piece, was 'fundamentally moral'. For Hackett, British policy under Lloyd George was illiberal and anti-democratic, reduced to reliance on the argument that holding Ireland was dictated by military necessity. In more than one sense, Hackett wrote, the war in Europe had left Britain too exhausted to deal with the rebellion in Ireland:

> [Everyone] knows that tiredness is moral as well as mental. It is the moral conflict which Ireland excites that accounts for British khaki-mindedness, petulance and fatigue. Sinn Féin, on the contrary has no rat in its moral wainscot. Sinn Féin is calm, keen and cool. This difference in temper is deeply significant…'[25]

Having asserted the moral superiority of Sinn Féin, Hackett attempted to argue that Irish nationalism should be a natural cause for American liberals. 'Is it Bolshevism?', he asked rhetorically. 'Is it syndicalism? Is it godlessness and irreligion? Is it anarchy? On the contrary, it is the most simple and elementary political proposal, about as wild as woman-suffrage.' The demand that a nation had the right to legislate for itself was nothing new: 'It involves an idea as old and as familiar, and as moss-grown, and as harmless, as the American Revolution of 1776.'[26]

The following week Hackett published in the *New Republic* a description of the workings of one of the local courts that Sinn Féin had established across Ireland as rivals to the Crown courts in an act both of usurpation and propaganda. Hackett began his article with a description of 'Mr W.', the Sinn Féin judge, selling sweets to children in his newsagents' shop in an undisclosed location: 'He was thin and worn, a seamed and grizzled man whose appearance had absorbed something of his stooped and ill-lit establishment.' We soon learn that the shopkeeper's health had been broken during a spell in prison in England after the 1916 Rising. While Hackett talks to Mr W., customers continue to arrive and, like the image of the children buying sweets at the outset, each transaction noted by Hackett establishes a picture of normality: a policeman (who obviously had no fear of entering a Sinn Féiner's shop) bought a sports paper and was served with 'perfect civility'; a young doctor – 'well-conditioned' – paid for sweets and English magazines.[27] An IRA man arrived to inform Mr W. that they were about to bring in a man who has been living rough in the woods and to ask if, in his capacity as judge, he could have an order ready to commit the tramp to the workhouse. Hackett gives no reason why the man in the woods had been 'exiled by his family and had for several years been living afoot like a hunted thing, half naked and famished and afraid'. However, the effect of this story of rescue is to portray Irish revolutionaries as benevolent agents of social reform, a compassionate militia subject to the due process of law administered by civilians.[28]

The next day Hackett goes to a session of the Sinn Féin court in a local village hall, still decorated from a recently staged play. The hall is crowded with people who, like the customers in Mr W.'s shop, encompassed the broad base of Sinn Féin's support: 'young men and old, shawled women, grannies and boys … artisans, labourers, publicans, farmers, shopkeepers. A late arrival was a curate who took his place in our row.'[29] Hackett is struck by the absence of formalities like oaths, constables and court attendants. When a row threatens to break out between a farmer and a shopkeeper who claimed his windows had been broken by the farmer's untended cattle, two IRA volunteers rise from the mass of people in the hall to gently enforce order. Later they restrain an enraged defendant but – in Hackett's telling – without crushing him: 'The Volunteers held their ground with insistence, but they gave play to this fiery human nature – which is their own nature, but disciplined and responsible and dignified, the nature that has made these Irish courts.'[30]

Aside from their undisguised partisanship, Hackett's articles on Ireland for the *New Republic* are clearly literary. His declared purpose not only to collect facts but to interpret them, his treatment of people and events through a series of novelistic scenes and the revelation of his political convictions in argument, show that he had no intention of being bound by the standard rules of mainstream American journalism. The fact that he was writing for an intellectual magazine and not a mass-circulation newspaper only partly accounts for his suppressed disdain for conventional report-age.[31] Much more germane is the fact that Hackett, in all his years in journalism, never became a professional reporter. He had no formal training in journalism of the kind that was then becoming popular in the USA.

Francis Hackett had arrived from Ireland in 1900 and at the age of 18 he came to the attention of an editor at the *Chicago American,* according to his colleagues, while selling neckties in the basement of one of the city's biggest department stores.[32] Hackett himself recounted how he was initially determined to succeed in the newsroom: 'I was inexhaustibly keen as a reporter. It demanded direct contact with people in the throes of action.'[33] The action of interest to the *Chicago American* was 'police news': dramatic human interest stories of crime and murder. Hackett struggled to deliver what was needed and was sacked because he refused to lie to obtain a photograph of a murder victim.[34] He managed to get himself a trial as a reporter on the *Chicago Evening Post* but after again failing to make an impression, concluded that he was only fit for writing editorials: 'I was not cut out to be a reporter. On the local American scene I was befuddled about unfamiliar issues that made news, nor had I the audacity to extract details on the surface.'[35] This explanation hints at how the job of the American reporter was becoming increasingly subject to formal procedures and was defined as the pursuit of a discrete set of details about a narrow set of issues.

At the time Hackett was trying to make his way in Chicago newspapers, mainstream American journalism was abandoning its identification with literary bohemianism: 'By the end of the nineteenth century the commercial popular press had transformed journalism into a business of news for the masses. A business model imposed on a craft had changed its practices and ethics.'[36] Journalism had become 'fact-centred and news-centred rather than devoted primarily to political commentary or preoccupied with literary aspirations' – as Francis Hackett was.[37] Rules were laid down in reporting manuals and new vocational courses emerged (the first journalism school opened in Missouri in 1908).[38] President Woodrow Wilson himself encouraged journalists to move towards professional respectability, noting disparagingly that before 1900 every newspaper was a 'law unto itself, without standards of either work or duty: its code of ethics, not yet codified like those of medicine or of law, had been, like its stylebook, individualistic in character'.[39] The first journalism textbook (published in 1894) clearly laid out what the new collective nostrum would be: 'It is the mission of the reporter to reproduce facts and the opinions of others, not to express his own.'[40]

Francis Hackett's early discomfiture in the city rooms of the big Chicago papers was provoked by his reluctance to grasp exactly how much this dictum had taken hold in American journalism. But the new discipline was certainly clear to other foreigners. In his study of political parties published in 1902, the German political scientist Moisei Ostrogorski observed that the American newspaper 'considers itself in the first place as a purveyor of facts, true, if such can be obtained, or otherwise…'.[41] And perusing an American textbook in 1913 a British press critic was appalled by how American journalists were all expected to conform to the same strict conventions:

> It conjured up in the mind's eye a vision of hundreds and hundreds of American towns, scattered over those vast States, producing similar newspapers on similar lines – hundreds and hundreds of newspapers training and sending out their professional journalists to carry on essentially the same work with the greater metropolitan papers - thousands and thousands of journalists migrating from newspaper to newspaper with the stamp of … reporter on their foreheads.[42]

This was not the kind of endorsement sought by Francis Hackett when he entered journalism; his repeated false starts in the Chicago newsrooms were largely a recoil against the kind of editorial regime that Michael Schudson has characterised as a form of 'industrial discipline'.[43] Hackett became literary editor of the *Chicago Evening Post* and later, before he joined the *New Republic*, the editor of a muckraking magazine.[44] Muckraking journalists prized facts but not – as one American reporter believed the public desired them – 'facts piled up to the point of dry certitude'.[45] The muckrakers deployed facts against organised interests and corrupt politicians in the service of their reforming convictions and in the belief that journalists 'had the potential – through the power of the press and public opinion – to overcome the weaknesses of political institutions'.[46] This was the sensibility that informed Hackett's articles on Ireland for the *New Republic*.

How did 'professional' American reporters treat the Irish revolution differently? A useful way of examining this question is to turn to the work of a prominent American foreign correspondent for an influential East Coast newspaper. Walter Lippmann placed Carl Ackerman of the Philadelphia *Public Ledger* on his list of first-rate foreign correspondents, 'men who know their way about the world'.[47] After graduating from Columbia University in 1913, Ackerman went to work for the United Press news agency in Washington to cover the White House, the State Department and foreign embassies. In 1915 he moved to Berlin for United Press International (UPI) and during the war he covered both the eastern and western fronts (and claimed to be one of the first American correspondents to fly over a battlefield in an army plane.) After the Russian Revolution he was a correspondent with the Allied intervention force in Siberia and also reported from China.[48] In early 1920 Ackerman was recruited by the *Public Ledger* to be the London correspondent for the paper's new foreign news service.

Until 1913 the *Public Ledger* was, in the words of a contemporary observer, 'one of the staidest of Philadelphia's institutions, a perfect embodiment of ... conservatism and propriety...'.[49] It was then bought by Cyrus H.K. Curtis, a successful magazine proprietor who aimed to turn it into an influential national newspaper, an American version of the *Manchester Guardian*.[50] It hired young reporters who were enthusiastic supporters of Wilsonian democracy. In 1918 the *Public Ledger* denounced American hostility towards the Russian Revolution, an editorial stance which provoked 'intense conflict between its liberal editors and its conservative readers...'.[51] However, after the Bolsheviks signed a peace treaty with Germany its editors 'reverted to a cautious conservatism'.[52] Thus, despite having 'a remarkable foreign service which it has widely syndicated'[53], the paper laid itself open to the charge of being 'a creature of many opinions but of no convictions...'.[54]

Ackerman began work as London correspondent for the *Public Ledger* at the beginning of March 1920 and, as he confessed to his editor, his early dispatches were largely composed from whatever news appeared in the London press while he waited to establish his own contacts.[55] On 20 March a dispatch from Ackerman appeared in the *Public Ledger* declaring Ireland was 'in a state of civil war', as demonstrated by the occurrence of 'a crop of crimes'. The evening newspapers in London, Ackerman reported, were 'crowded with news of riots, murders, robberies, hold-ups, raids and assassinations from Cork to Dublin'.[56]

Early the following month, Ackerman made his first visit to Ireland. The anarchy suggested by the news reaching London was not reflected in his initial dispatches from Dublin. Instead of a state of disorder he found a country in a ferment of convivial intellectual debate:

> As I saunter about the city meeting almost every hour some new leader or representative citizen, because all men of all factions and beliefs and parties are exceedingly approachable and cordial, I am impressed by the seriousness and firm convictions which all hold. Even those who pride themselves on their detached viewpoint become after fifteen minutes' conversation the most confirmed partisans. Like all revolutionary movements, this one in Ireland has its camp followers from every corner of the globe. There are Englishmen, Frenchmen, Americans, and maybe Germans for all I know, in every camp. Each leader has his satellites, who, over whisky and soda and champagne, sing the praises of each leader and his 'solution of the Irish problem' all based upon distrust of England.[57]

Travelling by train to Cork he was struck by the ubiquity of rebel sympathisers and described a city where the revolutionaries were in control:

> They ... drove me to my hotel; they served me in the restaurant; they showed me about the city; they talked revolution and independence late into the night; they greeted me again this morning. Everywhere I look, everywhere I go, I meet Sinn Féiners ... Everywhere people appear determined, defiant, confident.[58]

In contrast to the cocksure swagger of the revolutionaries, the police were portrayed by Ackerman as isolated, cowering figures, without authority:

> As I drove or walked about the city I met the same groups of eight, ten or twelve members of the Royal Irish Constabulary, huddled together in a corner of the post-office building or at a theatre or a street corner, armed with rifles, also defiant. But their defiance was pathetic. Last night eight of these policemen, armed with rifles and revolvers, were standing in a corner of two buildings near the post office, silent and, from outward appearance, terrified, while across the street crowds of young men, women and boys passed, avoiding the police as if they were contaminated.[59]

By the time of his next visit in July, Ackerman had reached an unequivocal conclusion: 'The facts about Ireland today are these: There are two governments, Sinn Féin and the British; there are two armies, Republican and royal.'[60]

Ackerman's reportorial eye, when engaged, could be keen and watchful. Arriving at the ferry port in Dublin he took note of how 'even Irish sailors showed feeling' towards the British troops, helping them to unload ships. But the railway station nearby was 'about as dead as some depots in Poland during the German invasion when all inhabitants had fled'.[61] In an unpublished draft of a magazine article he described how one day a car drove past him down the quay of the River Liffey with its roof torn to shreds:

> In the rear seat, behind the chauffeur, sat a Black-and-Tan trooper holding one of his comrades whose face, hands and green uniform were covered with blood. Death was running them a close race to the Royal Hospital on the hill.[62]

However, these vignettes were incidental to Ackerman's work. Investigating the war in more detail, beyond the scenes that were thrust in his path, held little interest for him. He stayed in the city; there are no accounts of visits to the scenes of ambushes or reprisals in rural areas or to civilians caught up in the war. And the tactics of the IRA or the Black and Tans – the obsessive focus of interest for British correspondents in Ireland, as we have already seen – rarely concerned him.

Ackerman's view of the conflict in Ireland was that of the disinterested yet appreciative spectator, observing a battle of wills with cool discrimination. A few months after Ackerman began his posting in London, he and his colleagues in other European capitals were chided by John J. Spurgeon, their editor in Philadelphia, for writing daily about 'a new move on the political chessboard' rather than thinking of 'news in the human sense'.[63] Revealingly, in an article specially commissioned by the *New York Times* to mark the truce in 1921, the chessboard is the analogy Ackerman himself chose to explain the Irish conflict. The war was rendered as a contest between two well-matched adversaries:

> No matter what the Irish did the equilibrium of British statesmanship was maintained, and each time the British Government made a move on the

chessboard of negotiation or warfare the Irish counter move was a master stroke. The Irish sense of humour and British poise prevented the checkmate until the hour arrived for the settlement of the century-old score.[64]

The depiction of a joust between 'Irish humour' and 'British poise' placed the war on a very different plane to that portrayed by Francis Hackett – who saw the issues at stake as 'fundamentally moral' – or the British and European correspondents for whom the campaign of reprisals by the Black and Tans called into question Britain's claim to be a beacon of civilisation in a barbarous world. How did Ackerman arrive at his particular understanding of the Irish revolution? One explanation is to be found in the intimate affinity between the beliefs of a generation of American foreign correspondents and Wilsonian ideology. Another derives from the idea of journalism and their own professional role held by Ackerman and his colleagues in the mainstream American press. As we shall see, both explanatory threads are intertwined.

Ackerman believed that being American endowed his work as a foreign correspondent with unique and desirable qualities. A brochure for prospective clients of the *Public Ledger* foreign news service informed them that it stood for 'fair play – for the broadest, bravest and most chivalrous Americanism'. Its correspondents, including Ackerman, had spent years acquiring expertise in European capitals but subscribers were assured that they had not been corrupted by exposure to Old World intrigues: they were 'native Americans who [would] see the Old World through American eyes' and they had been 'instructed to take no sides, play no favourites, reflect no prejudices'.[65] The brochure included a tribute paid to Ackerman by the American ambassador to Berlin during the war, who contrasted Ackerman's 'unimpaired Americanism' with the pro-German tendencies of the other correspondents, complimenting him on his 'splendid patriotism under fire'.[66] When he resigned from the *Public Ledger* in 1921, after a series of disputes with his editors, Ackerman wrote that he had wanted 'a foreign service which is all-American, which aims for accuracy and reliability first and which is free of propaganda and foreign entanglements...'.[67]

This depiction of specific professional ideals – fairness, accuracy, reliability – as inherently American is characteristically Wilsonian. In the sense that Wilson believed Americans brought a set of intrinsic ideals to politics,

Ackerman believed the same about the American contribution to journalism. And in his approach to international relations, Ackerman had revealed himself as a true Wilsonian long before he began to report on Ireland. In a series of books written out of his foreign assignments, Ackerman aligned himself with the policies of the Wilson administration. Covering the American intervention in Mexico he concluded that continuing guidance from Washington was indispensable if Mexico was to fulfil its potential to become a great nation.[68] He even identified a local whom he suspected of spreading pro-German propaganda as 'a trouble breeder, who might, with advantage, be watched by the [US] Department of Justice'.[69] After his time with the Allied forces in Siberia he dismissed Bolshevism as merely a passing fad and, in a somewhat tortured metaphor, conceived a vision of progress entirely commensurate with Wilson's doctrines:

> The pendulum of history has swung from reaction to revolution, but civilization has been advanced only when the pendulum swung backward and forward evenly over the arc of Time … It is the task of the peoples and governments of the world to generate the gravity which makes the pendulum swing ceaselessly and regularly, ticking the hours of progress which make the days of happiness and the centuries of advancement.[70]

The provision of facts to an enlightened public opinion would be the motor of this pacific evolution: 'The senseless demands of the radicals find no support among the great mass of people in any country where the facts can be shown. Facts are the deadliest arguments against reaction and revolution…'[71]

Perhaps most revealing of all is a note Ackerman made in the diary he kept while living in London (and which is mostly devoted to his work on Ireland). On 10 January 1921 he transcribed a passage from a book by an English traveller to the American colonies in the mid-eighteenth century:

> An idea, strange as it is visionary, has entered into minds of the generality of mankind, that empire is travelling westward and everyone is looking forward with eager and impatient expectation to that destined moment when America is to give law to the rest of the world. But if ever an idea was illusory and fallacious I will venture to predict that this will be so.[72]

Then Ackerman added his own gloss to this rash dismissal of eventual American hegemony: 'But was not this prophesy ... fulfilled in 1917, 1918, 1919? One hundred and fifty years for an idea to develop and be expressed.'[73] The notion that America would 'give law to the rest of the world' was central to Wilson's vision of the part he would play in a new post-war settlement.[74]

Ackerman's adherence to a Wilsonian worldview was not merely an intellectual position. In London he received daily guidance on his dispatches from Col. Edward House, President Wilson's former confidant and fixer, who had been retained by the *Public Ledger* as an advisor on diplomacy.[75] Several years earlier, when the *Public Ledger* was trying to establish itself as a major liberal paper, House had made friends with several of its young journalists, entertaining hopes of making the paper 'a semi-official organ of the Wilson administration'.[76] He may not have achieved this, but he did convince some key journalists that 'he represented the pinnacle of political wisdom'.[77] Certainly, Ackerman's diary reveals that during his time as London correspondent House had a major influence on his reporting. He refers to the ways in which he might make use of the colonel's analysis of world affairs in his own dispatches and plans how he will 'carry out Col. House ideas and carry on his work after he leaves Europe...'.[78]

Ackerman's reliance on House was not unconnected to his view of how he should collect news as a journalist; the idea that good journalism was the fruit of being on excellent terms with powerful contacts. In an unpublished magazine article Ackerman outlined his belief that

> every correspondent who has had foreign experience seeks to discover 'key men' in 'key positions' – men who know what is being privately discussed by cabinet officers, men who know what governmental policies are and when they are apt to be modified or changed.[79]

Ackerman professed more trust for these sources than for the views of ministers or heads of departments because 'influential statesmen too frequently have axes of their own to grind'.[80] In a letter written in March 1920 – ten days after the launch of the news service – Ackerman wrote to his boss in Philadelphia that he had been working assiduously on developing connections:

I think I have the American Embassy with me now. I have a good friend in the Foreign Office and for the moment I am working Downing Street. I find all English officials very reserved toward American correspondents because as my best friends explain they have been 'let down' frequently of late by American newspapermen and they are taking no chances. It may be a long uphill fight but, fortunately, this is not my first encounter with foreign government indifference, tinged with opposition. My first task, naturally, is to win their confidence even by sacrificing my work.[81]

As Ackerman intimates in his article, the idea that 'key men in key positions' should be the foundation for respectable journalism was a doctrine commonly held by American correspondents in Europe. The first American journalism textbook – referred to already for its dictum that the journalist should reproduce the opinions of others and not his own – emphasised the importance of authoritative sources.[82] By 1906 a new textbook for young journalists advised them to 'cultivate the friendship of influential citizens…'.[83] The ability to make prized contacts and passively await the transmission of 'inside' information was by then more valued in a reporter than a talent to explore an eclectic range of sources. In 1903 Julian Ralph, a New York *Sun* correspondent, observed that publishing an exclusive news story was 'growing to be more and more a product of intimate acquaintance with public men, and less and less a result of agility of mind and body'. Ralph chose a striking simile to illuminate contemporary journalism practice:

No one looks for news anymore. That is an old-fashioned idea which outsiders will persist in retaining. News is now gathered systematically by men stationed at all the outlets of it, like guards at the gate of a walled city, by whom nothing can pass in or out unnoticed.[84]

For Ackerman the gates of his own walled city were to be found at the American embassy, the Foreign Office and Downing Street. The combination of Ackerman's Wilsonian outlook – in which Ireland became a problem on the chessboard of international relations, to be solved by liberal pragmatism – and his belief that his credibility depended on his proximity to powerful sources is to be seen in how he set out his credentials in an article in the *New York Times* explaining how the British Government and the IRA came to agree a truce in 1921:

For nearly two years I have been in intimate contact with both British and Irish leaders. I have travelled frequently in Ireland and between that country and England. As a result of first-hand observations I propose to relate, for the first time, the inside story of the event which led to the truce and to the present conferences in London and Dublin.[85]

A year later, in a remarkable series of long articles in the *Atlantic Monthly*, Ackerman spelled out his role in even more detail. It was only partly a behind-the-scenes account of negotiations between the British government and the Irish rebels; it also explained how Ackerman himself became a participant in the negotiations as a mediator.

One of Ackerman's most reliable sources was Sir Basil Thomson, director of intelligence at Scotland Yard. Shortly after he started to work as a correspondent in London, Ackerman went to tea at the Foreign Office where he was advised by the under-secretary of state, William Tyrell, to call on Thomson 'because everything of a confidential nature relating to Ireland and from Ireland passed through his hands before it reached the Prime Minister'.[86] Soon Ackerman was calling at Scotland House every day. At their first meeting in May 1920 Thomson passed to him documents about Michael Collins, and Richard Mulcahy, the IRA chief of staff, seized during a raid in Dublin, as well as a copy of the constitution of the Irish Republican Brotherhood, the secret revolutionary organisation of which Collins was leader. Ackerman wrote an article about the documents for publication, which he sent to Thomson for revision.[87]

From Ackerman's account, Thomson intended that the leak would prepare the ground for negotiation with the IRA leaders, weakening the movement's appeal as the expressed will of the Irish people by disclosing its secret and sinister puppeteers. Ackerman wrote that Thomson believed it 'necessary for all parties to realize … that the real leaders of Sinn Féin were not the men then in the public eye'. However, Ackerman also wrote that Thomson was 'doubtful of the possibilities of suppressing the Sinn Féin movement by military means'.[88] As their relationship progressed, Thomson briefed Ackerman to carry messages to Sinn Féin and IRA leaders in Ireland, using Ackerman's journalistic missions as a cover for advancing an Irish settlement by negotiation.

After meeting Basil Thomson in London, Ackerman often went to Dublin to see General Sir Nevil Macready, the commander of British forces in Ireland. Ackerman met Macready on his first visit to Dublin at the beginning of April 1920.[89] He decided that Macready, like Thomson, was blessed with 'the traditional poise of the British people'.[90] Thomson gave Ackerman letters of introduction and it was Macready who facilitated his contacts with the underground leadership of the IRA.[91]

On the afternoon of 30 June 1920, Ackerman took tea with Macready at his headquarters in the Royal Hospital, Kilmainham, in Dublin – '[a] most beautiful old place with veterans of [the] Crimean war in their faded red, blue costumes hanging about everywhere'.[92] Macready said he would welcome some kind of mediation because 'something ought to be done … before [the] troops [got] out of hand'.[93] Thus, Macready gave Ackerman permission to make contact with IRA figures who would be captured if they appeared in public. This licence was granted at the behest of Thomson, who had chosen Ackerman as the conduit for 'a confidential exchange of views between representatives of the two peoples'.[94] The idea was that if the IRA was agreeable to the idea, Col. House could step in as a formal mediator.

In the days after his tea with Macready, Ackerman met Arthur Griffith, leader of Sinn Féin and the man considered by the British to be the leading moderate on the Irish side. Griffith told him he would accept mediation if Ireland could be recognised as the 'Switzerland of the seas'.[95] Ackerman returned to London to tell Basil Thomson at Scotland Yard that Sinn Féin was interested in a settlement. On the basis of this briefing, according to Ackerman, 'it was decided that steps should be taken to persuade the British Cabinet and the Dail to invite Colonel House [to be mediator]'. This involved Basil Thomson speaking directly to Lloyd George and enlisting the support of civil servants and leading politicians.[96]

Ackerman's sources mounted a concerted effort to argue for negotiations rather than a military solution, based on the information Ackerman had gathered on his reporting trip to Dublin. According to Ackerman, this remarkable campaign of persuasion almost bore fruit when Philip Kerr, Lloyd George's secretary, asked Col. House to become a mediator. The scheme foundered, however, when Sinn Féin decided 'that there could be no negotiations except between accredited representatives of the "Irish Nation" and official representatives of the British Government'.[97]

The collapse of the attempt at mediation did not mean that Ackerman's role as a go-between was over. In mid-August Desmond FitzGerald sent a telegram to Ackerman saying he had arranged an interview with Michael Collins and that he should come to Dublin at once.[98] Ackerman delayed his journey for four days so that he could have more consultations with Special Branch: 'Sir Basil was extremely anxious to know what kind of man [Collins] was; why he would not agree to independence within the British Commonwealth of Nations wherein lay his strength with the Irish army and people.'[99]

Shortly after his arrival in Dublin, Ackerman met FitzGerald at the Shelbourne Hotel in the centre of the city and they went on a walk which ended up at the front door of a Georgian house in nearby Fitzwilliam Square. After an elaborate series of coded knocks, Ackerman was admitted and taken to a back room on the third floor. A short while later Michael Collins 'boldly entered' and shook hands. 'I noticed that [he] was quite young', Ackerman later wrote, 'and expressed my surprise that a man who was supposed to have all [the] power he had in Ireland should still be in his thirties.'[100] Collins then indulged in a further piece of theatre, producing cuttings of articles Ackerman had written on the basis of his briefings from the Special Branch. 'I see you are publishing my private correspondence before it arrives,' Collins said.[101] Then he added, 'You see I know you better than you know me.'[102]

For two hours Collins and FitzGerald discussed Sinn Féin demands with Ackerman. Collins said there would be no compromise until the British government recognised Ireland as a republic. But later in the conversation he seemed to concede that a republic might not be achievable, saying that Sinn Féin's fundamental demands were that Ireland controlled finance, the courts, the police and the army.[103] When Ackerman returned to London he had several conversations with Thomson, trying to interpret which of Michael Collins' statements was the best reflection of the real position; in other words, whether the Irish revolutionaries should be regarded as absolutists or compromisers. Thomson asked Ackerman for a memorandum that could be shown to the Irish Secretary, Hamar Greenwood. Ackerman discounted the demand for the republic and favoured Thomson's assessment that Collins could deliver a settlement acceptable to the British government. However, Ackerman wrote later, the final decision rested with

Lloyd George, and the prime minister chose to interpret Collins' remarks as a renewed challenge. Ackerman blamed Lloyd George for the failure of these negotiations. In his *Atlantic Monthly* articles, Thomson and Macready on the British side and Collins and Griffith on the Irish side are portrayed as peacemakers. Lloyd George wanted a 'truce of surrender' and 'was not yet in favour of a "peace without victory"'.[104]

The Irish historian Paul Bew, who has used Ackerman's *Atlantic Monthly* articles in an appraisal of British policy in Ireland, believes he was co-opted by a network of British officials who 'had a clear picture of the [eventual] settlement ... and a confidence in their ability to deliver, in the end, the prime minister'.[105] Certainly, a closer examination of his private papers seems to support this view. Ackerman's job was to ascertain if the IRA leadership was ready for a compromise. On his visit to the Foreign Office as he was starting out in London, he had been told by C.J. Philips, Lord Curzon's chief assistant on Irish affairs, that 'within three years Ireland will be a republic in everything but name. Within less time than that all the British troops will be out of Ireland.'[106]

Bew notes that Curzon told his Cabinet colleagues in July 1920 that they had to negotiate with Sinn Féin since '[we] shall be driven to dominion home rule sooner or later'. To this Balfour replied, 'That won't solve the question. They will ask for a republic.'[107] Bew suggests that Curzon and the officials pushing for negotiation used Ackerman 'to find out, in effect, if Balfour's contention had substance'.[108] There is no sign that Ackerman's employers were aware of the secret work he had undertaken. In August 1920 Ackerman's editor, John J. Spurgeon, wrote to him expressing relief that Col. House had abandoned the idea of becoming a mediator in Ireland. The editor felt that for House, 'in his present capacity as a member of the Editorial staff of an American newspaper, such a role would be absolutely out of the question'.[109] If it was out of bounds for House to become a mediator on grounds of preserving editorial independence – even though he was an advisor to the *Public Ledger* and not a journalist – it must have been an equally forbidden path for Ackerman.

In Ackerman's account of his adventures, the one character who stands out is Basil Thomson of Scotland Yard. Thomson had taken over the Special Branch in 1913 after spending ten years in the Colonial Service in Fiji, New Guinea and Tonga and several years as a prison governor. He was a qualified barrister and had published novels and popular histories.[110] By the time he met Ackerman, Thomson was skilled at using journalists in his detective work. After journalists objected to Special Branch officers posing as reporters to get into syndicalist and suffragette meetings, Thomson won approval from the Home Secretary to pay a press agency to provide regular reports of the meetings.[111] And after the Easter Rebellion in 1916 Thomson persuaded the American journalist Arthur Bullard that the Irish rebels had merely been the dupes of a cynical German plot to divert British troops from Flanders to Dublin.[112]

There is no evidence that Ackerman was aware of Thomson's previous manipulations of journalists, or that it caused him any concern if he was aware of it. Ackerman's veneration for Thomson is expressed at length in an unpublished article entitled 'The house of a thousand mysteries'. Ackerman found Thomson to be 'the most painstaking, patient, persistent person I ever met ... the embodiment of British poise, that national characteristic which keeps the ship of state always on an even keel'.[113] This impression of imperturbability is at odds with an assessment of Thomson by a historian of the Special Branch who remarked on the 'exaggerated view of the sub-vertability of society' held by its detectives, a paranoia exemplified by 'the ludicrously extravagant accounts of their exploits' published by Thomson himself.[114] There is no sense in which any of this side of Thomson's character appears in Ackerman's appraisal.

Even more impressive for Ackerman than Thomson's self-assurance was the omniscience of the Special Branch; he portrays it as both a panoptic gatherer of information and the essential intelligence storehouse of the state. 'Without Scotland House', Ackerman wrote, 'the government of the day would be blind and deaf.'[115] Images of omniscience recur in his descriptions of the work of the Special Branch. The agency is 'the tower of observation' of strikes, rebellions and revolutionary plots, expert in 'mass psychology'.[116] The detectives who protect the prime minister are gifted with the ability to gaze into men's souls: 'Like eagle's eyes they penetrate beyond the mask of a facial expression. They sense men's motives and thoughts.'[117] Above all, Thomson makes his decisions on facts which 'can be fitted into the Chinese puzzles of politics or conspiracies with which he has to deal every day'.[118]

Ackerman listed the plots broken by Thomson's investigators: 'Bolshevist plots' in Ireland and India; the attempted assassination of Lloyd George by anarchists in Paris; the financing of uprisings in Mesopotamia and Egypt.[119] All of these schemes were allowed to proceed until the moment was right to cut them down. For Ackerman, the secret of the Special Branch's success was tolerance:

> It is this fact which those who predict revolution in England overlook. Liberty within the British Isles is more elastic than rubber. Is there any place in the world outside of Trafalgar Square, Hyde Park and the Marble Arch where anarchists, dreamers, religious fanatics, politicians, Communists, Scientists, Ministers and Whatnots may rant against the government, society, religion and the press without being molested?[120]

Ackerman's fascination with Thomson cannot be attributed to the reporter's desire to be 'close to and conversant with the "inside story" of political and economic life'.[121] In his discussion of the emergence of the interview as a form, Michael Schudson has also identified a complementary desire among reporters to be seen not, as the journalistic myth would have it, to speak truth to power but to speak 'close to power'.[122] And in the relationship revealed in Ackerman's notes and articles there is another dynamic at work, one identified by Christopher Lasch in describing Col. House's delight in watching his words being taken down by admiring reporters. This was the interviewee's self-conscious sense of being a figure in a big news story:

> In a world which manifests itself through the mass media, ambition is more likely to take the form of a kind of voyeurism directed in upon oneself, a longing to see oneself as one appears to the world, immortalised in the glare of publicity.[123]

But the source of Ackerman's enthusiastic approval of Thomson's method can also be located – as can the journalist's sense of his professionalism – in the prevailing popularity of scientific solutions to America's social problems. In the time of Wilson's presidency, 'many were increasingly emphasising the need for scientific expertise and administrative efficiency as the essential means to bring about ordered, benevolent change'.[124] This was as true in journalism as in other fields.

In 1920 Walter Lippmann was arguing that journalists should choose as models 'the patient and fearless men of science who have laboured to see what the world really is' and that 'good reporting requires the exercise of the highest of the scientific virtues'.[125] Louis Menand has suggested that this respect for professionalism, expertise and the efficiency of institutions had its origins in the attraction of these qualities for the generation which had been through the American civil war:[126] '[Pragmatists] spoke to a generation of academics, journalists, jurists, and policy makers eager to find scientific solutions to social problems, and happy to be given good reasons to ignore the claims of finished cosmologies.'[127] For Ackerman, Basil Thomson's composed and masterful manipulation of the facts allowed him to control fanatics and revolutionaries through the application of psychology rather than brute force; in the same scientific spirit, the director of intelligence at Scotland Yard was engineering peace and restoring order in Ireland (with the assistance of the correspondent from the *Public Ledger*).

Comparing the work of Francis Hackett and Carl Ackerman reveals not just two different approaches to coverage of the Irish revolution but two different conceptions of journalism. Both men were proud to identify themselves with American values, both were politically committed to liberalism and both shared a respect for fact and observation. However, one had an exalted sense of the importance of journalism as a profession whereas the other saw it as a way of advancing an argument. In a speech delivered after he had become dean of the Journalism School at Columbia University, Ackerman described the modern newspaper as 'a laboratory where man is portrayed as he is so that he may learn how to improve himself'.[128] Contrast this with Hackett's deeply sceptical notion that 'we pick up a paper without any suspicion that we are about to commit intellectual felony. We do not know that the news editor is in a conspiracy to play on our minds.'[129] Behind those two views lay widely divergent ideas of the relationship between journalism and power.

In Hackett's articles his political argument in favour of the Irish cause is overt and his reportage is naturalistic and first-hand, refusing to give any special authority to powerful sources. Ackerman's dispatches, by contrast, strive for apparent neutrality and their validity, by his own measure, rests on how conversant he has been with sources close to power. In Ackerman's view of journalism, the newspaper is an adjunct to the institutions of state:

> When ... the leaders of two belligerent peoples are unable to meet person-
> ally they frequently accept the press ... as a forum before which they can
> present their views ... This is the great service that the modern newspaper
> renders to the public ... It is more influential than parliaments and its
> verdict is as decisive as any recorded vote of elected representatives of the
> people.[130]

Hence his view of his mission in Ireland: '[Michael] Collins did not speak
*to* me but *through* me to the citizens of his own country, England and the
United States...'.[131]

The different ways in which Hackett and Ackerman positioned themselves in relation to figures of authority and political power in covering Ireland provides a snapshot of a key moment of transition in American journalism, from what Stephen Ward has characterised as 'active empiricism'
to 'passive empiricism'.[132] The era of the muckrakers – with which Hackett
was temperamentally aligned – was giving way to an age of professionalism,
exemplified by Ackerman. Or as Ward has put it, journalism turned from
'robust empiricism' in the nineteenth century into a 'careful, rule-bound
method of objectivity in the twentieth'.[133] The ideal of the journalist 'crusading against the "powers that be"' persisted in American journalism, but
the professional model became predominant.[134]

Ackerman's methods of reporting gradually became the norm for correspondents in the USA. The procedures of American reporters covering
foreign affairs examined by Bernard Cohen in the early 1960s were the
same as those Ackerman had practised in Ireland in the 1920s:

> The reporter's formal ideology of the press as the neutral link between the
> active participants in the policy-making process finds expression in a set of
> roles that have as their aim the more effective performance of the linkage
> function. In other words, these images of the reporter's role are designed
> to make the formal process work better, by improving the capacity of the
> political participants to act constructively...[135]

In his book on American media and the Vietnam War, Daniel Hallin
identified the incorporation of the American press as 'an integral part of
the governing process' as a phenomenon of the second half of the twentieth century.[136] However, Ackerman's reporting from Ireland suggests

this incorporation was well under way in the 1920s. Ackerman and the elite group of foreign correspondents who were his contemporaries were distinguished by their belief in Wilsonian ideology and their ties to the administration itself.[137] This is the beginning of a process by which the correspondents become 'deeply intertwined in the actual operation of government'.[138] As we have seen in Ackerman's case, elite correspondents won the confidence of government officials, who regarded them as a conduit to the public and other political groups; for their part, the correspondents regarded the officials as their most important source of information and often shared their 'inside' view of the political issues of the day with them.

What of the implications for the Irish revolution of Hackett and Ackerman's coverage? As with the reporting of the British correspondents and those from Europe, Hackett's focus on the morality of coercion and the rights of the Irish nation were entirely in accord with the message that Sinn Féin sought to project to the world. The Irish revolutionaries hoped it would sway President Wilson toward supporting their cause. However, as Hackett failed to get the *New Republic*'s editors to see Ireland through his eyes, Sinn Féin failed to move Wilson to act as their persuader with the British government. In March 1919 Wilson admitted that, despite the appearance he had given of making the Irish question a matter of disagreement between Britain and the USA, in reality it was 'a domestic affair of the British Empire and … neither he nor any other foreign leader [had] any right to interfere…'.[139] In June of that year when an Irish-American delegation in Paris challenged him as to why the doctrine of self-determination should not be applied to Ireland, the president's brush-off was expressed with almost comic gravity: 'You have touched on the great metaphysical tragedy of today.'[140]

Ackerman knew all along that the USA would never risk its relationship with Britain for the sake of Ireland's self-determination. He recalled irritating Michael Collins during their secret negotiations by repeatedly explaining to him 'why and how the American people would not go to war over Ireland…'.[141] The image of the bespectacled American correspondent haranguing Ireland's most wanted guerrilla leader is intriguing. However, for Ackerman journalism was important as much for the access it gave him to the powerful as the opportunities it gave him to publish.

# VII
# LITERARY TOURISTS:
# G.K. CHESTERTON, WILFRED
# EWART AND V.S. PRITCHETT
# AS REPORTERS

*Limerick lay under dust. It was hot. One found a baking station-yard and a long, straight main street suggestive of a Canadian prairie town. How ugly this place is and how shadeless! ... The abiding impression of Limerick was of the soldiers wandering through the streets in their curious patrol formation ... As to the lorry-loads of Black and Tans and the armoured cars, they were as numerous as in Dublin. And with what a clatter, with what a whirl of dust they careered along that arid main street on their way to or from the barracks! The old-fashioned Cruise's Hotel near the Town Hall had been taken over as temporary police barracks, so had a large building in Cecil Street, outside which Black and Tans lounged and smoked.*

Wilfred Ewart, *A Journey in Ireland 1921*

Gertrude Stein famously criticised Ernest Hemingway for spending too much time writing journalism rather than novels with the supercilious put-down, 'remarks are not literature'.[1] Despite their better judgement novelists have always been drawn to writing about current events, whether for money, publicity or, as Martin Amis once explained his motivation for taking on a reporting assignment, because it gets them out of the house. In a way that anticipated the response to the Spanish Civil War more than a decade later, literary writers were inspired by the publicity surrounding events in Ireland to go there to examine one of the great moral questions of the day: the justice of British rule. It is worth taking a look at the work of three British literary figures who came to Ireland at different stages of the revolution.

G.K. Chesterton published an account of a visit to Ireland just before Sinn Féin's sweeping victory in the 1918 election. Wilfred Ewart travelled through the country in the months before the signing of a truce in the summer of 1921. Both published their work in books, although Ewart's account of his journey was originally commissioned as a series of newspaper articles and Chesterton, of course, was a legendary newspaperman, a prolific columnist and 'one of the great exponents of the Fleet Street myth'.[2] V.S. Pritchett was the *Christian Science Monitor* correspondent in Ireland during the Civil War in 1923. The pieces Pritchett published in the *Monitor* at the beginning of his career as a writer are in many respects the precursor of his later travel books.[3]

All of the work published by these three writers is journalism, written to the moment but free of many of the routine occupational constraints on the regular newspaper correspondents. They share some of the practices of their less exalted colleagues (particularly in their reliance on some of the same sources) but they were free from the tyranny of daily news production and their work thus opens up a wider angle of observation of the events of the Irish revolution.[4]

Indeed, it is best, arguably, to look on this kind of journalism as a form of travel writing and to place it in the context of almost a century of attempts by British writers to describe Ireland for the general reader in London. There is a long line of English literary travellers who regarded Ireland as unexplored territory. In 1818, J.C. Curwen described Ireland as a country 'which, although almost within our view, and daily in our contemplation, is as little known to me, comparatively speaking, as if it were an island on the remotest part of the globe'. A contemporary of his, John Alexander Staples, who also published a travel book on Ireland, described it as 'a country that Englishmen in general know less about than they do of Russia, Siberia or the Country of the Hottentots'.[5] This sense of the neighbouring island as alien territory for the British writer surfaced in the newspaper reporting and this theme emerges again in the work of Chesterton, Ewart and Pritchett.

A sense of bizarre unfamiliarity possessed by a writer crossing the Irish Sea was usually accompanied by the prospect of excitement. The political turbulence that made Ireland a central issue for British politics in Edwardian and Victorian times promised for literary travellers rich material and a more attentive audience. Glenn Hooper notes that

> if travellers to the Orient went in search of exoticism or to Africa for adventure, then many came to Ireland for the simple pleasure of politics as an unfolding, almost theatrical experience. Everything, it would appear, was on offer; everything they had heard, especially how intractable the place was, seemed true. If travel writers journeying in other countries needed occasionally to enliven their narratives, travellers to Ireland had only to write up their experiences, like anthropologists on a field-trip.[6]

In placing Ireland for an audience back home, calculating the desires of its inhabitants and interpreting the claims of the separatists in the context of an otherwise entirely familiar Anglicised culture, British correspondents and writers would have been dealing with the currency of Anglo-Irish relations for centuries. Terry Eagleton has defined the question of Irish identity for Britons as 'a matter of some unthinkable conundrum of difference and identity in which the British can never decide if the Irish are their antithesis or mirror image, partner or parasite, abortive offspring or sympathetic sibling'.[7]

This was a problem for Irish nationalists as well. In their efforts to forge a pure national identity, they came up against the pervasive influence of the bigger island across the Irish Sea. Often these dilemmas have intruded on something as straightforward as the physical relationship between the two islands. The thinking of Conor Cruise O'Brien, a persistent critic of Irish nationalism, is encapsulated by his use of a geographical metaphor:

'The sea which we think of separating the two islands actually joins them.'[8] In his dense examination of British and Irish identity across two centuries, Oliver MacDonagh shows how maritime reasoning was similarly deployed in London:

> Seen in one geographic light Ireland could appear as the largest severed part of a single broken land mass, 'the British Isles', which themselves took on the form of an occidental Japan or an eastern-Atlantic New Zealand. In another geographic light however, Ireland could look to be a distinct and independent entity with the Irish Sea, as wide and deep a separating stretch as the North Sea or the English Channel.[9]

The task of placing Ireland in relation to Britain is fundamental in the work published by Chesterton, Ewart and Pritchett during the Irish revolution. However, at a time when the whole world order was being overturned by the settlement at Versailles and issues of democracy, nationalism and the struggle between capital and labour had become vital points of contention across Europe, other themes intrude on their preoccupation with the relationship between the two islands.

G.K. Chesterton's book *Irish Impressions* was published in 1919 in the months after Sinn Féin's sweeping victory in the general election and the establishment of Dail Eireann. It was based on material gathered by Chesterton during a speech-making visit to Ireland in late 1918 to recruit volunteers for the final push on the Western front (during which he also delivered a lecture at the Abbey Theatre at the behest of W.B. Yeats).[10] More than once, Chesterton apologises for the speed with which he has set down his thoughts for publication. He laments that his notes suffer 'all the stale scurry of my journalistic trade',[11] but his note-taking was not the only sign that in Ireland Chesterton played the journalist as much as the recruiting sergeant.

One of his important contacts in Dublin was George Russell – Æ – the poet, intellectual and controversialist who published the weekly newspaper the *Irish Homestead*, dedicated to promoting the material and intellectual development of rural Ireland, and who was an active sponsor of the agricultural cooperative movement. Russell's office in Merrion Square in the centre of Dublin was an essential stopping-off point for any writer or journalist looking for background on events in Ireland. Russell was not a member of Sinn Féin but his commitment to Irish self-determination made him a valuable ally of the movement and an articulate explainer of the cause.

The English writer Douglas Goldring (who lived in Dublin at the time and met Chesterton during his visit) recalled how Russell 'could … be relied upon to fire off a succession of quotable sayings for the benefit of any respectful caller at the Plunkett House in Merrion Square'.[12] And Russell as a literary figure was instantly appealing to visiting British writers; Nicholas Allen has noted how Russell's 'sense of mission was common to British intellectuals of the late nineteenth and early twentieth centuries … his compound interests in poetry, the occult and social organisation identify Russell as an Edwardian intellectual, albeit of Irish provenance'.[13] It would be Russell that Chesterton had in mind when he wrote of 'the stimulating society of the intellectuals of the Irish capital' and their opinions 'which moved both my admiration and amusement'.[14] Russell's championing of rural self-sufficiency would strike a chord with Chesterton's own political views.

For Chesterton, one of the most shocking features of Dublin was the extent of the British military presence:

> My first general and visual impression of the green island was that it was not green but brown; that it was positively brown with khaki … I knew, of course, that we had a garrison in Dublin but I had no notion that it was so obvious all over Dublin. I had no notion that it had been considered necessary to occupy the country in such force, or with so much parade of force.[15]

Alongside this visible British presence Chesterton was struck by *difference:* 'a stream of ten thousand things all pouring one way, labels, titles, monuments, metaphors, modes of address … that make an Englishman in Ireland know that he is in a strange land…'.[16] This quotidian distinctiveness stimulated his thinking about Irish nationality. He wrote that he had 'come to appreciate more imaginatively the importance of daily symbols like street names and pillar-boxes'[17] and argued that a sense of nationality was an eminently practical experience, inviting his English readers to imagine their irritation if such normal things like signs in railway carriages were written in German.[18] In this context Chesterton decried British recruiting efforts in Ireland. He repeated a story he was told of the display of a poster of the Union Jack bearing the legend, 'Is not this your flag? Come and fight for it' and recalls Latin grammar lessons 'about questions that expect the answer no...'.[19] Similarly, he cited a controversy over the prohibition of Irish children wearing green rosettes in schools: the effect, according to Chesterton, was to remind an Irish audience of past occasions when Britain was in the wrong and divert attention from a war for civilisation in which Britain was in the right.[20]

Chesterton's own approach to a recruitment speech was to acknowledge that Britain had been guilty of cruelty towards Ireland in the past and to try to convince his audience that the mass of English people were aware of wrongs done to Ireland: 'We stand here in the valley of our humiliation, where the flag we love has done very little that was not evil, and where its victories have been far more disastrous than its defeats.'[21] Chesterton then tried to pull a quick rhetorical move: the past behaviour of England towards Ireland was tyrannical, analogous to Prussianism. Therefore for the Irish to challenge tyranny they had to confront the real Prussians in the European war; to uphold the integrity of their fight against the British they were obliged to join Britain in war against Germany. For Chesterton, Irish nationalism had, by its very nature, to put Ireland on the side of Germany's opponents in the European war. Nationalism 'appeals to a law of nations'; it was naturally part of 'Christendom'.[22] It was also, he argued, an antidote to imperialism: 'It was exactly because Germany was not a nation that it desired more and more to be an empire ... A group of Teutonic tribes will not care how many other tribes they destroy or absorb...'[23] By contrast, Irish nationalism would be too aware of the need to preserve its own boundaries to indulge any desire to draw new ones. In a rhetoric suspiciously like flattery, Chesterton praised the restraint of 'the civilised Irish nation, a part and product of Christendom [which] has certainly no desire to be entangled with other tribes or have its outlines blurred with great blots like Liverpool and Glasgow, as well as Belfast'.[24]

This then was the basis of the recruitment appeal that Chesterton sought to put across on his journey to Ireland (although what hope recruitment had by 1918 is debatable).[25] What he saw and heard in Ireland, however, filled him with despair. It was not simply an issue of Britain making the wrong arguments for fighting the war against Germany; it was also the behaviour of the British forces themselves. Chesterton retold a story of a military plane dropping flares on a crowd of people attending an Irish music festival in Co. Cork.[26] From the context he appeared to have picked up this story from the newspapers or from friends in Dublin. The incident became, in Chesterton's eyes, a perfect metaphor for English Prussianism. The use of a plane to frighten a crowd of men, women and children with flares 'reproduced all the artificial accessories of the most notorious crimes of Germany' without any obvious point:

> It was as if the whole British army in Ireland had dressed up in spiked helmets and spectacles, merely that they might *look* like Prussians … These Christian peasants have seen coming westward out of England what we saw coming westward out of Germany. They saw science in arms; which turns the very heavens into hells.[27]

Here Chesterton was acknowledging the institutionalisation of air warfare and its deployment as a new form of policing in Ireland. At the outbreak of the First World War attacks on civilians from the air were regarded as beyond the rules of civilised combat. By the time Chesterton was writing, however, air power had become an indispensable tool in colonial control.[28] The use of a military plane in Cork was for him not only an act of stupidity that inflamed nationalist resentment but also a demonstration of how modern values had come to sanction tactics of warfare previously regarded as barbaric, Teutonic departures from the civilised norm. In Ireland, Chesterton was noticing – and resisting – the triumph of 'total war' as a military doctrine.

This was just one instance of how Chesterton made use of Ireland as the site of a continuous argument with the modern world. It was the theme to which he returned continuously on his journey through Ireland. The condition of the country was appropriated to this larger argument by a critique of the traditional view of 'the Irish Question'. Chesterton asserted that an Englishman entering Ireland had to discard his prejudices and pretend, if possible, that he was on an exotic island of which he knew nothing: 'the best thing a stranger can do is to forget the Irish Question and look at the Irish'.[29] Chesterton advised that the traveller appraise Ireland as a man in a fairytale would observe a fantastic and strange land of talking cows or walking haystacks; only then would the visitor be able to truly 'see' Ireland.

His argument was directed as much at English liberals who professed the greatest sympathy for Ireland as towards those hostile to Irish nationalism: 'What has been the matter with their Irish politics was simply that they were English politics. They discussed the Irish question; but they never seriously contemplated the Irish Answer.'[30] The Liberal declared that the Irish should not be prevented from having whatever law they liked, but he rarely contemplated what kind of society the Irish would choose because 'the law the Irish would like is as remote from what is called Liberal as from what is called Unionist'.[31] Ireland outside the union, Chesterton argued, would be neither lawless (as the naysayers warned) or free (in the sense understood by English Liberals and Radicals): 'it would be an orderly and even conservative civilisation like the Chinese'.[32]

Later, he came up with another geographical analogy: Ireland as Serbia, a nation of peasants set alongside an industrial power. For Chesterton, Ireland was part of a larger political drama: 'the real question ... [is] what is going to happen to the peasantries of Europe, or for that matter, the whole world?'[33] From this starting point Chesterton painted a picture of Ireland as an alternative to modern industrial society and it became for him a critique of his own society. In this sense he appropriated Ireland to his own sense of Englishness, which Patrick Wright has defined as 'a defensive stance adopted against the power of the state and transformations that follow in the wake of modernisation and change...'.[34]

It was on a drive through the countryside in the north-west ('slowed down to a solemn procession by crowds of families with their cattle and livestock going to market') that Chesterton observed a scene that would sum up his vision of Ireland as a prototype of a more desirable social organisation. He noted that on one side of the road the harvest had been gathered in 'neatly and safely', while on the other side 'it was rotting in the rain'.[35] The saved harvest was on land farmed by peasant proprietors; the wasted hay lay on the grounds of a large estate. Chesterton took this as a sign of the superiority of peasant values over those of the landowner and he projected it back towards the growing conflicts of industrial England and its competing ideologies:

England may seem to be rent by an irreconcilable rivalry between Capital and Labour; but the peasant across the road is both a capitalist and a labourer. He is several other curious things; including the man who got his crops in first; who was literally first in the field.[36]

The struggle between capital and labour was producing stalemate; in contrast the land of small-scale proprietors was vital and dynamic. What Chesterton saw in the north-west of Ireland he regarded as 'the flattest possible contradiction to all that is said in England, both by Collectivists and Capitalists about the efficiency of the great organisation'.[37]

Chesterton also saluted other features of Irish society, notably how, as he saw it, the family retained a 'corporate conception' connecting individuals to their communal past.[38] A peasant in a mud cabin in Co. Clare, Chesterton argued, possessed a superior knowledge of Christian history to a clerk in Clapham Common who was likely to be oblivious to the theological foundations of his own society: 'In the face of that simple fact, I have no doubt about which is the more educated man; and even a knowledge of the *Daily Mail* does not redress the balance.'[39] During the Dublin lockout in 1913, English socialists had offered to arrange for the strikers' children to be taken to England to be looked after by sympathetic families there. This was furiously resisted by priests and families in Ireland, despite assurances that care would be taken not to undermine the children's faith. Chesterton found this protectiveness entirely understandable; English socialists, he argued, did not understand religion as 'the world a man inhabits' and would have no idea therefore whether they were tampering with it or not.[40]

Chesterton believed the Irish wanted to be free of both liberalism and socialism: the series of Liberal reforms in the previous decade had been enacted 'at the expense of the independence of the family' and Ireland's demand for home rule was, at least partly, an expression of a desire 'to be emancipated from this emancipation'.[41] Thus the exemptions applied to Ireland exposed the supreme irony of British rule:

> that a man stands up holding a charter of charity and peace for all mankind; that he lays down a law of enlightened justice for all the nations of the earth; that he claims to behold man from the beginnings of his evolution equal, without any difference between the most distant creeds and colours;

that he stands as the orator of the human race, whose statute only declares all humanity must be human; and then slightly drops his voice and says, 'This Act shall not apply to Ireland.'[42]

Here Chesterton reached the nub of his argument that 'the real case against the Union [is] a case against the Universalists'.[43] When *Irish Impressions* was published in 1919 the terms of the debate over Ireland were being transformed swiftly. The guerrilla campaign of the IRA had not begun as Chesterton left Ireland to write up his book. In the years that followed, Ireland was to be the centre of a different debate in Britain about the morality of British statesmanship.

By the time that Wilfred Ewart wrote his book *Journey in Ireland 1921*, the war of reprisals had become notorious and, as we have seen in previous chapters, was cast by prominent English journalists as a stain on the British character. In the summer of 1921 Ewart was commissioned by the *Sunday Times* to write a series of articles about the war. He had just submitted the final draft of his Great War novel *Ways of Revelation*, which became a bestseller when it was published in the autumn of 1921 and was described by reviewers as 'the English *War and Peace*'.[44] The book is a melodramatic story of two friends who went to fight in France: one is killed, the wife of the other is seduced by a draft resister, becomes addicted to cocaine and dies. In a satisfying resolution, her former husband marries his dead friend's fiancée. The historian Hugh Cecil has noted that the ending signified that 'the sacrifice of good men and women had not been in vain ... This was a message that people wanted to hear just after the war; it was comforting but did not trivialise the calamity.'[45]

Ewart himself had endured plenty of experience of the war. He was wounded in 1915 and sent back to battle after six months' recuperation in England. He took part in the Battle of the Somme, developed gastroenteritis and was sent home again. In July 1917 he was returned to the front line in Flanders and was lucky to escape when his company was decimated in an attempt to take the town of Cambrai. He lay behind a tree, under fire from a German machine-gun, and watched German soldiers burning the British dead and wounded with phosphorus bombs.[46] Ewart also had some knowledge of Ireland. His father came from a well-known military family[47] and one of his closest childhood friends was the nephew of George Wyndham who, as chief secretary for Ireland, had authored the act that ended the Irish Land War in 1903 by committing government money to the purchase of landlord's estates.[48]

Ewart spent three weeks in Ireland, from mid-April to early May 1921. In the preface to *Journey to Ireland 1921* (published the following year) Ewart wrote that he had gone to assess 'the state of feeling in the country, as to which … propaganda and partisanship persistently vied … For my part I offer no conclusions, nor deliberately sought any.'[49] He spent time in Dublin, Cork and Belfast. He also traversed the countryside, undertaking a few twenty-mile walks along roads in the south and the midlands. Cecil suggests that Ewart was, like many other English literary figures of the time, a pantheist, whose writing came alive in his depictions of rural life.[50] Indeed, many pages in Ewart's book are devoted to lyrical descriptions of landscapes and nature, as he made his way, pilgrim-like, through the Irish countryside. Nevertheless, secreted within these passages of pastoral ecstasy are physical reminders of the troubles:

> After a while the sun came out and set the gorse aflame. Patches of barley and potatoes alternated with gorse and heather. Larks sang … There was a complete dearth of traffic. Every two or three miles occurred loose places in the road's surface, as though it had been dug up and replaced. A definite reminder of the realities of the countryside came beyond the village of Blackpool. Where a grey stone bridge crosses a stream which sings and ripples down a narrow ravine, a neat trench four feet deep by three broad had been dug across the road.[51]

This dissonance between normality and disturbance, gaiety and menace runs through Ewart's whole portrait of Ireland at war. Unlike the trenches in France, war in Ireland is fought on a terrain that is at first glance appealing and soothing:

> On fine afternoons the white-flannelled students play cricket on the grassy lawns of Trinity College, a stone's throw from Nassau Street. And as you stood, one of a group, watching them through the railings, through an opening in the foliage, you could not foresee that from here a fortnight hence revolver-shots would be fired or that the daisy-sprinkled bank would be stained by a girl's blood.[52]

In the Phoenix Park in Dublin on a hot April afternoon Ewart noted the following:

> old men dozing on seats and nurserymaids reading novelettes, and the children shouting and playing on grassy slopes for all the world as if Dublin herself were a playground. One passed out of the gates into the North Circular Road and lorries came tearing along at twenty-five miles an hour, their dark green or khaki loads bristling with rifles.[53]

In Ewart's prose, the Black and Tans regularly intrude as aliens on an otherwise tranquil landscape. At curfew hour in Dublin 'black motor-cars containing mysterious-looking men rushed out of College Green at breakneck speed like bats or night-insects'.[54] As Ewart sat discussing horse racing with a priest over breakfast on the train to Cork:

> four big Black and Tans with revolvers strapped to their thighs tramped in, sat down at the next table, and leant their rifles against the backs of their chairs. A prosperous-looking country fled by. The greenness of everything, the grazing cattle, the snug appearance of the white cottages and farmsteads against the sunlit landscape, protested against the presence of a spectre that stalked through the counties of the South.[55]

If the Black and Tans encroach suddenly on otherwise gentle surroundings, the IRA is an even more spectral presence in Ewart's account of his travels; a phantom army usually detectable by traces of its activities. Walking from Birr to Tullamore in the otherwise undisturbed midlands, Ewart came upon a barrier across the road as it curved around a hill at a point where it was shaded with trees; an excellent spot for an ambush: 'Four heavy beech-trunks interlaced with boughs had been thrown across it, forming a twelve-feet high obstacle not dissimilar to, though far more substantial than, a fence at Aintree.'[56]

Further along the road he noticed 'a figure [standing] on the skyline at some distance from the road, watching me intently'.[57] After an encounter with half-a-dozen youths outside a pub at a crossroads he was joined for a while by a middle-aged farmer who 'turned into a field and left me with, as I thought, a rather sinister grin'.[58] Shortly afterwards five young men on bicycles caught up with him shouting, 'Stop! Hands up!' He was searched and ordered to sit by the roadside until they decided he was unthreatening and allowed him to continue. The half-hour had not been pleasant for Ewart:

> Innocuous tourist though I was, friend of Ireland though I believed myself to be … my eyes repeatedly wandered to the bog and my thoughts to the number of people who had lately been found in bogs with brief notes attached to them.[59]

The mystery of revolutionary Ireland was not confined to menacing incidents on lonely country roads. Ewart confessed his difficulty with getting to grips with the whole idea of the IRA and its leadership. Even as he set out on his journey to Ireland it had seemed to him curious that 'while our "governing classes" had been stirred to the depths by the war in Ireland, the leaders of that war on the opposing side were all but unknown even by name'.[60]

In Dublin he followed the path of Chesterton and other writers and journalists to the house of George Russell in Merrion Square. Russell told Ewart that the rank-and-file members of the IRA were 'inspired by a mystical passion of nationality' and that they considered themselves as fighting for their country's integrity, as indeed did Ewart while fighting the Germans. 'As to murders,' Russell advised Ewart, 'you must have seen Germans shot in cold blood – prisoners for instance? Such things happen in war and always will.'[61] In Cork, Ewart met the Lord Mayor, Barry Egan, a Sinn Féiner who 'reminds one of certain symbolists of the French Revolution [with] the thin precise lips of – a doctrinaire?'[62] Egan argued for the morality of guerrilla strategy, telling Ewart that an ambush – the signature tactic of the IRA – was a legitimate act of war and he compared the Irish rebels to the Boers, who had also refused to fight in uniform.

Ewart never really came to his own conclusions about these arguments. He was genuinely bewildered by the type of warfare being practised in Ireland. Unlike Chesterton, he brought no ideological scheme to help him interpret the upheaval in Ireland. His template was the Great War, the clash of states and armies. He was puzzled by stateless nationalism and guerrilla tactics – a puzzlement that was possibly borne of the novelty of this form of struggle, with its combination of the familiar and the new and its intertwining loyalties (Ewart repeatedly met people who were unionists but opposed to the Black and Tans, or who managed to be pro-Sinn Féin as well as being landowners and imperialists, for example). The shape of the war in Ireland – reprisals and counter-reprisals between the Black and Tans and the IRA – was opaque compared with the fixed identities of the epic war in which Ewart had served.

After attempting to investigate the deaths of two Sinn Féin politicians in Co. Limerick (Sinn Féin said they had been killed by the Black and Tans, with the British military counter-claiming that they had been killed by Sinn Féiners), Ewart concluded that what had happened during the war in Ireland was only 'half known' and that 'much of it probably never will be known, that a man has to dig out and unearth the truth for himself, that, in short, the condition of the country during the insurrection was a "history within a history"'.[63]

The fascination of Ireland's war for literary travellers outlasted the truce agreed shortly after Ewart finished his journey. In July 1923 V.S. Pritchett, the Ireland correspondent for the *Christian Science Monitor*, published an article looking back at his first three months reporting from the newly independent country:

> Three months ago I landed at Kingstown, or, more correctly, Dun Laogaire [sic], wondering how exciting life would be in a country engaged in civil war. My luggage had been searched for arms at Holyhead; my person was searched on landing in Ireland. By the time I had arrived in Dublin itself, I was prepared for the wildest thrills, accompanied by a goodly share of what we Sassenachs call 'Irish humour'.[64]

Had Ireland matched up to his high expectations? His confession is a clue to two things: first, how Ireland since the Easter Rising of 1916 had become a country where things happened, a place of intense interest to newspaper readers and, second, how remote it could seem to a visitor from England, even someone with Pritchett's literary sensibility. Pritchett describes in his memoirs how in 1922 he had gone about Fleet Street seeking commissions to begin his life as a writer. Finally a Mr Bassellthorpe, the London editor of the *Christian Science Monitor*, returned his call:

What, he said, did I know about Ireland? Almost nothing I said. All I knew was that the Irish Treaty had been signed and that, as was foreseen, the Irish were fighting one another ... The war was dragging on. Why, I did not know.[65]

Mr Bassellthorpe reassured him that the readership of the *Monitor* was mostly Protestant and that they would be sure to be interested in Ireland.

The *Monitor* had been established by the founder of Christian Science, Mary Baker Eddy, in 1908. In a manifesto published on the anniversary of its first issue in November 1909 the paper said its mission was 'not only to keep its readers informed of events all over the world, but to interpret those events in a way to show their relation to the great movements that are of significance to the human race'.[66] Despite the intimation that the *Monitor* might align itself with movements of social change, one historian concluded that, on the contrary, its editorial philosophy exuded 'contentment with the established order of political and economic arrangements'.[67]

However, Pritchett's sardonic observation that in those days the *Monitor* 'was really more of a daily magazine than a daily newspaper' reveals how this woolly commitment to explain world events did mean that the paper offered its contributors freedom to write.[68] Pritchett himself confessed that he was 'untrained and innocent', an unlikely candidate for the role of roving reporter at a time of civil disturbance: 'I had never been in a newspaper office. I did not know how one gathered news. I did not know that one could actually call on a government office or a politician. I knew no one in Ireland.'[69]

When Pritchett went to Ireland its intractability – from a British point of view – was on full display. Under the treaty signed in London in December 1921 to end the Anglo-Irish War, the Irish Free State – covering twenty-six of the thirty-two counties of Ireland – was granted Dominion status within the British Empire and a provisional government was established in Dublin. However, within days of the treaty being signed, a significant minority of the nationalist movement rejected it because of the failure to achieve the aim of a thirty-two-county republic.

It was a bitter but reluctant split. For several months in 1922, leaders from both sides tried to find an accommodation that would avoid all-out conflict. The most charismatic IRA figure during the War of Independence,

Michael Collins – who had signed the treaty – tried to devise a constitution that would be acceptable to those who opposed the treaty. However, 'British opposition, oblivious of the human cost to Ireland, and at least in some quarters, relishing the prospect of civil war among the wretched natives, compelled him to modify the constitution in accordance with the Treaty.'[70] The opponents of the treaty regarded the Free State government as 'a military junta set up and armed by England' to crush the true army of the republic established in 1919 by the Dail Eireann.[71] *The Times* judged that with 'the passing of British responsibility ... Irishmen are shown at death grips with the monster their own folly has begotten'. The conflict developing between the pro- and anti-treaty factions was 'none other than that between human progress and the resurgent powers of a darker age'.[72]

In June 1922 the civil war began when government troops assaulted the Four Courts building in Dublin which had been occupied by anti-Treaty fighters. The British government demanded that the new leadership in Dublin put an end to the rebellion or face re-occupation for being in breach of the treaty: 'This was virtually an ultimatum requesting one set of Irishmen to fire on another set of Irishmen at the behest of the British cabinet.'[73] By the time Pritchett arrived in Dublin in early 1923 the dissidents, known as 'Irregulars', had been pushed out of the main towns and cities; their numbers had dwindled and their campaign was heading towards defeat.

However, the cost in lives and property over the previous nine months had exceeded that incurred during the two-year War of Independence. There is still no definitive figure for civilian and military deaths, although 4,000 is the accepted (though probably exaggerated) estimate.[74] The methods used by the provisional government to suppress the threat to its authority represented an even more vicious version of the reprisal tactics that had been used on its leaders by Lloyd George and the Black and Tans. The republicans assassinated members of the new Free State parliament; in response the government began executing prisoners – seventy-seven were killed before the war ended. It was an irony not lost on those who had supported the Irish nationalist cause in Britain. C.P. Scott remarked to Asquith's wife: 'Who would have believed that, having got rid of us, the Irish would start a terror of their own?'[75]

In his earliest dispatches from Ireland, V.S. Pritchett was keen to show that the terror there was the responsibility of a minority obsessed by a warped patriotism that was itself fast becoming an anachronism. A little over a month after his arrival in Ireland, full of expectation of adventure, Pritchett published the second of his pieces in the *Christian Science Monitor.* It occupied most of a column on the back page and was signed with his initials, 'V.S.P.'. His first piece, an account of a disrupted rail journey from Dublin to Cork in the south-west, had been more concerned with scenery and the weather than with politics. In his second article, however, he established his point of view by gazing from his window overlooking one of the main streets in Cork city: 'My window is one of the little windows of the world, a peephole into southern Irish life.'[76] In contrast to the wild thrills for which he had prepared himself, and the expectations of his readers who associated Ireland with war and revolution, Pritchett's first snapshot of the disturbed country highlighted a resilient normality and the triumph of commerce over political passion:

> Cattle are driven through the streets; lorries turn down the side roads towards the quays where ships are loading and unloading; farmers' carts are coming to town and going away; there are businessmen in the hotels from all parts of the country; there is a pleasant hum of activity everywhere. The pleasure seeker is here as well. There is golf if you want it; and football whether you want it or not. At night the theatres and cinemas are crowded. There has been a two weeks' Shakespeare season, the popularity of which attests a love for the finer things in human thought.[77]

Pritchett argued that the very appearance of normality, as he described it, was a reliable indicator of the pacific intentions of the majority of Irishmen. This majority retained only a 'theoretical' sympathy for Republicanism and none at all for its methods. They were indifferent to 'the occasional spell of firing at night', which was all the republicans could now manage. If only people had developed self-awareness, Pritchett believed, and had not been inhibited by 'a trait of suspicion in Irish character generally', there could already have been peace.[78]

With the possibility of a settlement growing, the Irish people were ready to close ranks behind their government. However, Pritchett suggested that once peace was established, not only the romantic idealism of the Republicans but even the conservative nationalism of the pro-treaty government might become passé:

> It is remarkable how closely associated with beautiful poetic expression the movement for Irish self-government has been. The patriots have given a poetical halo to their country's tradition; but with law and order established, the turn of the patriots will have been served.[79]

The fighting poets and patriots would be supplanted by an economic elite. Pritchett reported that he had been told by 'responsible men' that in elections over the next decade the entire political class that brought about the retreat of the British administration would be replaced 'by men who have a stake in the country'.[80] He was convinced by this prognosis. His summing up at the end of his second dispatch for the *Monitor* is remarkably assured for somebody who only a few months previously confessed to knowing 'almost nothing' about Ireland:

> There are broadly speaking, two types of Irishman today. The one who will not easily forget old differences, a dweller in a melancholy and ineffectual past, perpetuating the old myth that an Irishman is never happy unless he is fighting; the other, one who sees the apathy and evils to be met and is enthusiastic and practical enough to suggest remedies. I believe that in the new Ireland the word will be to him.[81]

One can trace how Pritchett arrived at his conclusion from the autobiographical sketches he published decades later. Pritchett's reflections on Ireland appear in his memoir *Midnight Oil* (published in 1971) and his book *Dublin* (published in 1967). Here he explains that at the time he came to Ireland he still retained the views of his family who were 'firm *Manchester Guardian* liberals and Home Rulers'. These views should have made him sympathetic to Irish nationalism. However, he suggests that even sympathetic British liberal notions had little resonance in Ireland: his inherited views 'condemned me from the start' in a country 'which is innately illiberal' – a conclusion similar to Chesterton's.[82]

Writing almost half a century after his time as Ireland correspondent for the *Monitor*, Pritchett reflected on his personal identification with Irish rebellion:

I had easily rid myself of the common English idea that Ireland was a piece
of England that for some reason or other would not settle down and had
run to seed ... I ardently identified Irish freedom with my own personal
freedom which had been hard to come by. A revolutionary break? I was for
it. Until you are free you do not know who you are.[83]

Using Ireland for such a purpose, as an unshaped reality that could allow
for experimentation with new identities, is a pattern identified by Roy Foster: 'From an early period disaffected British people used Ireland for dreams
or ideas or insecurities too uncomfortable for home.'[84]

Pritchett's elation was heightened by the knowledge that he was being
paid to observe and write up 'the first modern defeat of colonialism'. Watching the debates in Dail Eireann from the press gallery was, he remembered,
'like being at school taking a course in the foundation of states'.[85] However,
despite his predetermined sympathy for the cause of Irish nationalism and
his youthful enthusiasm for upheaval and flux, Pritchett equally confessed
to a sense of estrangement: 'I realized what a social revolution was, although
I was (inevitably as an Englishman and Protestant) much more in the old
Anglo-Irish society, the majority of whom reluctantly accepted the new
regime, than among the rising Catholic middle class.'[86]

Forty years after the revolution Pritchett appeared to be ambivalent
about the people towards whom he naturally gravitated socially. He judged
that during his time in Ireland he had become 'sensitive, snobbish and fey'
as a consequence of 'this easy going life in a Victorian lagoon' (an image
which conveys a sense of a whole society being lost or marooned).[87] But
he also claimed credit for clear sightedness, for recognising that 'the Irish
Troubles were, in an important sense, a continuation of the European revolution caused by the European war'. Both the Irish working class and the
Anglo-Irish – whom he considered 'more European than they were patriots'
– had been bypassed by the nationalists.[88]

The idea of the Anglo-Irish and working classes being 'European' is
likely to have been Pritchett's retrospective term to characterise what in
June 1923 he regarded as a commonsense aversion to republicanism. This
theme emerged in his dispatches to the *Monitor* in June. On a visit to the
midlands Pritchett's driver, Paddy O'Brien, recounted an exchange with
an Irregular who had claimed to have played a large role in 'pushing the

British Empire into the sea'. Mr O'Brien told Pritchett that after listening patiently to the IRA man's story he had replied: 'So it's after pushing the British Empire into the sea, you are, is it? Sure, you couldn't push a little pussy cat into the sea!'[89]

The Anglo-Irish landowners were similarly derisive of the efficacy of the revolutionaries but their crisis was acute; Pritchett noted that the owners of the country estates were losing money and influence: 'Many of them are saddled with mansions built for more spacious times when their owners were more prosperous; and when such an idea as the eventual decay of the "country gentleman" as an institution was never entertained...'.[90] In the civil war these mansions were being burned down, and many former Unionists were choosing to leave the Irish Free State. Pritchett understood the despair of an entire class: 'It is not altogether unnatural – nor, perhaps, unreasonable – that the country folk, pestered about their estates, should become pessimistic about the country.'[91]

Pritchett himself was struck by the divergence between the national ideals expounded by the revolutionary leaders and the state of social organisation in the Irish countryside:

> When one sees the scattered cottages, the tumble-down farms, the strange-eyed unkempt peasantry, the 'backward' little towns ... the station masters who will keep a train for you half an hour if necessary, the national school with its thirty or forty pupils, who attend when it pleases their parents, one wonders what all this has to do with the 'national consciousness' and 'the splendour of the Gael' about which so much is written and spoken in Dublin.[92]

However, just as in his earlier dispatch from Cork, Pritchett predicted that a practical Irish mentality was in the ascendant, a spirit in which the local schoolteacher – though apparently surrounded by an apathetic peasantry – would replace the man of action as a hero figure in a new, enlightened Ireland:

> Education will destroy superstitions – religious, pagan and social; and while pessimists with hundreds of acres make despairing epigrams about what is called the Irish temperament, men like the national schoolmaster think that the salvation of the country lies in the educating of its consciousness.[93]

Pritchett considered that an obsession amongst the Irish about their history was inhibiting the creation of that new consciousness. He embarked on another train journey from Dublin to Belfast, passing over a bridge that had been blown up during the fighting but had been repaired and was now protected by a special corps of troops whose job was to keep the railways running. An hour out of Dublin the train crossed the River Boyne as it entered the town of Drogheda. The Boyne was the site of the famous battle in which the army of William of Orange defeated James II in 1691, the iconic defeat of Catholics by Protestants. Crossing the Boyne, Pritchett was reminded of one of his 'favourite theories about Ireland' that 'it is the country of old history books'.[94] This is a visual trope for an enduring motif in English writing about Ireland: the fixation with history, an immersion in the wrongs of the past inimical to utilitarian optimism:

> I could take you to a second-hand bookshop in Dublin where there are books on Irish history from all possible points of view between bigotry and blarney, piled from floor to ceiling. If the Irish would go back to Cuchulain and the giants of Ulster there might not be any objection; but they stop at Cromwell or William of Orange.[95]

Later, Pritchett discovered a more benign Irish approach to history, more in tune with his vision for a practical future. In early summer he went to Trinity College in Dublin for the annual end-of-term celebrations. Trinity had always been identified as one of the most important institutions of the Protestant ascendancy in Ireland; indeed, to some nationalist ideologists it was 'the chief agent of English culture in Ireland'.[96] Trinity's position in the new state was precarious and this sense of displacement was conveyed by Pritchett's account of the visit of the Governor General to the college during Trinity Week. The college authorities were in a quandary as to what tune to play for his arrival – 'God Save the King' and 'Rule Britannia' were deemed unsuitable (even though the Governor General was the King's representative in Dublin). In the end, 'the Governor General arrived and scarcely anyone knew what the band was playing'.[97]

Pritchett noted the irony of how Trinity, though 'an emblem of loyalty', had produced nationalist leaders and key figures of the Irish Literary Revival as well as serving as the custodian of some of the prized antiquities of Irish literature. The secret of Trinity's endurance, Pritchett concluded, was that it remained aloof from the events unfolding outside its walls: 'The fact is, history may have made Trinity; but Trinity has never made history. Her attitude has been that of the scholar rather than that of the politician. She has been more concerned with ideas than with agitations.'[98]

Now that scholarly detachment, cultivated over the centuries, would be a boon to the new Ireland. Pritchett observed how Trinity, like the English universities, had become less the property of a particular class; farmers' sons and 'boys of similar standing' were now being admitted to what had once been the preserve of the gentry. Pritchett exulted at how liberal education might eventually permeate all ranks of society:

> There is an urbanity in the history which shelters in Trinity's quadrangles and rests under its academic elms. It has a leavening influence in a country which has too often been on the one hand lulled into ignorance, and on the other sharpened into bigotry. Trinity stands for tolerance.[99]

After a few months in Ireland, Pritchett believed that tolerance, level headedness and an interest in the practical were winning out over the romantic visionaries and their violence. The Irregular campaign had badly faltered, reduced to 'wordy threats', and Ireland was in transition from civil war to normal life.[100] Pritchett even regarded the eruption of a series of strikes (particularly those by agricultural labourers seeking better conditions from the big farmers) as a sign of progress. Unlike Chesterton, who believed that Irish peasant society offered an alternative to industrialism, Pritchett saw Ireland moving towards modern norms – and he approved of it. 'Before', Pritchett held, 'the country was governed by what was more or less of a benevolent despotism, which created a state of society in many respects feudal.' In post-independence Ireland 'you have democracy with a vengeance'.[101]

This last phrase suggests a degree of violence in the imposition of civility on a disordered country, and is probably unwittingly suggestive of the part that score-settling and retaliation played in the restoration of order during and after the civil war. There is no doubt that Pritchett admired the leaders of the Free State government in the struggle to assert their authority. In his memoirs he writes of W.T. Cosgrave, the leader of the government, as 'the clever and dogged little Cosgrave' who astonished people by his political aptitude:

He was the perfect exemplar ... of the ordinary man suddenly elevated to high office, who had the inborn moral character that is required for rule. It was a delight to hear this little fighter with the gay brushed-up hair, in debate.[102]

This preference for the pro-treaty politicians ran through his dispatches to the *Monitor*. There is no sustained analysis of the Free State government's opponents, no humanising pen portraits of its leaders or followers. Mostly the views of the Republicans are dismissed as visionary rhetoric: wild, irrelevant or – increasingly as 1923 wore on – shopworn. In Pritchett's dispatches, the Republican position is almost always compared unfavourably with the flux of ordinary life and the creative endeavours of state-building.

A typical example of Pritchett's attitude was given by his account of a visit to Clare in the west of Ireland in the autumn of 1923. The spectacular electoral success in Co. Clare in 1917 of the Republican leader Eamon De Valera had put Sinn Féin on the political map. In the general election of August 1923 De Valera came out of hiding to stand in Clare and was arrested in dramatic fashion as he tried to address an election meeting in the county's main town, Ennis. Pritchett wrote of his journey to Clare:

It was difficult to believe, as one trotted among these bare green hills, with their patchwork of little fields, and their fierce stone walls, their scraps of bogland, and those misty mountains lying all around, that the inhabitants of each innocent-eyed cottage were violent politicians.[103]

However, Pritchett discovered that Co. Clare's reputation for violence was exaggerated. He met local people, some of whom he thought were 'wild-looking', but found no hostility towards him as an Englishman. Indeed, he discovered that the people in Clare were 'children' who had lived in a kind of prelapsarian state of anarchy throughout the revolution and were finding it difficult to readjust to a new era of civic responsibility:

Lawlessness became the law; revenge was the only form of justice; and the simple men of Clare and of all the counties of Ireland became 'free'. In those days no-one was 'agin the government'; there was no government in authority to be 'agin'. But now that has changed or is changing; law and order are returning and with them has returned the old tradition of being 'agin' the Government – this time an Irish Government.[104]

In another report from Clare, published two weeks later, Pritchett noted the observations of the novelist William Thackeray, who had visited Ennis in the mid-nineteenth century. Thackeray had remarked that Ennis was 'foreign-looking' and Pritchett concurred, adding that parts of Ireland possess qualities of charm that he associated with France. He visited the town's main square where De Valera had been arrested in such dramatic circumstances in August and tried to imagine the emotion of that day. However, he concluded that the enthusiasm of the locals for De Valera was feckless and misguided – another symptom of their flight from civic duty:

> [The] only side the people of Ennis see is that De Valera is a 'grand speaker' who has been carried off by the same tyrannous soldiers who chased the poor young boys up into the hills. Incidentally, De Valera has not tried to make them pay rents, and taxes and rates; but has succeeded in being the most talked-about person in Clare.[105]

V.S. Pritchett's dispatches from Ireland throughout 1923 consistently returned to one theme: that republicanism was a political dead end, that the people knew this and that Ireland was about to embrace a liberal future. Thus he attempted to confound a perennial British view of Ireland as politically intractable, forever given to dissension. (At the same time, however, he employed a familiar Victorian conceit about the 'childlike' Irish.[106]) Pritchett repeatedly cautioned against pessimism and predicted the triumph of distinctly liberal values. However, he was soon disappointed. Years later, recalling his return to Ireland in the late 1920s after two years in Spain, Pritchett confesses to a surprisingly bitter disillusionment: 'One could smell the coming reaction and the dullness of growing religious obduracy.'[107]

The work of Chesterton, Ewart and Pritchett examined here shares many common themes. One of the most consistent is the difficulty of truly knowing Ireland. Chesterton claims that many people in Britain have misunderstand Ireland; Ewart is constantly surprised by the differences he encounters; Pritchett goes there slightly ashamed at his ignorance. Perhaps because Ireland is exotic to them it becomes, for all three writers, a place to rework imaginatively some personal or political argument that began before they left Britain. For Chesterton the state of Ireland provides evidence for his case against industrialism. Ewart too questions the morality of modern warfare. And for Pritchett – aged twenty-three – the revolution in Ireland become synonymous with his own bid for personal freedom. All of them note the paradox of revolution in a society that otherwise appears stable. Both Chesterton and Pritchett characterise Ireland as illiberal; Ewart is struck by the irony of normality and practicality persisting side by side with risk and menace.

Most importantly, however, all of them place Ireland outside the context of the Union. Chesterton highlights how the predominance of the peasantry equates Ireland with Serbia or Slovenia. Pritchett suggests that the Irish uprising is a continuation of the European revolution. Ewart perceives Ireland through the prism of the Great War. Thus, as with the newspaper reports from Britain and the USA, literary travellers to Ireland sought to explain the conflict that convulsed the country between 1919 and 1923 in the context of the forces changing the whole world as 'the great edifice of nineteenth century civilisation crumpled in the flames of world war as its pillars collapsed'.[108]

# CONCLUSION

*The best description that has been given of [British government] policy was given by a French journalist after a tour through Ireland. He said that the British Government was trying to subdue a people as intelligent as any in Europe, by the means that European Governments use for the correction of Berbers.*

J.L. Hammond, *The Terror in Action*

The Irish revolution coincided with the birth of mass democracy, in an age when the press was perceived to be a decisive factor in shaping the political world. The newspaper reader – 'audience man' – had become an active figure in history.[1] This was nowhere clearer than in Ireland, where newspapers had been the lifeblood of agrarian agitation and the movement for home rule in the late nineteenth century.

Newspaper culture also connected Ireland to the opinions of the wider world; the nationalist press quoted extensively from British newspapers to authenticate their favourable assessment of Charles Stewart Parnell's performance as leader of the Irish Parliamentary Party in the House of Commons.[2] Debates about the influence of the press, whether it was pernicious or uplifting, flourished among politicians, intellectuals and journalists. This was as true for Ireland as for the USA, Britain and the rest of Europe. In a contribution to the national debate about how the ancient Irish nation could cope with modernity, W.B. Yeats argued that journalese was the most debased form of English and thereby a corrosive component of Anglicisation.[3] Ironically, he pursued this argument in voluminous contributions to newspapers and journals where controversy raged on the future course of cultural and political nationalism.

By the end of the First World War another debate about the press had begun in London, which would have a profound impact on how the Irish revolution would be covered. From 1914 to 1918 the mainstream press in Britain had been co-opted for the war effort. Newspaper proprietors acquiesced in the system of censorship and their journalists followed suit. British propaganda had been so successful that many voices questioned whether the press had been turned into a lying machine.

Particular targets of the critics were the special correspondents, whose reputation depended on being fearless witnesses. The correspondents who tried to report independently from northern France in the early days of the war were arrested and expelled. Soon afterwards, official war correspondents were sanctioned to send the news back to London. They were carefully escorted to the front and the dispatches they wrote in the specially appointed villas situated well behind the lines were only sent out after being scrutinised and passed by military censors; they could hardly be said to have witnessed the war in any real sense.

The memoirs of Philip Gibb, Henry Wood Nevinson and Hamilton Fyfe show how influential correspondents were acutely aware that the recognition they achieved for their war coverage was undercut by their collusion with censorship, and that they gradually began to feel they had betrayed their calling. This sense of shame was accentuated by the emergence in Britain of a wider post-war critique of the perils of propaganda, which assimilated fears that the press had become the political tool of powerful interests seeking political advantage. Hilaire Belloc's complaint that an oligarchy controlling the press had 'come to believe that it can suppress any truth and suggest any falsehood' was not untypical.[4] Contemporary journalistic memoirs show how this critical perspective on the role of correspondents during the war was incorporated by many of them into their view of what journalism should aspire to achieve.

On the eve of the war in Ireland a notion that the reputation of the press had been tarnished by collaboration with the government had taken hold. Correspondents for major London newspapers, whose professional self-image was based on the idea that they reported what they saw, went to Ireland in the context of complaints that journalists had compromised their integrity and that reporters were frauds because they had not been doing the job that the public had been led to expect of them.

In their coverage of the early stages of the war the correspondents who went to Ireland appeared to maintain a general respect for the government view. They were prepared to take on trust the official line that the Sinn Féin MPs, who had inaugurated their own parliament in Dublin rather than taking their seats in the House of Commons in London, would soon come to their senses. However, as the volunteer army that became the IRA stepped up its guerrilla campaign during 1919, the reporting from Ireland grew more sceptical of official explanations, openly questioning whether the Irish administration had the ability or the means to contain it. When the Black and Tans and the Auxiliaries were introduced in 1920 to bolster the disintegrating Irish police force, the reporting of the British campaign became even more hostile.

What was unusual about this was that Ireland was but one of a series of revolts around the empire that coincided with the signing of the Versailles treaty. Britain was confronted with uprisings in Egypt, Afghanistan, India and the new protectorate of Mesopotamia as 'a new and more elaborate set of crises marched indefatigably on through the body politic of Empire, like gout through the enfeebled frame of a toper'.[5] It was Ireland, however, that received an inordinate amount of attention in the press.

Indeed, the campaign in Ireland generated more critical coverage than most of the foreign expeditions that preceded it. In his survey of nine-teenth- and twentieth-century war reporting Joseph Matthews noted that although small imperial wars regularly provoked internal political dissent in Britain, France and Germany, 'none of this ... was reflected in news dispatches from the field'.[6] Correspondents might criticise specific tactics or a shortfall in provision for the troops, but the essential thrust of their reporting 'was one of wholehearted belief in the blessings of civilisation that were being carried to the heathen for the good of the heathen and for the good of the conquerors'. These battles were usually 'set in romantic sur-roundings, far removed from the troublesome controversies at home, and the reporters took care that the two did not meet'.[7]

Ireland was different. Here, doubts and disagreements about the correct course of action were publicly exposed and dissected in a fashion hardly ever equalled in the case of small wars in more distant lands. The war in Ireland changed the terms of that engagement for the British reporters be-cause its proximity and the ambiguity of Ireland's status combined to make the conflict a highly visible test of some of the most cherished imperial illu-sions. No doubt one reason for this was that Ireland's status was associated by British politicians with 'the integrity of the British state itself'.[8] Unlike the First World War, when the entire nation was mobilised, the Irish con-flict was small-scale, which offered 'wider scope for diversity of perception' and space for arguments over its purpose.[9] This presented British corre-spondents in particular with an opportunity to respond to the major assault on their own cherished sense of independence.

Once the arguments began, controlling perceptions became more dif-ficult. In a typical gambit in the House of Commons the Irish Secretary, Hamar Greenwood, tried to portray the sister island as largely serene and loyal. 'In two-thirds, or nearly three-fourths of Ireland, there is as great peace as there is in the county of Kent', Greenwood insisted, dismissing the remaining fraction of the country (anything from one-third to one quarter) as a manageable area of distemper infected by sedition with foreign roots.[10]

However, as the war of reprisals became the focus of coverage in the London (and international) press, it was hard to portray Ireland convincingly as a peaceful corner of the kingdom beset by bandits; as with Vietnam nearly half a century later, there came a point when 'events themselves … could not longer be rationalized or suppressed or distorted by "progress reports".[11]

Coverage of the IRA campaign confounded the idea that Ireland was in the grip of a temporary disturbance. And coverage of reprisals by the Crown forces provided evidence that an incompetent administration had become lawless as well. Correspondents such as Hugh Martin travelled the country to interview witnesses to atrocities. The presence of the Black and Tans and Auxiliaries and the notoriety they attained through their indiscipline opened a new vista for the reporting from Ireland. They were disliked and shunned by the many correspondents who regarded them as neither proper soldiers nor gentlemen.

By contrast, the revolutionary movement was regarded as a legitimate and honourable source of news. British correspondents would have been intimately familiar with Irish nationalism. The Irish question had been a staple of metropolitan politics for generations and representatives of the Irish cause enjoyed a status and authority beyond the reach of other contemporary anti-colonial nationalist movements: it should be remembered that the deputies in the first Dáil Eireann had been returned to the House of Commons in a British general election. British correspondents would also have been personally familiar with Irish concerns because London journalism had been colonised by the Irish. And much Irish history was played out in London – the reporting of Terence McSwiney's funeral procession from Brixton Prison, where he died on hunger strike, to Euston Station in October 1920 made the point that Sinn Féin flags and uniforms were treated with respect by the crowds lining the streets.

The ability of the British government to prevent correspondents from presenting Sinn Féin's view of the war was also fatally undermined by the emergence of critics of Lloyd George's strategy within the government itself and in the wider political elite. Members of the Cabinet and senior officials in London and Dublin combined a sensitivity towards public opinion with distaste for the tactics of reprisals. The reality of powerful dissenting voices at the highest level in London and in the Irish administration in Dublin Castle extended the limits of legitimate political controversy and meant that Sir Hamar Greenwood – whose sole aim according to T.P. O'Connor was 'publicity and more publicity and still more publicity' – lost control of the press in Ireland.[12]

The British government thus failed to monopolise the interpretation of the news. As the war of reprisals in Ireland worsened, powerful figures in the political elite – both inside and outside the Cabinet – took issue with its conduct. At the same time the British correspondents began to challenge directly the official presentation of events, a case in point being Hugh Martin's adversarial reporting, which directly contradicted Sir Hamar Greenwood's explanations in parliament. The conceits of British, European and American correspondents (such as the idea that British forces were engaged in a policy of Prussian frightfulness in Ireland) were reproduced by prominent figures such as Asquith in political debate in London.

Running through the correspondents' dispatches was also a fear that Ireland might be an experiment in maintaining public order that could eventually be re-imported to Britain itself at a time of deep insecurity. In 1920, at the height of the Irish troubles, W.B. Yeats – an avid imbiber of the zeitgeist – wrote to Lady Gregory of his fear that

> everywhere governments and military power are let do much what they like. People speak quite calmly of a large part of Europe sinking back into barbarism and compare it to the break up of civilization at the fall of the Roman Empire. They cling to any authority.[13]

The Labour Party was alive to the possibility that repression in Ireland might inspire emulation in Britain. Its leaders 'believed that reactionary groups within the government were exploiting unrest in Ireland as an excuse to develop a paramilitary force that could be mobilized against labour militancy at home'.[14] This idea was not new: in his classic tract on imperialism published at the turn of the century, J.A. Hobson had warned that autocratic mentalities fostered among British administrators in the colonies were being introduced to Britain on their return: 'It is indeed, a nemesis of Imperialism that the arts and crafts of tyranny, acquired and exercised in our unfree Empire, should be turned against our liberties at home.'[15] These arguments all played a part in how the news from Ireland was conceived by British correspondents.

News had become the chief currency of the commercial press for a mass audience. Becoming newsworthy or receiving favourable treatment in the news was a fundamental aim of political movements. Sinn Féin was no different. The chief representatives of the revolutionaries whom correspondents first encountered when they arrived in Dublin – Desmond FitzGerald and Erskine Childers – were themselves British-born, urbane and well connected to the media world in London. They in turn opened doors to intellectual advocates for the Sinn Féin cause such as George Russell and the popular historian Alice Stopford Green, whose outlook was essentially the same as English liberals. An official at Dublin Castle is reputed to have surprised a visiting correspondent by describing in detail the itinerary the journalist had already been taken through by Sinn Féin:

> You went to ... the home of Sir Horace Plunkett and you had a couple of hours with George Russell at Plunkett House. Desmond FitzGerald called on you at the Shelbourne Hotel, and with an elaborate show of secrecy arranged an interview with Arthur Griffith. One or two harmless young Catholic priests fell into conversation with you at the Shelbourne. You had invitations to tea from Mrs Erskine Childers, Maud Gonne MacBride and Mrs Stopford Green, who described atrocities they claim to have seen...[16]

Historians who have written about Sinn Féin's propaganda effort have dealt with it in isolation, often regarding it as an ingenious sales pitch. However, it must be looked at in tandem with British efforts to influence journalists in a very modern struggle to define the news. Writing in 1936, the historian and journalist R.C.K. Ensor argued that the relationship between journalism and politics had changed in the previous fifty years: in the nineteenth century 'propaganda was made by open argument' whereas in the twentieth century it was achieved by 'the doctoring of news'.[17] Ensor's insight appeared to be borne out by the observation by one of Britain's propagandists during the First World War, Sir Gilbert Parker, to the effect that he and his colleagues had been more successful than the Germans because they used the 'objective' language of news to mobilise opinion rather than crude propaganda.[18]

During the Anglo-Irish War, both sides realised that influencing the news was vital to controlling public perceptions of the conflict. Echoing

Parker, the head of the News Bureau at Dublin Castle, Basil Clarke, tried to persuade his political and military masters that news was a more effective propaganda weapon than argument:

> Whereas *views* like a quack medicine, must be 'pushed' with influence, with petitions and grovelling only to find a niggardly resting place in a single journal ... news travels of its own volition without need of any further expenditure of energy on the part of the original transmitter, and pokes its own way into journals home and foreign, friendly and unfriendly, the world over.[19]

He argued that labelling news as 'official' would give it a 'hallmark' that would trump whatever opinions were held by the correspondents and guarantee publication.[20] What he had not accounted for was that Sinn Féin propagandists were also well aware of what journalists needed to write their stories. Describing his day-to-day encounters with correspondents in a letter to his fiancée, Frank Gallagher wrote that he strived to 'give them *news*' [my italics].[21] To Basil Clarke's dismay, many correspondents who went to cover the war in Ireland proved reluctant to regard 'official' news as the only legitimate news.

Sinn Féin's focus on publicity was consistent with the approach of other insurgent groups in the new media age. Prior to the American intervention in Cuba in 1898, Cuban exiles in New York had helped journalists from the major papers there to write about the scorched-earth tactics being practised by the Spaniards in the effort to suppress Cuban nationalism.[22] And during the Mexican revolution Pancho Villa used the press to disseminate 'ready-made perceptions of him and his struggle in terms of three fundamental issues – his morality, his and the United States' mutual self-interest, and American pragmatism'.[23] He regularly gave interviews to American newspaper correspondents, including John Reed, and provided a special carriage on his military train for journalists.[24] One of Villa's lieutenants, Pablo Lopez, once gave an interview to a correspondent of a Texan newspaper after he discovered that the reporter was Irish by birth. 'Ah', said Lopez, 'you are not then a gringo. Well, that makes a little difference; you have revolutions in your own land. Is it not so? Yes, my friends keep me posted on outside news.'[25]

This story points to the success of a fundamental strategy of the Irish revolutionaries: the attempt to universalise their cause and thus invite visiting journalists to locate their struggle within greater historical world dimensions. By claiming the right to self-determination the Irish revolutionaries were connecting themselves to the idea being promoted by President Woodrow Wilson as a prophylactic against future imperial wars. This 'allowed Sinn Féin to represent itself to the world as more than just a physical force party'.[26] It also associated the struggle in Ireland with nascent anti-colonial nationalisms around the world. Sinn Féin was thus attempting to 'persuade the English that nationalism was not a vile Irish disease but a natural and irresistible phenomenon'.[27] In a memorandum written in 1922, George Gavin Duffy – the Minister for Foreign Affairs in the new Free State government – argued that Ireland could be a force to be reckoned with in the League of Nations because it was regarded as standing for 'democratic principles, against Imperialism and upon the side of liberty throughout the world'.[28] This was the master narrative that Sinn Féin pressed on journalists covering the Anglo-Irish War.

Champions of the empire had their own master narrative: many of them 'believed that the strength of the Empire lay not in its territorial magnitude but in its liberalism, its moral greatness'.[29] Condemnation of German militarism had been at the core of Allied propaganda during the First World War: 'Liberal supporters of the war needed a just peace to vindicate their position.'[30] In the immediate aftermath of the war, Lloyd George's government advanced legal arguments for prosecuting German war criminals according to British standards of justice.[31] This opened the way for any other state to object to British methods of warfare in its colonies.[32] Such a political climate influenced the reporting from Ireland and it is in this context that we should read the repeated references in correspondents' dispatches as to how the methods of the Black and Tans were undermining Britain's right to be the arbiter of universal morality and its post-war standing, as *The Times* put it, as 'the proved champion of civilisation'.[33]

International press coverage spread the notoriety of the war of reprisals in Ireland around the globe; descriptions of a British *freikorps* who self-consciously modelled themselves on the gunslingers of the Wild West were little aid to the image that the British government was trying to project to the world.[34] After a visit to the USA, Henry Wood Nevinson wrote that it was 'a terrible thing to feel ashamed of the country one loves. It is like coming home and finding one's mother drunk upon the floor.'[35]

The nature of this sustained press critique and the extent to which it both reflected and encouraged dissenting opinion within Britain's political elite lends weight to the argument that 'the actions of liberal states ... cannot be explained convincingly without an account of their principled ideas...'.[36] Indeed, Gary Peatling has maintained that the force of these ideas ultimately prevented the deployment of overwhelming military force to crush the rebellion in Ireland:

> [The] idea of a self-governing Ireland and resistance to the coercion of nationalist Ireland, obtained substantial, ready and ultimately decisive support from longstanding and self-consciously 'British' traditions ... [It] must be conceded that without such assistance, Irish nationalists would have found it much harder to establish the Irish Free State, not to mention the Republic.[37]

The desire of British correspondents to reinvigorate the myth of their independence from the state was one tradition that helped resistance to coercion in Ireland. For once there was a grain of truth in the journalistic legend. Thus the war in Ireland allowed the journalists who had been under attack for their collusion with government propaganda during the First World War to reassert their identity as truth tellers. This return to the ideals made famous by *The Times*' coverage of the Crimean War was not only proclaimed by the newspapers themselves (in articles such as the *Manchester Guardian* editorial claiming that the only way of knowing the truth of events in Ireland was by reading the correspondents' dispatches).[38] More important was the consecration offered by the repetition of these dispatches by the government's critics in the House of Commons.

In his study of the political press, Stephen Koss noted how politicians 'sedulously fostered newspapermen's self-images' as representatives of the Fourth Estate.[39] Coverage of the war in Ireland was a classic case in point. The persistent quotation in parliament of the reports written by British, American and European correspondents covering the war seemed to vindicate the myth of the vigilant press. The authority of journalists as honest witnesses had always been important to their self-image, but this watchdog role was reinvested with validity during the Anglo-Irish War.

In his memoirs Philip Gibbs took up this theme of valiant crusading for truth by suggesting that there was 'a boycott of news' from Ireland but that a few courageous newspapers broke through 'this conspiracy of silence'.[40] At the same time, and with no apparent sense of contradiction, he also managed to argue that it was at least a year after the end of the Anglo-Irish War before admissions were made in the House of Commons and 'facts [published] in papers like *The Times*'.[41] As well as suiting his thesis that the God-fearing Englishman would never have condoned the activities of the Black and Tans had he known about what was going on in Ireland, Gibbs's torturous argument encompasses the idea of a small band of journalistic heroes redeeming their much traduced profession.

The British and American journalists had in common an irresistible in-clination to place their coverage of the Irish revolution within a context of other issues that they found more pressing. Sometimes implicitly, some-times explicitly, their interpretations of events in Ireland are interventions in debates about their own societies. In the passage quoted earlier from Hugh Martin's dispatch, written as he returned to London for Armistice Day in 1920, Martin represents Ireland as a theatre where British morality was be-ing put to the test on a stage visible only to newspaper correspondents, who watched the drama unfold as stand-ins for the public.[42] G.K. Chesterton was able to use the vigorous upsurge of Irish nationalism to make his case against industrialism and collectivism. For V.S. Pritchett, being a correspon-dent in revolutionary Ireland was a personal liberation from the stultifying horizons of his lower-middle-class family. And Carl Ackerman saw Ireland in terms of the anti-revolutionary creed of Wilsonian democracy.

A particularly enduring conceit among the British journalists is the abandonment of supposed norms of virtuous governance. Thirty years after the Irish revolution the *Daily Mirror* began to carry reports by James Cam-eron criticising the conduct of the war in Kenya (in which he compared the Mau Mau to Sinn Féin).[43] Cameron wrote that Britain had to protect 'our good name ... our reputation' as much as the white settlers.[44] In an editorial in support of Cameron's exposé, the *Mirror* argued that although the Mau Mau was 'a vicious organisation', the greater issue was 'the ruin of Colonial goodwill and the strange sad corruption of British rule'; the conflict essentially came down to 'our own morality as rulers'.[45] It was as if the debate on Ireland had never happened.

This tendency among many liberal British correspondents to view the Irish troubles overwhelmingly in terms of their implications for the ethics of British rule is partly responsible for what some see as a distorted account of the conflict enduringly popularised by Sinn Féin apologists. Robert Kee has argued that the success of Sinn Féin publicity made it appear that the IRA had merely acted in response to the ruthlessness of British mercenaries, whereas the reality was that many of the Crown forces killed were Catholic Irishmen, not Black and Tans.[46] Kee observed that

> so much efficient propaganda about reprisals was made on behalf of the Sinn Féin cause that it can now be too easily forgotten that a strong element of civil war was involved in the events of 1920–1; it accounted for much of the peculiar savagery.[47]

It is true that correspondents from *The Times*, the *Manchester Guardian* and the *Daily News* were so focused on documenting reprisals that the IRA's campaign virtually escaped scrutiny, save for a periodic totting up of 'outrages', a practice that gave the impression that assassinations and ambushes were merely an incidental backdrop to the reprisals themselves. There was hardly any attempt to explain IRA tactics or its practice of kidnapping magistrates and shooting informers. This kind of news usually appeared in the pro-Unionist *Morning Post*, albeit often in the form of the verbatim recycling of press statements from Dublin Castle. However, it did at least partially reflect a feature of the war that the other papers deemed unimportant.

The same fate mostly befell other specifically local dimensions of the revolution: language, religion and the nature of Irish nationalism itself were rarely explored in their own right. The work of foreign correspondents covering the Irish revolution was mainly about other things besides Ireland.[48]

# NOTES

## INTRODUCTION

1   H.V. Brasted, 'Irish nationalism and the British Empire in the late nineteenth century', in Oliver MacDonagh, W.F. Mandle and Pauric Travers (eds), *Irish Culture and Nationalism 1750–1950* (London: Macmillan, 1983), p.84.

2   Corelli Barnett, *The Collapse of British Power* (London: Eyre Methuen, 1972), p.184.

3   Jan Morris, *Farewell the Trumpets* (London: Faber, 1978), p.219.

4   Michael Laffan, *The Resurrection of Ireland: The Sinn Fein Party 1916–1923* (Cambridge: CUP, 1999), p.295.

5   Barnett: *Collapse of British Power*, p.185.

6   Dorothy Macardle, *The Irish Republic* (London: Corgi, 1968), p.407.

7   Ibid., p.330.

8   Ibid., *passim*, but see for example p.278 and p.302.

9   Michael Hopkinson, *The Irish War of Independence* (Dublin: Gill and Macmillan, 2002), p.45.

10  Richard Bourke, *Peace in Ireland: The War of Ideas* (London: Pimlico, 2003), p.121.

11  Kevin Myers, 'An Irishman's diary', *Irish Times*, 16 September 2003. Bourke later replied, 'Mr Myers drew the conclusion that because I mentioned the reporting of such outrages I must be implying that they did not in fact take place – which, of course, they did.' (*Irish Times*, 10 February 2004).

12  D.G. Boyce, *Englishmen and Irish Troubles: British Public Opinion and the Making of Irish Policy* (London: Jonathan Cape, 1972), pp.200–1.

13  Arthur Mitchell, *Revolutionary Government in Ireland: Dail Eireann 1919–22* (Dublin: Gill and Macmillan, 1995), pp.101–2.

14   See for example Conor Cruise O'Brien, *Parnell and His Party 1880–90* (Oxford: Clarendon Press, 1957) and T.W. Moody, *Davitt and Irish Revolution 1846–82* (Oxford: Clarendon Press, 1981).

15   David Fitzpatrick, *Politics and Irish Life: Provincial Experience of War and Revolution* (Togher: Cork University Press, 1998).

16   David Fitzpatrick, *Harry Boland's Irish Revolution* (Togher: Cork University Press, 2003), p.402, n. 100.

17   Quoted in Brendan Dooley, 'From literary criticism to systems theory in early modern journalism history', *Journal of the History of Ideas* 51/iii (1990), p.461.

18   Kate Campbell, 'On perceptions of journalism', in Kate Campbell (ed.), *Journalism, Literature and Modernity: From Hazlitt to Modernism* (Edinburgh University Press, 2000), p.1.

19   J.A. Hobson, *Confessions of an Economic Heretic* (London: George Allen and Unwin, 1938), pp.85–6.

20   Herbert Gans, *Deciding What's News* (New York: Pantheon, 1979); Gaye Tuchman, *Making News* (New York: Free Press, 1978); and Jeremy Tunstall, *Journalists at Work* (London: Constable, 1971).

21   James Curran, *Media and Power* (London: Routledge, 2002), p.46.

22   Michael Schudson, *Origins of the Ideal of Objectivity in the Professions: Studies in the History of American Journalism and American Law 1830–1940* (New York: Garland, 1990); Jean Chalaby, *The Invention of Journalism* (London: Macmillan, 1998); and Mark Hampton, *Visions of the Press in Britain, 1850–1950* (Urbana: University of Illinois Press, 2004).

23   Phillip Knightley, *The First Casualty: The War Correspondent as Hero, Propagandist and Myth Maker* (London: Quartet, 1982).

24   See Stephen Koss, *The Rise and Fall of the Political Press in Britain* (London: Fontana, 1990) and *Fleet Street Radical: A.G. Gardiner and the Daily News* (London: Allen Lane, 1973).

25   Quoted in Niall Ferguson, 'Virtual history: towards a "chaotic" theory of the past', in Niall Ferguson (ed.) *Virtual History: Alternatives and Counterfactuals* (London: Picador, 1997), pp.58–9.

26   Hampton: *Visions of the Press*, pp.76–7.

27   Max Weber, 'Politics as a vocation', in H.H. Gerth and C. Wright Mills (eds), *From Max Weber: Essays in Sociology* (London: Routledge, 1991), p.97.

28   Daniel C. Hallin and Paolo Mancini, *Comparing Media Systems: Three Models of Media and Politics* (Cambridge: CUP, 2004), p.35.

29   Ibid., p.40.

30   E.H.L. Watson, *Hints to Young Authors* (London: Brown, Langham and Co., 1906), quoted by Kate Campbell, 'Journalistic discourses and construction

of modern knowledge', in Laurel Brake, Bill Bell and David Finkelstein (eds), *Nineteenth Century Media and the Construction of Identities* (London: Palgrave, 2000), p.42.

31    R.A. Scott-James, *The Influence of the Press* (London: S.W. Partridge, 1913), p.11.

32    Hamilton Fyfe, *Sixty Years of Fleet Street* (London: W.H. Allen, 1949), p.168.

33    Sydney Brooks, 'The press in war-time', *North American Review* CC (December 1914), p.858.

34    Anne Olivier Bell (ed.), *The Diary of Virginia Woolf*, vol. ii: 1920–1924 (London: Hogarth, 1978), pp.72–3.

35    Ibid., p.100.

36    Joseph Conrad, *Notes on Life and Letters* (London: J.M. Dent, 1921), p.112.

37    J.G. Farrell, *Troubles* (London: Phoenix, 1993), p.102.

38    Ibid.

39    Ibid., p.290.

40    Ibid., p.318.

41    Ibid., p.84.

42    Kevin Barry (ed.), *James Joyce: Occasional, Critical and Political Writing* (Oxford: OUP, 2000), p.146.

43    David Hogan (Frank Gallagher), *The Four Glorious Years* (Dublin: Irish Press, 1953), p.62.

44    Hampton: *Visions of the Press*, p.9.

45    Ibid., pp.9–10.

46    Ibid., p.13.

47    Quoted in Hampton: *Visions of the Press*, p.109.

48    F.H. Hayward and B.N. Langdon-Davies, *Democracy and the Press* (Manchester: National Labour Press, 1919), p.4.

49    Quoted in Gary Bass, *Stay the Hand of Vengeance: The Politics of War Crimes Tribunal* (Princeton, NJ: Princeton University Press, 2000), p.73.

50    His most recent biographer has affirmed: 'Throughout his career Lloyd George took the press very seriously ... he was ever conscious that the press and those who controlled it had unique resources for interpreting and influencing public opinion.' Note that this view takes in both the educational and the representative ideal (John Grigg, *Lloyd George: War Leader, 1916–1918* (London: Allen Lane, 2002), p.614).

51    Edwin Lawrence Godkin, *Unforseen Tendencies of Democracy* (London: Constable, 1898), quoted in Gaetano Quagliariello, *Politics Without Parties: Moisei Ostrogorski and the Debate on Political Parties on the Eve of the Twentieth Century* (Aldershot: Avebury, 1996), p.158, n. 5.

52   C.A. Bayly, *The Birth of the Modern World 1780–1914* (Oxford: Blackwell, 2004), p.484.

53   Niall Ferguson, *The Pity of War* (New York: Basic Books, 1999), p.212.

54   David Welch, *Germany, Propaganda and Total War, 1914–1918: The Sins of Omission* (London: Athlone Press, 2000), p.1.

55   Quoted in Knightley: *The First Casualty*, p.93.

56   Philip Elliott, 'All the world's a stage or what's wrong with the national press', in James Curran (ed.), *The British Press: A Manifesto* (London: Macmillan, 1978), p.143.

57   Norman Angell, *The Press and the Organisation of Society* (London: Labour Publishing Company, 1922), p.20.

58   Walter Raleigh, *The War and the Press* (Oxford: Clarendon Press, 1918), pp.9–10.

59   Ibid., p.18.

60   Letter from Desmond FitzGerald to Dail Eireann, 1 January 1920, *Desmond FitzGerald Papers*, Archive Department, University College Dublin, P80/14/1.

61   Angell: *The Press and the Organisation of Society*, pp.37–8.

62   Ibid., p.16.

63   Ibid., p.17.

64   Ibid., p.137.

65   Hugh Brogan, *The Life of Arthur Ransome* (London: Jonathan Cape, 1984), p.227.

66   Anthony Smith, 'War and ethnicity: the role of warfare in the formation, self-images and cohesion of ethnic communities', *Ethnic and Racial Studies* 4/iv (1981), p.387.

67   Mark Mazower, *Dark Continent: Europe's Twentieth Century* (London: Allen Lane, 1998), p.45.

68   Toby Dodge, *Inventing Iraq: The Failure of Nation Building and a History Denied* (London: Hurst, 2003), p.5.

69   John Dunn, *Modern Revolutions: An Introduction to an Analysis of a Political Phenomenon* (Cambridge: CUP, 1972), p.xii.

70   Ben Levitas, *The Theatre of Nation: Irish Drama and Cultural Nationalism 1890–1916* (Oxford: Clarendon Press, 2002), p.91.

71   C.A. Bayly, 'Representing copts and muhammadans: empire, nation and community in Egypt and India, 1880–1914', in Leila Tarazi Fawaz and C.A. Bayly (eds), *Modernity and Culture from the Mediterranean to the Indian Ocean* (New York: Columbia University Press, 2002), p.160.

72   Moody: *Davitt and Irish Revolution*, p.142.

73    Brasted: 'Irish nationalism and the British Empire', p.89.
74    Quoted in Donal Lowry, 'New Ireland, old empire and the outside world, 1922–49: the strange evolution of a "dictionary republic"', in Mike Cronin and John Regan (eds), *Ireland: The Politics of Independence, 1922–49* (London: Macmillan, 2000), p.173.

## I – THE EDUCATION OF THE WAR CORRESPONDENTS

1     See James Curran and Jean Seaton, *Power Without Responsibility: The Press and Broadcasting in Britain* (London: Routledge, 1988), pp.46–63 and D.G. Boyce, 'Crusaders without chains: power and the press barons 1896–1951', in James Curran, Anthony Smith and Pauline Wingate (eds), *Impacts and Influences: Essays on Media Power in the Twentieth Century* (London: Methuen, 1987).
2     Michael Schudson notes that in the USA it was at the turn of the twentieth century that 'reporters were for the first time actors in the drama of the newspaper world' (Michael Schudson, *Origins of the Ideal of Objectivity in the Professions: Studies in the History of American Journalism and American Law 1830–1940* (New York: Garland, 1990), p.162).
3     Jean Chalaby, *The Invention of Journalism* (London: Macmillan, 1998), p.79.
4     Ibid., p.84.
5     Oron J. Hale, *Publicity and Diplomacy – With Special Reference to England and Germany 1890–1914* (New York: D. Appleton-Century Co., 1940), quoted in Philip Taylor, 'Publicity and diplomacy: the impact of the First World War upon Foreign Office attitudes towards the press', in David Dilks (ed.), *Retreat from Power: Studies in Britain's Foreign Policy of the Twentieth Century*, vol. i (London: Macmillan, 1981), p.45.
6     John Hohenberg, *Foreign Correspondence: The Great Reporters and Their Times* (New York: Columbia University Press, 1964), p.113.
7     Tom Clarke, *My Northcliffe Diary* (London: Victor Gollancz, 1931), p.42.
8     Lucy Brown, 'The treatment of the news in mid-Victorian newspapers', in *Transactions of the Royal Historical Society*, 5th series, vol. xxvii (1977).
9     Hamilton Fyfe in a private letter to Lord Northcliffe, 13 October 1913, *Northcliffe Papers*, British Library, London, Add. 62206/fos. 87–8.
10    Roger T. Stearn, 'War correspondents and colonial war, c. 1870–1900', in John M. MacKenzie (ed), *Popular Imperialism and the Military 1850–1950* (Manchester University Press, 1992), pp.239, 151.
11    F. Lauriston Bullard, *Famous War Correspondents* (London: Sir Isaac Pitman, 1914), p.23.

12   Henry W. Nevinson, *Changes and Chances* (London: James Nisbet, 1923), p.167.

13   Frank Scudamore, *A Sheaf of Memories* (London: T. Fisher Unwin, 1925), pp.285–6.

14   Stearn: 'War correspondents', p.142.

15   William Maxwell, 'The war correspondent in sunshine and eclipse', *The Nineteenth Century and After*, no. 433 (March 1913), pp.620–1.

16   Quoted in Robert W. Desmond, *The Information Process: World News Reporting to the Twentieth Century* (University of Iowa Press, 1978), p.325.

17   Philip Gibbs, *Adventures in Journalism* (London: William Heinemann, 1923), p.179.

18   Philip Gibbs, *The Pageant of Years: An Autobiography* (London: William Heinemann, 1946), p.71.

19   Ibid., p.1.

20   Ibid., pp.1–2.

21   Jean Seaton, *Carnage and the Media: The Making and Breaking of News About Violence* (London: Allen Lane, 2006), p.289.

22   Quoted in Bullard: *Famous War Correspondents*, p.22.

23   Stearn: 'War correspondents', p.145.

24   Ibid.

25   Maxwell: 'The war correspondent', p.623.

26   Stearn: 'War correspondents', pp.147, 149.

27   See Bullard: *Famous War Correspondents*, pp.320–35 for a summary of Churchill's career as a war correspondent.

28   Quoted in Bullard: *Famous War Correspondents*, p.29.

29   Stearn: 'War correspondents', pp.146–7.

30   Bullard: *Famous War Correspondents*, p.29.

31   Ibid., p.156.

32   Stearn: 'War correspondents', p.150.

33   John S. Ellis, '"The methods of barbarism" and the "Rights of small nations": war propaganda and British pluralism', *Albion* 30/i (spring 1998), pp.49–62.

34   Philip Gibbs: *The Pageant of Years*, pp.94–5.

35   Angela V. John, *War, Journalism and the Shaping of the Twentieth Century: The Life and Times of Henry W. Nevinson* (London: I.B.Tauris, 2006), pp.85–90, 161–4.

36   H.W. Nevinson in the *Nation*, 20 April 1907, quoted in ibid., pp.162–3.

37   James Duffy, *A Question of Slavery* (Oxford: Clarendon Press, 1967), pp.186–98. Nevinson published his reports as a book: *A Modern Slavery* (London: Harper, 1906).

38    Henry W. Nevinson, *Changes and Chances* (London: James Nisbet, 1923), p.202.

39    Ibid., p.203.

40    Ibid., p.235.

41    John: *War, Journalism*, p.162.

42    Ibid.

43    Maxwell: 'The war correspondent', p.609.

44    Scudamore: *A Sheaf of Memories*, p.223.

45    Maxwell: 'The war correspondent', p.608.

46    Bullard: *Famous War Correspondents*, p.2.

47    Ibid., p.28.

48    Deian Hopkin, 'Domestic censorship in the First World War', *Journal of Contemporary History*, 5/iv (1970), pp.152–3.

49    Sir George Cockerill in *The Times*, 23 May 1905, quoted in Gary S. Messinger, *British Propaganda and the State in the First World War* (Manchester University Press, 1992), p.102.

50    Hopkin: 'Domestic censorship', pp.152–3.

51    Ibid., p.153, and Niall Ferguson, *The Pity of War* (New York: Basic Books, 1999), p.223.

52    Alice Goldfarb Marquis, 'Words as weapons: propaganda in Britain and Germany during the First World War', *Journal of Contemporary History* 13/iii (July 1978), p.495.

53    Sir Edward Cook, *The Press in War-Time*, (London: Macmillan, 1920), p.51.

54    Ibid., pp.4–5.

55    Ibid., p.9.

56    Phillip Knightley, *The First Casualty: The War Correspondent as Hero, Propagandist and Myth Maker* (London: Quartet, 1982), p.69.

57    Philip Gibbs, *The Pageant of Years: An Autobiography* (London: William Heinemann, 1946), pp.141–2.

58    Philip Gibbs, *Realities of War* (London: Hutchinson, 1929), p.11.

59    Cook: *The Press in War-Time*, p.48.

60    Gibbs: *The Pageant of Years*, p.162.

61    Philip Knightly also suggests the Cabinet was swayed by a letter from the former American President Theodore Roosevelt saying the only real war news written by Americans was coming from the German side, and that the refusals by British and French censors was harming their cause in America. See Knightley: *The First Casualty*, p.79.

62    Ibid., pp.229–30.

63    C.E. Montague, *Disenchantment* (London: Chatto and Windus, 1922), p.97.

64   Ted Bogacz, '"A tyranny of words": language, poetry and antimodernism in England in the First World War', *Journal of Modern History*, 58/iii (September 1986), p.643.

65   Quoted in Ferguson: *The Pity of War*, p.234.

66   Quoted in Samuel Hynes, *A War Imagined: The First World War and English Culture* (London: Pimlico, 1992), p.110.

67   Gibbs describes the working conditions of the correspondents in *Realities of War*, pp.15–26, and *The Pageant of Years*, pp.163–7.

68   C.E. Montague observed: 'In the first few months of the war our the General Staff ... treated British war correspondents as pariah dogs [but after the war] all the regular pariah dogs were offered knighthoods' (Montague: *Disenchantment*, pp.94–5).

69   Gibbs: *Realities of War*, pp.27–8.

70   Ibid.

71   Ibid.

72   Gibbs: *The Pageant of Years*, pp.207–8.

73   Quoted in Marquis: 'Words as weapons', p.482.

74   Gibbs: *The Pageant of Years*, p.226.

75   Ibid., p.242.

76   Hynes: *A War Imagined*, p.284.

77   Bogacz: 'A tyranny of words', p.665.

78   Hynes: *A War Imagined*, p.284. Philip Gibbs resigned from the *Daily Chronicle* 'and the best salary I had ever earned in Fleet Street' in 1919 in protest against Lloyd George's policy in Ireland. The *Chronicle* had been bought by a syndicate acting on behalf of Lloyd George in 1918. The paper's new Irish policy was to support the dispatch to Ireland of the gendarmerie known as the Black and Tans. Gibbs felt he could no longer work for the *Chronicle* because 'it seemed to me shameful ... that after a war which was supposed to be for liberty and the self-determination of peoples, we should hire a lot of young thugs and let them loose upon the Irish'. See Gibbs: *The Pageant of Years*, p.266.

79   Montague: *Disenchantment*, p.98.

80   Ibid., p115.

81   Norman Angell, *The Press and the Organisation of Society* (London: Labour Publishing Company, 1922), p.69.

82   Hamilton Fyffe, *Sixty Years of Fleet Street* (London: W.H. Allen, 1979), p.172.

83   Quoted in Ferguson: *The Pity of War*, pp.240–1.

84   Gibbs: *The Pageant of Years*, p.72.

85   Marquis: 'Words as weapons', pp.495–6.

86  The phrase is used by Montague in *Disenchantment*, p.118, as well as by others.

87  Hilaire Belloc, *The Free Press* (London: George Allen and Unwin, 1918), p.29.

## II – REVOLUTION IN THE MAKING

1  Jose Harris, *Private Lives, Public Spirit: A Social History of Britain 1870–1914* (Oxford: OUP, 1993), p.204.

2  Richard English, *Irish Freedom: The History of Nationalism in Ireland* (London: Macmillan, 2006), p.210.

3  Benedict Anderson, *Imagined Communities: Reflections on the Origins and Spread of Nationalism* (London: Verso, 1991), p.36.

4  Mary Louise Legg, *Newspapers and Nationalism: The Irish Provincial Press, 1850–1892* (Dublin: Four Courts Press, 1999), p.72.

5  Ibid., p.148.

6  Quoted in James Loughlin, 'Constructing the political spectacle: Parnell, the press and national leadership, 1879–86', in D. George Boyce and Alan O' Day (eds), *Parnell in Perspective* (London: Routledge, 1991), p.225.

7  Ibid., p.224.

8  J.B. Hall, *Random Records of a Reporter* (Dublin: Fodhla Printing Co., 1928), p.226.

9  Frank Callanan, *T.M. Healy* (Togher: Cork University Press, 1996), p.14.

10  Hugh Heinrick, *A Survey of the Irish in England* (London, 1872), quoted in Fintan Cullen and R.F. Foster, *'Conquering England': Ireland in Victorian London* (London: National Portrait Gallery, 2005), pp.14–15.

11  Ibid., p.12.

12  *The Times*, 11 October 1887, quoted in Legg: *Newspapers and Nationalism*, p.158.

13  Legg: *Newspapers and Nationalism*, pp.114–18.

14  Ibid., p.116–17.

15  Loughlin: 'Constructing the political spectacle', p.227.

16  Ibid.

17  Quoted in R.V. Comerford, *Ireland* (London: Hodder Arnold, 2003), p.139.

18  Damien Kiberd, *Inventing Ireland: The Literature of the Modern Nation* (London: Vintage, 1996), p.145.

19  Comerford: *Ireland*, p.140.

20  Ibid., p.144.

21  Quoted in Conor Cruise O'Brien, *Parnell and His Party 1880–90* (Oxford: Clarendon Press, 1957), p.194, n. 3.

22   Paul Bew, *Ideology and the Irish Question: Ulster Unionism and Irish National-ism 1912–1916* (Oxford: Clarendon Press, 1994), p.53.

23   J.J. Lee, *Ireland 1912–1985* (Cambridge: CUP, 1989), p.18.

24   Norman Angell, *After All: The Autobiography of Norman Angell* (London: Hamish Hamilton, 1951), p.17.

25   Stanley Morison, *The History of* The Times: *The 150th Anniversary and Be-yond, 1912–1948*, vol. iv, part 2 (London: The Times, 1952), p.541.

26   Quoted in David Fitzpatrick, *Politics and Irish Life: Provincial Experience of War and Revolution* (Togher: Cork University Press, 1998), p.53.

27   D.G. Boyce, *Ireland 1828–1923: From Ascendancy to Democracy* (Oxford: Blackwell, 1992), p.80.

28   Quoted in Keith Jeffery, *Ireland and the Great War* (Cambridge: CUP, 2000), p. 12.

29   Charles Townshend, *Easter 1916: The Irish Rebellion* (London: Allen Lane, 2005), p.73.

30   Mark Tierney, Paul Bowen and David Fitzpatrick, 'Recruiting posters', in David Fitzpatrick (ed.), *Ireland and the First World War* (Dublin: Lilliput Press and Trinity History Workshop, 1988), pp.54–6.

31   Kevin Myers, 'The Irish and the Great War: A case of amnesia', in Richard English and Joseph Morrison Skelly (eds), *Ideas Matter: Essays in Honour of Conor Cruise O'Brien* (Dublin: Poolbeg Press, 1998), pp.103–4.

32   Quoted in Jeffery: *Ireland and the Great War*, p.70.

33   Mark Bence-Jones, *Twilight of the Ascendancy* (London: Constable, 1993), p.187.

34   Fitzpatrick: *Politics and Irish Life*, p.56.

35   David Fitzpatrick, 'The overflow of the deluge: Anglo-Irish relationships, 1914–1922', in Oliver MacDonagh and W.F. Mandle (eds), *Ireland and Irish-Australia: Studies in Cultural and Political History* (London: Croom Helm, 1986), p.86.

36   Boyce: *Ireland 1828–1923*, p.88.

37   Townshend: *Easter 1916*, pp.71–2.

38   Canon Hannay (the novelist, George Birmingham), quoted in Townshend: *Easter 1916*, pp.75.

39   Garret FitzGerald, 'The meaning of the rising', *Irish Times*, 13–18 July 1991, quoted in Bew: *Ideology and the Irish Question*, p.xvii.

40   Michael Laffan, *The Resurrection of Ireland: The Sinn Fein Party 1916–1923* (Cambridge: CUP, 1999), p.224.

41   Ibid., p.11.

42   Ibid., pp.11–33.

43   Townshend: *Easter 1916*, p.63.

44   Ibid., pp.78–9.

45   Ibid., p.77.

46   F.S.L. Lyons, *John Dillon: A Biography* (London: Routledge and Keegan Paul, 1968), p.366.

47   On 22 April 1916 – two days before the Rising took place – Nathan wrote to his boss Augustine Birrell: 'I see no indications of a rising' (ibid., p.368).

48   British naval intelligence were made fully aware of the conspirator's plans by intercepted German naval codes but kept officials at Dublin Castle in the dark for fear of revealing to the Germans that their codes were compromised. However, the fact that the Dublin administration seemed oblivious to the Rising contributed to its reputation for incompetence. See Laffan: *The Resurrection of Ireland*, pp.36–40.

49   F.S.L. Lyons, *Ireland Since the Famine* (London: Fontana, 1976), pp.334–9.

50   R.F. Foster, *Modern Ireland 1600–1972* (London: Allen Lane, 1988), p.479.

51   Ruth Dudley Edwards, *James Connolly* (Dublin: Gill and Macmillan, 1998), p.123.

52   Laffan: *The Resurrection of Ireland*, p.46.

53   Quote from the diary of J.R. Clark, cited in ibid.

54   F.A. MacKenzie, *The Irish Rebellion: What Happened and Why* (London: C. Arthur Pearson, 1916), pp.105–6.

55   Jeffery: *Ireland and the Great War*, p.53.

56   Lyons: *John Dillon*, p.380.

57   Ibid., p.373.

58   Ibid., p.375.

59   Warre B. Wells and N. Marlowe, *A History of the Irish Rebellion of 1916* (London: Maunsel, 1916), pp.204–5.

60   Henry W. Nevinson, *Last Changes, Last Chances* (London: James Nisbet, 1928), p.87.

61   Lyons: *Ireland Since the Famine*, p.369.

62   Lyons: *John Dillon*, pp.381–2.

63   Ibid.

64   Ibid., p.395.

65   Owen Dudley Edwards and Fergus Pyle, *1916: The Easter Rising* (London: MacGibbon and Kee, 1968), p.243.

66   Wells and Marlowe: *A History of the Irish Rebellion*, pp.203–4.

67   Townshend: *Easter 1916*, p.302.

68   Quoted in ibid., p.308.

69   Ibid., p.307.

70   Callanan: *T.M. Healy*, p.518.

71    David Fitzpatrick: *Politics and Irish Life*, p.8.
72    Quoted in Lyons: *John Dillon*, p.391.
73    Townshend: *Easter 1916*, p.369.
74    Alan J. Ward, 'Lloyd George and the 1918 Irish Conscription Crisis', *The Historical Journal*, 17/I (1974), p.108.
75    Ibid., pp.110–14.
76    Ferriter: *The Transformation of Ireland*, p.182.
77    Mansion House Declaration, 23 April 1918, quoted in Arthur Mitchell and Padraig O'Snodaigh (eds), *Irish Political Documents 1916-1949* (Dublin: Irish Academic Press, 1985), pp.41-2.
78    Ward: 'Lloyd George and the 1918 Irish conscription crisis', pp.118-20.
79    Ibid., p.126.

## III – THE MORAL ACCOUNTANT

1    R.F. Foster: *Modern Ireland 1600–1972* (London: Allen Lane, 1988), p.489.
2    *Daily News*, 22 January 1919, p.1.
3    Ibid.
4    *Manchester Guardian*, 22 January 1919, p.5.
5    *Daily Mail*, 22 January 1919, p.5.
6    *Manchester Guardian*, 22 January 1919, p.5.
7    *The Times*, 23 January 1919, p.11.
8    *Daily Mail*, 22 January 1919, p.5.
9    *Manchester Guardian*, 22 January 1919, p.5.
10   Ronan Fanning, Michael Kennedy, Dermot Keogh and Eunan O'Halpin (eds), *Documents on Irish Foreign Policy*, vol. i, 1919-1922 (Dublin: Royal Irish Academy, 1998), p.1.
11   Ibid., p.2.
12   Ibid.
13   *Daily Mail*, 22 January 1919, p.5.
14   *Manchester Guardian*, 21 January 1919, p.5.
15   Lord French to Walter Long, 12 January 1919, quoted in Eunan O'Halpin, *The Decline of the Union: British Government in Ireland 1892-1920* (Dublin: Gill and Macmillan, 1987), p.180.
16   *The Times*, 23 January 1919, p.11.
17   *The Times*, 8 January 1919.
18   *Manchester Guardian*, 6 January 1919, p.4.
19   *Daily Mail*, 20 January 1919, p.3.
20   D.G. Boyce, *The Irish Question and British Politics, 1868-1996* (London: Macmillan, 1996), p.67.

21    Quoted in O'Halpin: *The Decline of the Union*, p.187.

22    Ibid.

23    *Manchester Guardian*, 6 January 1919, p.4.

24    *Manchester Guardian*, 23 January 1919.

25    *The Times*, 23 January 1919.

26    *Daily Mail*, 23 January 1919.

27    *Daily News*, 16 January 1919, p.5.

28    See accounts in the *Daily News*, 22 and 23 January 1919, p.5 and p.3; *Daily Mail*, 22 January, p. 5 and 23 January 1919, p.5.

29    *Manchester Guardian*, 23 January 1919, p.6. In a book published more than twenty years later, Desmond Ryan, a journalist sympathetic to Sinn Féin, bore out the *Guardian*'s insight: 'Even the Dublin volunteers, that is to say the more militant section … criticised Soloheadbeg sharply … they believed the capture of arms and gelignite could have been made without loss of life…' (Desmond Ryan, *Sean Treacy and the Third Tipperary Brigade IRA* (Tralee: Anvil Books, 1945), p.59.

30    Ibid.

31    *Daily News*, 24 January 1919.

32    *Daily Mail*, 7 May 1919, p.6.

33    *Morning Post* , 6 May 1919, p.7.

34    *Daily Mail*, 12 May 1919.

35    *Morning Post*, 13 May 1919, p.7.

36    *Daily News*, 15 May 1919, p.2.

37    *Daily Mail*, 19 May 1919; *Manchester Guardian*, 14 May 1919.

38    *Morning Post*, 15 May 1919, p.7.

39    *Daily Mail*, 19 May 1919, p.51.

40    Sheila Lawlor, *Britain and Ireland 1914–23* (Dublin: Gill and Macmillan, 1983), p.39.

41    *Manchester Guardian*, 22 May 1919, p.5.

42    *Daily News*, 30 May 1919, p.4.

43    Ibid.

44    *Morning Post*, 8 September 1919, p.8; *Daily News*, 8 September 1919, p.1.

45    *Morning Post*, 9 September 1919, p.7.

46    *The Times*, 9 September 1919, p.12.

47    *Daily Mail*, 10 September 1919, p.5; *Daily News*, 10 September 1919, p.5; *The Times*, 10 September 1919, p.10.

48    *Daily News*, 10 September 1919, p.5.

49    See reports in *The Times*, the *Morning Post* and the *Daily News* from 10 September 1919.

50    *Manchester Guardian*, 10 September 1919, p.4.

51   Quoted in D.W. Hayward, 'The British press and Anglo-American relations with particular reference to the Irish question 1916–1922' (unpublished MA thesis, University of Manchester, 1960), p.163.

52   *The Times*, 10 September 1919, p.11.

53   Charles Townshend, *Political Violence in Ireland: Government and Resistance since 1848* (Oxford: Clarendon Press, 1983), p.67.

54   David Fitzpatrick, *Politics and Irish Life: Provincial Experience of War and Revolution* (Togher: Cork University Press, 1998), pp.412, 417.

55   Darell Figgis, *Recollections of the Irish War* (London: Ernest Benn, 1927), p.282.

56   Charles Townshend, 'Policing insurgency in Ireland', in David M. Anderson and David Killingray (eds), *Policing and Decolonisation: Politics, Nationalism and the Police 1917–65* (Manchester University Press, 1992), p.36.

57   Ibid., p.60.

58   Notes of a conversation at Downing Street, 30 April 1920, Cabinet minutes, National Archives, Kew, CAB 23/21/62.

59   Richard Hawkins, 'Dublin Castle and the Royal Irish Constabulary', in T. Desmond Williams (ed.), *The Irish Struggle 1916–1926* (London: Routledge and Kegan Paul, 1966), p.180.

60   See the conclusions of the conference at Downing Street, Cabinet minutes, 11 May 1920, National Archives, Kew, CAB 23/21/141.

61   See F.S.L. Lyons, *Ireland Since the Famine* (London: Fontana, 1976), pp.415–16.

62   Townshend: 'Policing insurgency in Ireland', p.26.

63   Quoted in Richard Bennett, *The Black and Tans* (New York: Barnes and Noble, 1995), p.37.

64   Lyons: *Ireland Since the Famine*, p.415.

65   Robert Kee, *The Green Flag: A History of Irish Nationalism* (London: Weidenfeld and Nicolson, 1972), p.667.

66   Joost Augustejin, *From Public Defiance to Guerrilla Warfare: The Experience of Ordinary Volunteers in the Irish War of Independence 1916–1921* (Dublin: Irish Academic Press, 1996), pp.202–3.

67   Quoted in Peter Hart, *The IRA and its Enemies: Violence and Community in Cork 1916–1923* (Oxford: Clarendon Press, 1998), p.82.

68   Brian Inglis, *West Briton* (London: Faber and Faber, 1962), p.31. It is noteworthy that Inglis uses classic Sinn Féin terminology – 'the sweepings of British jails' – to present the views of his family's Protestant friends.

69   Jon Lawrence, 'Forging a peaceable kingdom: war, violence, and fear of brutalization in post-First World War Britain', *Journal of Modern History*, 75 (September 2003), p.577.

70    Peter Clarke, *Liberals and Social Democrats* (Cambridge: CUP, 1978), p.213.

71    Laurence does acknowledge that there were 'many incidents of reprisal before Balbriggan hit the  news' (Laurence: 'Forging a peaceable kingdom', p.577, n. 92).

72    *Daily News*, 16 January 1919.

73    Francis Hackett, 'The price of being Irish', *New Republic*, 23 March 1921, p.94. Hackett reported that after Martin left, the Mayor's wife declared that 'he's a nice man and you can trust him but he's an English Liberal and he won't face the truth'.

74    Macready quoted by Sir Hamar Greenwood, Chief Secretary for Ireland in the House of Commons, 4 November 1920, Hansard, HC (series 5), vol. 134, col. 720.

75    Lord Decies, 'Report on censorship for December 1918', National Archives, Kew, CO 904/167/370–1.

76    *Daily News*, 28 October 1920, p.3.

77    *Daily News*, 21 October 1920, p.3.

78    *Daily News*, 25 October 1920, p.1.

79    *Daily News*, 3 November 1920, p.1 and 4 November 1920, p.1.

80    See the dispatch of a French correspondent reprinted in the *Daily News*, 5 November 1920.

81    *Daily News*, 4 November 1920.

82    *Daily News*, 5 November 1920.

83    H.W. Nevinson Journals, 5–6 October 1920, in *Henry Wood Nevinson*, Bodleian Library, Oxford, e621/4.

84    Ibid., 8 October 1920.

85    Ibid., 13–18 November 1920.

86    Ibid., 19 November 1920.

87    Editorial in the *Manchester Guardian*, 23 October 1920, p.8.

88    Mark Hampton, 'The press, patriotism and public discussion: C.P. Scott, the *Manchester Guardian*, and the Boer War, 1899–1902', *Historical Journal*, 44/i (2001), pp.187, 189.

89    Ibid., p.189.

90    *Daily News*, 11 November 1920, p.3.

91    Mark Hampton: 'The press, patriotism and public discussion', p.191.

92    Larry Zuckerman, *The Rape of Belgium: The Untold Story of World War I* (New York: NYUP, 2004), p.132.

93    Ibid., pp.23, 121.

94    Ibid., p.120.

95    Gary Bass, *Stay the Hand of Vengeance: The Politics of War Crimes Tribunal* (Princeton, NJ: Princeton University Press, 2000), p.73.

96 Philip Gibbs, *The Hope of Europe* (London: William Heinemann, 1921), p.70.

97 Modris Eksteins, *Rites of Spring: The Great War and the Birth of the Modern Age* (New York: Mariner Books, 2000), p.158.

98 For examples see 'The proclamation of anarchy' in the *Nation*, 2 October 1920, pp.4–5, and Robert Lynd in the *Daily News*, 16 November 1920.

99 Hugh Martin, *Ireland in Insurrection* (London: Daniel O'Connor, 1921), p.42.

100 Peter Clarke, *Liberals and Social Democrats* (Cambridge: CUP, 1978), p.177.

101 Ibid., p.181.

102 Laurence: 'Forging a peaceable kingdom', pp.578–9.

103 Ibid., p.580.

104 Henry Wood Nevinson, 'The Anglo-Irish War', *The Contemporary Review*, 120 (July 1921), pp.22–3.

105 Quoted in David Ayerst, *The Guardian: Biography of a Newspaper* (London: Collins, 1971), p.423.

106 *Manchester Guardian*, 29 October 1920, p.7.

107 Ibid.

108 Ibid., p.6.

109 *Daily News*, 29 October 1920, p.1.

110 Ibid.

111 The killings and the reprisal that followed that afternoon when Auxiliaries fired into a crowd at a football match killing 11 spectators and one of the players, are described in Lyons: *Ireland Since the Famine* (London: Fontana, 1976), pp.418–19.

112 *Daily News*, 22 November 1920, p.1.

113 *Morning Post*, 22 November 1920, p.6.

114 *Manchester Guardian*, 26 November 1920, p.9.

115 *The Times*, 27 November 1920, p.10.

116 Ibid.

117 *Morning Post* , 27 November 1920, p.7.

## IV – SEEING THE SUN AT NOON

1 From Dan H. Laurence (ed.), *Bernard Shaw Collected Letters*, vol. iii, 1911–1925 (London: Max Reinhardt, 1985), p.697.

2 Editorial, *Manchester Guardian*, 22 September 1920.

3 Hansard, HC (series 5), vol. 133, col. 946 (20 October 1920).

4 Robert Skidelsky, *Oswald Mosley* (London: Macmillan Papermac, 1981), p.93.

5    Hansard, HC (series 5), vol. 133, cols 1326–7 (25 October 1920).

6    Ibid., col. 1327.

7    Ibid., cols 1327–8.

8    Ibid., col. 1328.

9    Hansard, HC (series 5), vol. 135, col. 658 (24 November 1920).

10   Hansard, HC (series 5), vol. 134, col. 700 (4 November 1920).

11   Hansard, HC (series 5), vol. 135, col. 489 (24 November 1920).

12   Hansard, HC (series 5), vol. 134, col. 687 (4 November 1920).

13   Ibid., col. 687.

14   Hansard, HC (series 5), vol. 134, cols. 359–60 (3 November 1920).

15   Hansard, HC (series 5), vol. 134, col. 719 (4 November 1920).

16   Ibid., cols 720–1.

17   Jean Chalaby, *The Invention of Journalism* (London: Macmillan, 1998), pp.79, 110.

18   Hansard, HC (series 5), vol. 133, cols 935–6 (20 October 1920).

19   Ibid. Unlike Hugh Martin these unamed journalists were, apparently, not pretending to be heroes.

20   Hansard, HC (series 5), vol. 134, col. 719 (4 November 1920).

21   Harvey Molotch and Marilyn Lester, 'News as purposive behaviour: on the strategic use of routine events, accidents and scandals', *American Sociological Review* 39 (1970), p.105.

22   Hansard, HC (series 5), vol. 135, col. 497 (24 November 1920).

23   Hansard, HC (series 5), vol. 135, col. 502 (24 November 1920).

24   Hansard, HC (series 5), vol. 134, col. 719 (4 November 1920).

25   Hansard, HC (series 5), vol. 134, col. 726 (4 November 1920).

26   Ibid., col. 517.

27   Hansard, HC (series 5), vol. 136, col. 603 (21 February 1921).

28   Ibid., col. 606.

29   Hansard, HC (series 5), vol.134, col. 692 (4 November 1920).

30   Robert B. Self (ed.), *The Austen Chamberlain Diary Letters: The Correspondence of Sir Austen Chamberlain with His Sisters Hilda and Ida 1916–1937*, vol. v (Cambridge: CUP, 1995), pp.138–9.

31   Cabinet minutes for 13 August 1920, National Archives, Kew, CAB 23/22/116.

32   Thomas Jones, *Whitehall Diary*, vol. i, 1916–1925 (Oxford: OUP, 1969), pp.36–7.

33   Major-General Sir C.E. Callwell, *Field-Marshall Sir Henry Wilson: His Life and Diaries*, vol. ii (London: Cassell, 1927), p.256.

34   Ibid., p.251.

35   Ibid., p.263.

36   Ibid., p.255.

37   Ibid., pp.253–4.

38   H.A.L. Fisher, 'The position in Ireland: note by the president of the Board of Education', 1 March 1921, National Archives, Kew, CAB 24/120/CP 2656.

39   Jones: *Whitehall Diary*, p.69.

40   Ibid., p.66.

41   Ibid., p.68.

42   John M. McEwen, 'The press and the fall of Asquith', *The Historical Journal*, 21/iv (1978), p.865.

43   George Boyce, 'The Fourth Estate: the reappraisal of a concept', in George Boyce, James Curran and Pauline Wingate (eds), *Newspaper History from the Seventeenth Century to the Present Day* (London: Constable, 1978), pp.27–8.

44   Stephen Koss, *The Rise and Fall of the Political Press in Britain* (London: Fontana, 1990), p.712.

45   Chandrika Kaul, *Reporting the Raj: The British Press and India, c. 1880–1922* (Manchester: MUP, 2003), p.100.

46   Ibid., p.139.

47   Ibid., p.100.

48   A.B. Lowell, *Public Opinion in War and Peace* (Cambridge, MA: Harvard University Press, 1923), pp.260–1.

49   It was later taken up by the Labour Party and the cross-party campaigning group, the Peace with Ireland Council (whose secretary was Oswald Mosley).

50   Quoted in Mark Hampton, *Visions of the Press in Britain, 1850–1950* (Urbana: University of Illinois Press, 2004), pp.147–8.

51   Philip Elliott, 'All the world's a stage or what's wrong with the national press', in James Curran (ed.), *The British Press: A Manifesto* (London: Macmillan, 1978), p.143.

52   Daniel C. Hallin, *The 'Uncensored War': The Media and Vietnam* (New York: OUP, 1986), p.10.

53   Peter Clarke, *Hope and Glory: Britain 1900–1990* (London: Allen Lane, 1997), pp.98–9.

54   John McColgan, *British Policy and the Irish Administration 1920–22* (London: Allen and Uynwin, 1983), p.2.

55   Ibid., p.8.

56   Ibid., p.14.

57   'Periscope' (G.C. Duggan), 'The last days of Dublin Castle', *Blackwood's Magazine*, August 1922, p.152.

58    Michael Hopkinson (ed.), *The Last Days of Dublin Castle: The Diaries of Mark Sturgis*, (Dublin: Irish Academic Press, 1999), p.101.

59    Olive Anderson, *A Liberal State at War: English Politics and Economics During the Crimean War* (London: Macmillan, 1967), p.70.

60    Melissa Fegan, *Literature and the Irish Famine: 1845–1919* (Oxford: Clarendon Press, 2002), p.35.

61    *The Times*, 10 June 1854; ibid.

62    Paddy Scannell and David Cardiff, *A Social History of British Broadcasting: 1922–1939 – Serving the Nation*, vol. i (Oxford: Basil Blackwell, 1991), p.11.

63    *The Times*, 21 March 1921.

64    F.W. Hirst, *The Six Panics and Other Essays* (London: Methuen, 1913), p.156.

65    Henry Wickham Steed, *Through Thirty Years 1892–1922: A Personal Narrative* (London: William Heinemann, 1924), pp.351–2.

66    J. Lee Thompson, *Northcliffe: Press Baron in Politics, 1865–1922* (London: John Murray, 2000), p.341.

67    Letter from John Walter to Lord Northcliffe enclosing the 'letter from a friend', 19 May 1920, *Northcliffe Papers*, British Library, London, Add. 62239/fos. 51–4.

68    Letter from John Walter to Lord Northcliffe, 1 December 1920, *Northcliffe Papers*, British Library, London, Add. 62239/fos. 78–9.

69    Stanley Morison, *The History of The Times: The 150th Anniversary and Beyond, 1912–1948*, vol. iv, part 2 (London: The Times, 1952), p.523.

70    *The Times*, 13 December 1920, p.12.

71    *The Morning Post*, 14 December 1920, p.6.

72    Ibid., p.573.

73    Philip Geyelin, 'Vietnam and the press: limited war and an open society', in Anthony Lake (ed.) *The Vietnam Legacy: The War, American Society and the Future of American Foreign Policy* (New York: NYUP, 1976), p.169.

74    Max Boot, *The Savage Wars of Peace: Small Wars and the Rise of American Power* (New York: Basic Books, 2002), p.340.

75    Mark Jacobsen, '"Only by the Sword": British counterinsurgency in Iraq, 1920', *Small Wars and Insurgencies*, 2/ii (August 1991), pp.323, 335, 338.

76    Kaul: *Reporting the Raj*, p.209. On 19 April, six days after the massacre, the London papers published a communique from the India office to the effect that troops had come into 'collision' with 'a rioting mob' and that 'there were 200 casualties among the rioters' (ibid., p.200).

77    Thomas R. Mockaitis, *British Counterinsurgency, 1919–1960* (London: Macmillan, 1990), p.17.

78    George Dangerfield, *The Strange Death of Liberal England* (London: Paladin, 1970), p.21.

79    Stuart Hall and Bill Schwarz, 'State and society, 1880–1930', in Langan and Schwarz (eds): *Crises in the British State*, p.13.

80    Quoted in John Gallagher, 'Nationalisms and the crisis of empire, 1919–1922', *Modern Asian Studies*, 15/ii (1981), p.362.

81    Addressing the House of Commons on the Amritsar scandal, Montagu asked the members: 'Are you going to keep your hold upon India by terrorism, racial humiliation and subordination, and frightfulness, or are you going to rest it upon the goodwill, the growing goodwill, of the people of your Indian Empire?' Quoted in Chandrika Kaul, 'Press and empire: the London press, government news management and India circa 1900–22' (unpublished PhD thesis, University of Oxford, 1999), p.153.

82    Derek Sayer, 'British reaction to the Amritsar massacre 1919–1920', *Past and Present*, 131 (May 1991), p.153.

83    Ibid., p.154.

84    Ibid., p.159.

85    Glenn R. Wilkinson, *Depictions and Images of War in Edwardian Newspapers, 1899–1914* (London: Palgrave Macmillan, 2003), p.39.

86    Quoted in Jan Dalley, *Diana Mosley* (New York: Alfred A. Knopf, 2000), p.105.

87    Joseph Devlin noted that 'one of the curious paradoxes of modern British life [is] that the highest moral note has been sounded for freedom by Tories'. Hansard, HC (series 5), vol. 138, col. 664 (21 February 1921).

88    Ibid., col. 675.

89    Ibid., col. 679.

90    See Sayer: 'British reaction to the Amritsar massacre', p.141.

91    Declan Kiberd has suggested that '[t]he problem never fully confronted by the English was that much of their history had happened overseas, and so they could easily deflect attempts to discuss its meaning' (Damien Kiberd, *Inventing Ireland: The Literature of the Modern Nation* (London: Vintage, 1996), p.32).

92    Philip Gibbs, *The Hope of Europe* (London: William Heinemann, 1921), p.71.

93    Ibid., pp.73–4.

94    Ibid., pp.124–5.

95    Gary Peatling, *British Opinion and Irish Self-Government 1865–1925: From Unionism to Liberal Commonwealth* (Dublin: Irish Academic Press, 2001), p.180.

96    Dan H. Laurence (ed.), *Bernard Shaw: Collected Letters, 1911–1925*, vol. iii
      (London: Max Reinhardt, 1985), p.697.
97    Kaul: *Reporting the Raj*, p.136.

## V – THE PROPAGANDA WAR

1     Letter from Maxwell H.H. MacCartney to Desmond FitzGerald, 19 August
      1921, in *Desmond FitzGerald Papers*, Archives Department, University Col-
      lege Dublin, P80/43.
2     Ronan Fanning, Michael Kennedy, Dermot Keogh and Eunan O'Halpin
      (eds), *Documents on Irish Foreign Policy*, vol. i, 1919–1922 (Dublin: Royal
      Irish Academy, 1998), pp.3–4. Faith in Wilson turned out to be misplaced
      (see Chapter 7).
3     Donal Lowry, 'New Ireland, old empire and the outside world, 1922–49:
      the strange evolution of a "dictionary republic"', in Mike Cronin and John
      Regan (eds), *Ireland: The Politics of Independence, 1922–49* (London: Mac-
      millan, 2000), p.166.
4     Margaret MacMillan, *Peacemakers: The Paris Conference of 1919 and Its At-
      tempt to End War* (London: John Murray, 2002), p.65.
5     Fanning et al. (eds): *Documents on Irish Foreign Policy*, p.8.
6     Ibid., p.10.
7     Ibid., p.14.
8     Ibid., p.32.
9     Ibid., pp.18, 34.
10    Ibid., p.38.
11    Keiko Inoue, 'Propaganda II: propaganda of Dail Eircann, 1919–21', in
      Joost Augusteijn (ed.), *The Irish Revolution, 1913–1923* (London: Palgrave,
      2002), p.88.
12    Lawrence Ginnell was in the post for a few months before he was arrested in
      May 1919, but Desmond FitzGerald is seen as the first post-holder to have
      any real impact.
13    Garret FitzGerald in interview with the author, Dublin, 20 January 2003.
      He recalled that when he was in the European movement, agitating for Irish
      membership of the EEC in the early 1960s, he would brief foreign journal-
      ists and take them to meet the Irish prime minister, Sean Lemass. Some
      of the older journalists told him they had been briefed by his father in the
      Shelbourne Hotel. They said the waiters would always warn if the Black and
      Tans were coming.
14    'Notes on Desmond FitzGerald', *Desmond FitzGerald Papers*, Archives De-
      partment, University College Dublin, P80/1453(1).

15    Kathleen Napoli McKenna, 'Wielding words and other weapons for the cause', *Irish Times*, 24 December 1979, p.10.

16    Todd Andrews, *Dublin Made Me: An Autobiography* (Cork: The Mercier Press, 1979), p.177.

17    'An Irishman's diary', by 'Nichevo', *Irish Times*, 12 April 1947, in *Desmond FitzGerald Papers*, Archives Department, University College Dublin, P80/1452(4).

18    Unsigned obituary, *Manchester Guardian*, 10 April 1947, in *Desmond FitzGerald Papers*, Archives Department, University College Dublin, P80/1452/(2).

19    Michael McInerney, *The Riddle of Erskine Childers* (Dublin: E. and T. O'Brien, 1971), pp.18–25.

20    Erskine Childers, *The Form and Purpose of Home Rule* (London: Simpkin, Marshall, Hamilton, Kent and Co., 1912), pp.32–3.

21    Quoted in Jim Ring, *Erskine Childers* (London: John Murray, 1996), p.208.

22    Robert Brennan, *Allegiance* (Dublin: Browne and Nolan, 1950), p.244.

23    Ibid., p.244.

24    Tom Cox, *Damned Englishman: A Study of Erskine Childers, 1870–1922* (New York: Exposition Press, 1975), p.108.

25    Desmond Ryan, *Remembering Sion: A Chronicle of Storm and Quiet* (London: Arthur Barker, 1934), pp.283–4.

26    Ring: *Erskine Childers*, p.211.

27    Quoted in Andrew Boyle, *The Riddle of Erskine Childers* (London: Hutchinson, 1977), p.252.

28    Ibid., p.253.

29    Arthur Mitchell, *Revolutionary Government in Ireland: Dail Eireann 1919–22* (Dublin: Gill and Macmillan, 1995), p.100.

30    Ring: *Erskine Childers*, p.207.

31    'Account of the Department of Publicity submitted by Desmond FitzGerald', August 1921, *Ernest Blythe Papers*, Archives Department, University College Dublin, P24/19.

32    Kathleen Napoli McKenna, 'The Irish Bulletin', in *The Capuchin Annual* (Dublin, 1970).

33    Charles Townshend, *The British Campaign in Ireland, 1919–1921* (Oxford: OUP, 1975), p.67.

34    See 'List of the acts of aggression committed in Ireland by the police and military of the usurping English government, as reported in the daily press, for the week ending: Saturday, July 10th, 1920', *Irish Bulletin Summaries 1919–21*, National Library of Ireland, Dublin.

35    McKenna: 'Wielding words and other weapons', p.10.

36    Ernest Blythe in the *Sunday Independent*, 13 April 1947, in *Desmond FitzGerald Papers*, Archives Department, University College Dublin, P80/1452(6).

37    McKenna: 'Wielding words and other weapons', p.10.

38    Ibid.

39    Kathleen Napoli McKenna, 'A battle of wits for publicity', *Irish Times*, 25 December 1979, p.10; 26 December 1979, p.10; and 27 December 1979, p.10.

40    Ibid.

41    Ibid.

42    Letter from Frank Gallagher to Cecilia Saunders, 13 November 1921, in *Frank Gallagher Papers*, Trinity College Archives, Dublin, fo. 132.

43    Ibid.

44    McKenna: 'A battle of wits', p.10.

45    Ibid.

46    Boyle: *The Riddle of Erskine Childers*, p.257.

47    *Erskine Childers Papers*, Trinity College Archives, Dublin, manuscripts 7811, diaries, p.43.

48    Ibid., p.55.

49    Ibid., p.69.

50    Ibid., p.73.

51    Ibid., p.79.

52    Memo from Art O'Brien to Erskine Childers, 29 March 1921, in *Art O'Brien Papers*, National Library of Ireland, Dublin, MS 8421/43.

53    Memo from Art O' Brien to Erskine Childers, 19 April 1921, in *Art O'Brien Papers*, National Library of Ireland, Dublin, MS 8421/45.

54    Memo from Erskine Childers to Art O'Brien, 2 May 1921, in *Art O'Brien Papers*, National Library of Ireland, Dublin, MS 8421/46.

55    Memo from Art O'Brien to Erskine Childers, 3 May 1921, in *Art O'Brien Papers*, National Library of Ireland, Dublin, MS 8421/45.

56    Ibid.

57    Quoted in Ian Ousby, *The Road to Verdun: France, Nationalism and the First World War* (London: Pimlico, 2003), p.18.

58    Michael Laffan, *The Resurrection of Ireland: The Sinn Fein Party 1916–1923* (Cambridge: CUP, 1999), p.16.

59    Ben Novick, *Conceiving Revolution: Irish Nationalist Propaganda during the First World War* (Dublin: Four Courts Press, 2001), p.167.

60    Ibid., pp.132–3.

61    Ibid. For Belgium see pp.104–7; for the *Lusitania* pp.72–6; and for the danger of a German invasion see pp.120–5.

62   Quoted in ibid., p.107.

63   Mitchell: *Revolutionary Government in Ireland*, p.99.

64   Kieran Flanagan, 'The chief secretary's office 1853–1914: a bureaucratic enigma', *Irish Historical Studies*, xxiv (1984–5), p.198.

65   Hugh Martin, *Daily News*, 16 January 1919, p.5.

66   Quoted in K.D. Ewing and Conor Gearty (eds), *The Struggle for Civil Liberties, Political Freedom and the Rule of Law in Britain 1914–45* (Oxford: OUP, 2000), p.340.

67   Novick: *Conceiving Revolution*, p.36, and Lord Decies's memorandum to the under secretary for Ireland, 10 July 1917, *Press Censorship Records 1916–1919*, National Archives of Ireland, Dublin, 3/722/3 (34).

68   Lord Decies to the chief secretary, 17 January 1917, *Press Censorship Records 1916–1919*, National Archives of Ireland, Dublin, 3/722/4 (160).

69   Memo from Lord Decies to the under secretary for Ireland, 26 February 1917, *Press Censorship Records 1916–1919*, National Archives of Ireland, Dublin, 3/722/3 (34).

70   Ibid.

71   Letter to Lord Decies, 20 July 1917, *Press Censorship Records 1916–1919*, National Archives of Ireland, Dublin, 3/722/3 (146).

72   Lord Decies, *Report on Censorship for December 1918*, National Archives, Kew, CO 904/167/371-372.

73   Ibid., CO 904/167/370-371.

74   Sir Basil Clarke, 'An outlaw on the Western Front', *World's Press News*, 15 November 1934, p.2.

75   Basil Clarke memo, 18 April 1921, National Archives, Kew, CO 904/168/832-836.

76   Ibid.

77   Ibid., CO 904/168/841.

78   *Daily News*, 29 April 1921, p.3.

79   *Daily News*, 30 April 1921, p.3.

80   Ibid.

81   Egon Larsen, *First with the Truth: Newspapermen in Action* (London: Baker, 1968), pp.66–7.

82   *Daily News*, 2 May 1921, p.1.

83   Letter from Basil Clarke to Colonel Foulkes, 10 August 1921, National Archives, Kew, CO 904/168/577.

84   Ibid.

# VI – An Old World Fight

1    Paul Kennedy, *The Realities Behind Diplomacy: Background Influences on British External Policy 1865–1980* (London: Fontana, 1985), p.148.

2    J. Lee Thompson, *Politicians, the Press and Propaganda: Lord Northcliffe and the Great War 1914–1919* (Kent, OH: Kent State University Press, 1999), p.160.

3    N. Gordon Levin Jr, *Woodrow Wilson and World Politics: America's Response to War and Revolution* (Oxford: OUP, 1968), p.5.

4    Margaret MacMillan, *Peacemakers: The Paris Conference of 1919 and Its Attempt to End War* (London: John Murray, 2002), p.18.

5    Levin Jr.: *Woodrow Wilson and World Politics*, p.18.

6    Niall Ferguson, *Colossus: The Rise and Fall of the American Empire* (London: Penguin, 2005), p.63.

7    Francis M. Carroll, *American Opinion and the Irish Question 1910–1923* (Dublin: Gill and Macmillan, 1978), p.55.

8    Ibid., p.59.

9    Ibid., pp.103–4.

10   Thomas E. Hachey, 'British Foreign Office and new perspectives on the Irish issue in Anglo-American relations 1919–1921', *Eire-Ireland* 7/ii (1972), p.5.

11   Oliver Gramling, *AP: The Story of News* (New York: Farrar and Rinehart, 1940), p.299.

12   Joe Alex Morris, *Deadline Every Minute: The Story of the United Press* (New York: Doubleday, 1957), pp.114–15.

13   George Seldes, *Tell the Truth and Run* (New York: Greenberg, 1953), p.89. Seldes confesses, with vitriolic disillusion, that he later soured on Ireland's revolution, finding to his dismay that a thing of beauty had been 'altered and perverted into a shoddy middle-class stupid conservative uninspired unpoetic unromantic Free State and finally an independent Republic devoted to nothing more noble than the perpetuation of middle class respectability and the *status quo*' (p.90).

14   American Commission on Conditions in Ireland, *Evidence on Conditions in Ireland: The American Commission on Conditions in Ireland* (Washington, DC: Bliss Building, 1921), p.141.

15   Robert A. Rosenstone, *Romantic Revolutionary: A Biography of John Reed* (Cambridge, MA: Harvard University Press, 1990), pp.206–7.

16   Charles Forcey, *The Crossroads of Liberalism: Croly Weyl, Lippmann and the Progressive Era 1900–1925* (New York: OUP, 1961), p.183.

17   Edmund Wilson, *The Twenties: From Notebooks and Diaries of the Period* (New York: Farrar, Straus and Giroux, 1975), p.100.

18   Forcey: *The Crossroads of Liberalism*, p.230.

19   Ibid., p.90.

20   Ibid., p.260.

21   Editorial, *New Republic*, 27 October 1920, p.207.

22   Francis Hackett, open letter, *New Republic,* 28 April 1920, pp.283–4.

23   Ibid.

24   American Commission on Conditions in Ireland: *Evidence on Conditions in Ireland*, p.140.

25   Francis Hackett, *New Republic*, 13 October 1920, p.161.

26   Ibid., p.163.

27   Francis Hackett, *New Republic*, 20 October 1920, p.188.

28   Ibid., p.189.

29   Ibid., p.189.

30   Ibid., p.190.

31   Some of this disdain was explicit in Hackett's wife's account of an interview they conducted with the editor of a unionist newspaper in Belfast. The editor, she said, 'thought we were typical American journalists, and he gave us what we considered to be the regular dope for American journalists. Much of it we knew ... was not true' (American Commission on Conditions in Ireland: *Evidence on Conditions in Ireland*, p.175).

32   Floyd Dell, *Homecoming: An Autobiography* (New York: Farrar and Rinehart, 1933), p.195.

33   Francis Hackett, *American Rainbow: Early Reminiscences* (New York: Liveright, 1971), p.172.

34   Ibid., p.176.

35   Ibid., p.182.

36   Stephen J.A. Ward, *The Invention of Journalism Ethics: The Path to Objectivity and Beyond* (Montreal: McGill-Queen's University Press, 2004), p.212.

37   Michael Schudson, 'The objectivity norm in American journalism', *Journalism*, 2/ii (August, 2001), p.157.

38   Ward: *The Invention of Journalism Ethics*, p.209.

39   Quoted in ibid., p.226.

40   Quoted in ibid., p.210.

41   Moisei Ostrogorski, *Democracy and the Organization of Political Parties*, vol. ii (London: Macmillan, 1902), p.321.

42   R.A. Scott-James, *The Influence of the Press* (London: S.W. Partridge, 1913), pp.255–6.

43   Schudson: 'The objectivity norm in American journalism', p.162.

44   Forcey: *The Crossroads of Liberalism*, p.174.

45    Michael Schudson, *Origins of the Ideal of Objectivity in the Professions: Studies in the History of American Journalism and American Law 1830–1940* (New York: Garland, 1990), p.168.

46    Morris Janowitz, 'Professional models in journalism: the gatekeeper and the advocate', *Journalism Quarterly*, 52/iv (winter, 1975), p.622.

47    Walter Lippmann, *Liberty and the News* (New York: Harcourt, Brace and Howe, 1920), p.79.

48    Brochure on *Philadelphia Public Ledger*, Foreign News Service, p.5, in Box 173, *Carl W. Ackerman Papers*, Library of Congress, Washington DC.

49    Oswald Garrison Villard, *Some Newspapers and Newspaper-men* (New York: Alfred A. Knopf, 1926), p.151.

50    Ibid., pp.151–2.

51    Christopher Lasch, *The American Liberals and the Russian Revolution* (New York: Columbia University Press, 1962), p.77.

52    Ibid., p.88.

53    Villard: *Some Newspapers*, p.153.

54    Ibid., p.169.

55    Letter from Carl Ackerman to John J. Spurgeon, 10 March 1920, Spurgeon file, Box 131, *Carl W. Ackerman Papers,* Library of Congress, Washington DC.

56    Carl Ackerman, *Philadelphia Public Ledger*, 20 March 1920.

57    Carl Ackerman, *Philadelphia Public Ledger*, 4 April 1920.

58    Carl Ackerman, *Philadelphia Public Ledger*, 6 April 1920.

59    Carl Ackerman, *Philadelphia Public Ledger*, 6 April 1920.

60    Carl Ackerman, *Philadelphia Public Ledger*, 20 July 1920.

61    Entry for 30 June 1920 in 'London notes', *Carl W. Ackerman Papers*, Box 1, Library of Congress, Washington DC.

62    Typescript entitled 'When Ireland's freedom hung by a thread', Speech/Article/Book File, Box 174, *Carl W. Ackerman Papers*, Library of Congress, Washington DC.

63    John J. Spurgeon in communications to Carl Ackerman, 25 May 1920, Spurgeon file, Box 131, *Carl W. Ackerman Papers*, Library of Congress, Washington DC.

64    *New York Times*, 7 August 1921.

65    Ledger Syndicate News Service brochure, p.1, Box 173, *Carl W. Ackerman Papers*, Library of Congress, Washington DC.

66    Ibid., pp.4–5.

67    Carl Ackerman to Cyrus H.K. Curtis, *Philadelphia Public Ledger*, 8 July 1921, Curtis file, Box 133, *Carl W. Ackerman Papers*, Library of Congress, Washington DC.

68   Carl W. Ackerman, *Mexico's Dilemma* (New York: George H. Doran, 1918), p.136.

69   Ibid., p.59.

70   Carl Ackerman, *Trailing the Bolsheviki: Twelve Thousand Miles with the Allies in Siberia* (New York: Scribners, 1919), pp.xi–xii.

71   Ibid., p.258.

72   Ackerman: 'London notes', entry for 10 January 1921.

73   Ibid.

74   The British historian and diplomat H.A.L. Fisher wrote that at Versailles 'the American president shone … with the lustre of a Messiah'. Quoted by Ronan Brindley, 'Woodrow Wilson, self determination and Ireland 1918–1919: a view from the Irish newspapers', *Eire-Ireland* 23/iv (winter 1988), p.69.

75   Ray Stannard Baker characterised House as 'a liberal by instinct though not at all a thinker. He is a conciliator and arranger' (quoted in Inga Floto, *Colonel House in Paris: A Study of American Policy at the Paris Peace Conference 1919* (Princeton, NJ: Princeton University Press, 1980), p.28). Walter Lippmann described the service House rendered to Wilson: 'The things which Colonel House did best, meeting men face to face and listening to them patiently and persuading them gradually, Woodrow Wilson could hardly bear to do at all … Lacking all intellectual pride, having no such intellectual cultivation as Woodrow Wilson, he educated himself in the problems of the day by inducing men of affairs to confide in him.' Quoted in Ronald Steel, *Walter Lippmann and the American Century* (London: The Bodley Head, 1980), p.108.

76   Christopher Lasch, *The New Radicalism in America 1889–1963: The Intellectual as a Social Type* (New York: W.W. Norton, 1965), p.234.

77   Ibid., p.235.

78   Ackerman: 'London notes', entry for 27 June 1920.

79   Carl Ackerman, unpublished version of 'Ireland – from my Scotland Yard notebook', p.2, Box 1, *Carl W. Ackerman Papers*, Library of Congress, Washington DC.

80   Ibid.

81   Carl Ackerman in communication to John J. Spurgeon, editor of the *Philadelphia Public Ledger*, 10 March 1920, Spurgeon file, Box 131, *Carl W. Ackerman Papers*, Library of Congress, Washington DC.

82   Ward: *The Invention of Journalism Ethics*, p.210.

83   Quoted in Dan Schiller, *Objectivity and the News: The Public and the Rise of Commercial Journalism*, (Philadelphia: University of Pennsylvania Press, 1981), p.182.

84   Ibid., p.183.

85   Carl Ackerman, 'Inside Irish parley: new light on quiet negotiations that led up to conference – peace is probable', *New York Times*, 7 August 1921.

86   Carl Ackerman, typescript of 'The house of a thousand mysteries', p.5, Box 1, *Carl W. Ackerman Papers*, Library of Congress, Washington DC.

87   Thomson wrote back: 'I have made one or two slight alterations which I have no doubt you will accede to, otherwise I think your cable is excellent' (Carl Ackerman, 'Ireland from a Scotland Yard notebook', *Atlantic Monthly*, April 1922, pp.434–5.

88   Ibid., p.434.

89   Ibid.

90   Ackerman: 'Ireland from a Scotland Yard notebook', p.436.

91   Ackerman: 'London notes', entry for 28 June 1920.

92   Ackerman: 'London notes', entry for 30 June 1920.

93   Ibid.

94   Ackerman: 'Ireland from a Scotland Yard notebook', p.435.

95   Ibid., p.437.

96   Ibid., p.437.

97   Ibid., p.438.

98   Ackerman: 'London notes', entry for 18 August 1920.

99   Ackerman: 'Ireland from a Scotland Yard notebook', p.439.

100  Ackerman: 'London notes', entry for 23–25 August 1920.

101  Ibid.

102  Ackerman: 'Ireland from a Scotland Yard notebook', p.440.

103  Ibid.

104  Carl Ackerman, 'The Irish education of Mr Lloyd George', *Atlantic Monthly*, May 1922, p.606.

105  Paul Bew, 'Moderate nationalism and the Irish revolution, 1916–1923', *The Historical Journal* 42/iii (1999), p.743.

106  Carl Ackerman, 'Janus-headed Ireland', *Atlantic Monthly*, June 1922, p.812.

107  Bew: 'Moderate nationalism', p.743.

108  Ibid., p.744.

109  Letter from John J. Spurgeon to Carl Ackerman, 6 August 1920, Spurgeon file, Box 131, *Carl W. Ackerman Papers*, Library of Congress, Washington DC.

110  Rupert Allason, *The Branch: A History of the Metropolitan Police Special Branch 1883–1983* (London: Secker and Warburg, 1983), p.34.

111  Bernard Porter, *The Origins of the Vigilant State: The London Metropolitan Police Special Branch Before the First World War* (Woodbridge: The Boydell Press, 1987), p.175.

112   Carroll: *American Opinion and the Irish Question*, p.60.

113   Carl Ackerman, 'The house of a thousand mysteries', p.5, Box 1, *Carl W. Ackerman Papers*, Library of Congress, Washington DC.

114   Porter: *The Origins of the Vigilant State*, p.147. Poise was hardly in evidence either in the incident that ended Thomson's public career when he was arrested in Hyde Park in December 1925 on charges of 'fondling' a prostitute. He said he had been researching a newspaper article but was found guilty and fined (Allason: *The Branch*, p.87).

115   Ackerman: 'The house of a thousand mysteries'., p.1.

116   Ibid., p.6.

117   Ibid., p.3.

118   Ibid., p.5.

119   Ibid., pp.2, 4, 5.

120   Ibid., p.6.

121   Schudson: *Origins of the Ideal of Objectivity*, p.257.

122   Michael Schudson, *The Power of News* (Cambridge, MA: Harvard University Press, 1995), p.92.

123   Lasch: *The New Radicalism in America*, p.244.

124   Edward A. Purcell, *The Crisis of Democratic Theory: Scientific Naturalism and the Problem of Value* (Lexington: University Press of Kentucky, 1973), pp.24–5.

125   Walter Lippmann, *Liberty in the News* (New York: Harcourt, Brace and Howe), p.82.

126   Louis Menand, *The Metaphysical Club* (London: Flamingo, 2002), p.59.

127   Ibid., p.372.

128   Carl Ackerman, remarks at a conference called 'The Press and Crime Prevention', Albany, 2 October 1935, see Box 160, *Carl W. Ackerman Papers*, Library of Congress, Washington DC.

129   Francis Hackett, *The Invisible Censor* (New York: Books for Libraries Press, 1968), pp.48–9.

130   Ackerman: 'Ireland from a Scotland Yard notebook', p.441a.

131   Ibid.

132   Ward: *The Invention of Journalism Ethics*, p.197.

133   Ibid., p.219.

134   Daniel C. in, *The 'Uncensored War': The Media and Vietnam* (New York: OUP, 1986), p.68.

135   Bernard C. Cohen, *The Press and Foreign Policy* (Princeton, NJ: Princeton University Press, 1963), p.22.

136   Hallin: *The 'Uncensored War'*, p.69.

137 American reporters who acted as emissaries included Raymond Swing, sent to Europe by Col. House in 1917 to explore a negotiated peace, and Ray Stannard Baker, sent to Ireland by the State Department in 1918. Morrell Heald, *Transatlantic Vistas: American Journalists in Europe, 1900–1940* (Kent, OH: Kent State University Press, Ohio, 1988), p.137, and Robert C. Bannister Jr, *Ray Stannard Baker: The Mind and Thought of a Progressive* (New Haven: Yale University Press, 1966), pp.177–9.

138 Hallin: *The 'Uncensored War'*, p.8.

139 Michael Hopkinson, 'President Woodrow Wilson and the Irish Question', *Studia Hibernica*, 27 (1993), p.96.

140 Carroll: *American Opinion and the Irish Question*, p.136.

141 Carl Ackerman, unpublished draft of 'When Ireland's freedom hung by a thread' speech, article and book file 1922, *Carl W. Ackerman Papers*, Library of Congress, Washington DC.

# VII – LITERARY TOURISTS

1 Quoted in Robert O. Stephens, *Hemingway's Nonfiction: The Public Voice* (Chapel Hill: University of North Carolina Press, Chapel Hill, 1968), p.5.

2 John Gross, *The Rise and Fall of the Man of Letters: Aspects of English Literary Life Since 1800* (London: Penguin, 1991), p.237.

3 His biographer has described Pritchett's journalism as 'serial autobiography'. Jeremy Treglown, *V.S. Pritchett: A Working Life* (London: Chatto and Windus, 2004), p.11.

4 'Essentially, daily publication cuts things out of a larger reality in order to dispose of them and clear the decks for tomorrow's edition. There can be little historical or philosophical scale in such reports, because every day's events must be presented as deserving of equal attention' (C. John Somerville, *The News Revolution in England* (Oxford: OUP, 1996), p.4).

5 Curwen and Staples are both quoted in Glenn Hooper (ed.), *The Tourist's Gaze: Travellers to Ireland 1800–2000* (Togher: Cork University Press, 2001), p.xx.

6 Ibid., p.115.

7 Terry Eagleton, *Heathcliff and the Great Hunger* (London: Verso, 1995), p.127.

8 Conor Cruise O'Brien, *Neighbours: The Ewart-Biggs Memorial Lectures* (London: Faber, 1980), p.33.

9 Oliver MacDonagh, *States of Mind: A Study of Anglo-Irish Conflict 1780–1980* (London: Allen and Unwin, 1983), p.31.

10   For Yeats's invitation see R.F. Foster, *W.B. Yeats: A Life*, vol. ii: *The Arch-Poet 1915–1939* (Oxford: OUP, 2003), p.131.

11   G.K. Chesterton, *Irish Impressions* (London: W. Collins, 1919), p.25.

12   Douglas Goldring, *The Nineteen Twenties: A General Survey and Some Personal Memories* (London: Nicholson and Watson, 1945), p.117.

13   Nicholas Allen, *George Russell and the New Ireland 1905–30* (Dublin: Four Courts Press, 2003), pp.20–1.

14   Chesterton: *Irish Impressions*, pp.8–9.

15   Ibid., p.69.

16   Ibid., p.204.

17   Ibid., pp.193–4.

18   Ibid., pp.196–7.

19   Ibid., pp.119–20.

20   Ibid., p.122.

21   Ibid., p.110.

22   Ibid., p.147.

23   Ibid., p.150.

24   Ibid., pp.150–1.

25   By the time that Chesterton made his journey to Ireland the horror of the war and the scale of its casualties may have been a bigger obstacle to recruiting than Irish nationalism per se. Ben Novick notes that by 1918 Sinn Féin was attracting voters because Ireland was 'increasingly war weary'. See Ben Novick, *Conceiving Revolution: Irish Nationalist Propaganda during the First World War* (Dublin: Four Courts Press, 2001), pp.67–71.

26   Chesterton: *Irish Impressions*, p.128.

27   Ibid., pp.130–1.

28   In October 1914 the Entente powers regarded a German air raid on Paris in which three civilians died as 'an … unacceptable broadening of the forms of warfare' (Modris Eksteins, *Rites of Spring: The Great War and the Birth of the Modern Age* (New York: Mariner Books, 2000), pp.158–9). By 1921, however, Britain ruled Iraq through the RAF – see Toby Dodge, *Inventing Iraq: The Failure of Nation Building and a History Denied* (London: Hurst, 2003), p.132.

29   Chesterton: *Irish Impressions*, pp.22–3.

30   Ibid., p.24.

31   Ibid.

32   Ibid., p.25.

33   Ibid., p.33.

34   Patrick Wright, 'Last orders', *Guardian Review*, 4 April 2005, pp.4–6.

35   Ibid., p.29.

36    Ibid.
37    Ibid., p.30.
38    Ibid., p.51.
39    Ibid., pp.52–3.
40    Ibid., p.79.
41    Ibid., pp.64–5.
42    Ibid., pp.65–6.
43    Ibid., p.65.
44    Hugh Cecil, *The Flower of Battle: How Britain Wrote the Great War* (Hanover, NH: Steerforth Press, 1996), p.168.
45    Ibid., p.139.
46    Ibid., pp.153–66.
47    Ibid., p.140.
48    Ibid., p.145. Despite this, Wyndham nearly suffered a nervous breakdown from dealing with the problems in Ireland and ended up being 'driven from office into lasting and ignominious obscurity' (F.S.L. Lyons, *John Dillon: A Biography* (London: Routledge and Keegan Paul, 1968), p.273).
49    Wilfred Ewart, *A Journey in Ireland 1921* (London: G.P. Putnam's Sons, 1922), p.ix.
50    Cecil: *The Flower of Battle*, pp.142–3. By the age of 18, Ewart was an expert on poultry.
51    Ewart: *A Journey in Ireland 1921*, p.55.
52    Ibid., p.7.
53    Ibid., p.6.
54    Ibid., p.2.
55    Ibid., p.26.
56    Ibid., p.125.
57    Ibid., p.126.
58    Ibid., p.127.
59    Ibid., p.128.
60    Ibid., p.34.
61    Ibid., p.20.
62    Ibid., p.35.
63    Ibid., p.102.
64    V.S. Pritchett, 'Three months in Ireland', *Christian Science Monitor*, 23 July 1923.
65    V.S. Pritchett, *Midnight Oil* (London: Chatto and Windus, 1971), p.108.
66    Quoted in Lawrence N. Strout, *Covering McCarthyism: How the* Christian Science Monitor *Handled Joseph R. McCarthy 1950–1954* (Westport, CT: Greenwood Press, 1999), p.xiv.

67    Bryan R. Wilson, *Sects and Society: A Sociological Study of Three Religious Groups in Britain* (London: William Heinemann, 1961), p.125. Quoted in Treglown: *V.S. Pritchett*, p.21.

68    Pritchett: *Midnight Oil*, p.109.

69    Ibid., p.109.

70    J.J. Lee, *Ireland 1912–1985* (Cambridge: CUP, 1989), p.59.

71    Bill Kisssane, *The Politics of the Irish Civil War* (Oxford: OUP, 2005), p.30.

72    Editorial: 'Irishmen in conflict', *The Times*, 21 April 1922.

73    F.S.L. Lyons, *Ireland Since the Famine* (London: Fontana, 1976), p.461.

74    See Lee: *Ireland 1912–1985*, p.69.

75    Quoted in Michael Hopkinson, *Green Against Green: The Irish Civil War* (Dublin: Gill and Macmillan, 1988), p.276.

76    V.S. Pritchett, 'A glimpse at a southern Irish town', *Christian Science Monitor*, 6 March 1923.

77    Ibid.

78    Ibid.

79    Ibid.

80    Ibid.

81    Ibid.

82    V.S. Pritchett, *Dublin: A Portrait* (London: The Bodley Head, 1967), p.4.

83    Pritchett: *Midnight Oil*, p.118.

84    R.F. Foster, *Paddy and Mr Punch: Connections in Irish and English History* (London: Allen Lane, 1993), p.282.

85    Pritchett: *Midnight Oil*, p.119.

86    Ibid., p.119.

87    Pritchett: *Dublin: A Portrait*, p.4, and *Midnight Oil*, p.120.

88    Pritchett: *Dublin: A Portrait*, pp.6–7.

89    V.S. Pritchett, 'In the Queen's county', *Christian Science Monitor*, 5 June 1923.

90    Ibid.

91    Ibid.

92    Ibid.

93    Ibid.

94    V.S. Pritchett, 'Northward bound', *Christian Science Monitor*, 29 June 1923.

95    Ibid.

96    Terence Brown, *Ireland: A Social and Cultural History 1922–79* (London: Fontana, 1981), p.115.

97    V.S. Pritchett, 'Trinity – past and present', *Christian Science Monitor*, 13 July 1923.

98   Ibid.

99   Ibid.

100  V.S. Pritchett: 'Three months in Ireland'.

101  Ibid.

102  Pritchett: *Dublin: A Portrait*, p.6.

103  V.S. Pritchett, 'Men of Clare', *Christian Science Monitor*, 13 October 1923.

104  Ibid.

105  Pritchett: 'Men of Clare'.

106  'The equation of the Irishman with the child in Victorian thinking was based on the fear of the inner child within many adult males. It is this that had led to a ferocious disciplining of their offspring' (Declan Kiberd, *Irish Classics* (London: Granta Books, 2000), p.326).

107  Pritchett: *Midnight Oil*, p.173.

108  Eric Hobsbawm, *The Age of Extremes: A History of the World 1914–1991* (New York: Pantheon Books, 1994), p.22.

## CONCLUSION

1   Charles Maier, *Recasting Bourgeois Europe: Stabilization in France, Germany and Italy in the Decade After World War I* (New Haven: Princeton University Press, 1975), p.585.

2   James Loughlin, 'Constructing the political spectacle: Parnell, the press and national leadership, 1879–86', in D. George Boyce and Alan O'Day (eds), *Parnell in Perspective* (London: Routledge, 1991), p.230. According to Charles Townshend the term 'land war' was invented by journalists (see Charles Townshend, *Easter 1916: The Irish Rebellion* (London: Allen Lane, 2005), p.2).

3   Ben Levitas, *The Theatre of Nation: Irish Drama and Cultural Nationalism 1890–1916* (Oxford: Clarendon Press, 2002), p.49.

4   Hilaire Belloc, *The Free Press* (London: George Allen and Unwin, 1918), p.37.

5   John Gallagher, 'Nationalisms and the crisis of empire, 1919–1922', *Modern Asian Studies* 15/ii (1981), p.355.

6   Joseph J. Mathews, *Reporting the Wars* (Minneapolis, MN: University of Minnesota Press, 1957), p.139.

7   Ibid., p.140.

8   Stephen Howe, *Ireland and Empire: Colonial Legacies in Irish History and Culture* (Oxford: OUP, 2000), p.65.

9   Paddy Griffith, 'Small wars and how they grow in the telling', *Small Wars and Insurgencies*, 2/ii (August 1991), pp.216–17.

10   Hansard, HC (series 5), vol. 135, col. 494 (24 November 1920).

11   Geyelin: 'Vietnam and the press', p.171.

12   Quoted in 'Periscope' (G.C. Duggan), 'The last days of Dublin Castle', *Blackwood's Magazine*, August 1922, p.156.

13   Quoted in R.F. Foster, *W.B. Yeats: A Life*, vol. ii: The Arch-Poet 1915–1939 (Oxford: OUP, 2003), p.184.

14   Jon Lawrence, 'Forging a peaceable kingdom: war, violence and fear of brutalization in post-First World War Britain', *Journal of Modern History*, 75/iii (September 2003), p.582.

15   J.A. Hobson, *Imperialism: A Study* (London: James Nisbet, 1902), p.160.

16   Richard Bennett, *The Black and Tans* (New York: Barnes and Noble, 1995) p.100.

17   R.C.K. Ensor, *England 1870–1914* (Oxford: Clarendon Press, 1985), p.144. However, Lucy Brown and others have contended that the 'doctoring of news' was not as absent from the nineteenth-century press as Ensor made out (Lucy Brown, *Victorian News and Newspapers* (Oxford: Clarendon Press, 1985)).

18   Mark Hampton, *Visions of the Press in Britain, 1850–1950* (Urbana: University of Illinois Press, 2004), p.153.

19   Basil Clarke, undated memo, National Archives, Kew, CO/904/168/915.

20   Basil Clarke, National Archives, Kew, CO/904/168/843.

21   Letter from Frank Gallagher to Cecilia Saunders, 13 November 1921, *Frank Gallagher Papers,* Trinity College Archives, Dublin, p.132.

22   Richard Gott, *Cuba: A New History* (New Haven: Yale University Press, 2004), pp.93–5, 100.

23   Mark Cronlund Anderson, *Pancho Villa's Revolution by Headlines* (Norman, OK: University of Oklahoma Press, 2000), p.44.

24   Friedrich Katz, *The Life and Times of Pancho Villa* (Palo Alto, CA: Stanford University Press, 1998), p.322.

25   Ibid., pp.559–60.

26   Bill Kissane, *The Politics of the Irish Civil War* (Oxford: OUP, 2005), p.46.

27   Ibid., p.97.

28   Quoted in Donal Lowry, 'New Ireland, old empire and the outside world, 1922–49: the strange evolution of a "dictionary republic"', in Mike Cronin and John Regan (eds), *Ireland: The Politics of Independence, 1922–49* (London: Macmillan, 2000), pp.173–4.

29   Gary Peatling, *British Opinion and Irish Self-Government 1865–1925: From Unionism to Liberal Commonwealth* (Dublin: Irish Academic Press, 2001), pp.61–2.

30   Peter Clarke, *Liberals and Social Democrats* (Cambridge: CUP, 1978), p.180.

31   Gary Bass, *Stay the Hand of Vengeance: The Politics of War Crimes Tribunal* (Princeton, NJ: Princeton University Press, 2000), p.73.

32   Brian A.W. Simpson, *Human Rights and the End of Empire: Britain and the Genesis of the European Convention* (Oxford: OUP, 2001), p.322.

33   Editorial, *The Times*, 3 November 1920.

34   One former Auxiliary officer recalled how, influenced by Western films, they wore revolvers in holsters 'slung low on the thigh'. Quoted in David Leeson, 'The Black and Tans: British police in the first Irish War, 1920–1' (unpublished PhD thesis, McMaster University, Ontario, 2003), p.122.

35   Quoted in Gary Peatling, *British Opinion and Irish Self-Government 1865–1925: From Unionism to Liberal Commonwealth* (Dublin: Irish Academic Press, 2001), p.93.

36   Bass: *Stay the Hand of Vengeance*, p.280.

37   Peatling: *British Public Opinion*, p.175.

38   Editorial in the *Manchester Guardian*, 23 October 1920, p.8.

39   Stephen Koss, *The Rise and Fall of the Political Press in Britain* (London: Fontana, 1990), p.445.

40   Philip Gibbs, *The Hope of Europe* (London: William Heinemann, 1921), p.73.

41   Ibid., p.74.

42   Hugh Martin, *Daily News*, 11 November 1920.

43   Joanna Lewis, '"Daddy wouldn't buy me a mau mau": the British popular press and the demoralization of empire', in E.S. Atieno Odhiambo and John Lonsdale (eds), *Mau Mau and Nationhood: Arms, Authority and Narration* (Oxford: James Currey, 2003), pp.234–5.

44   Ibid., p.238.

45   *Daily Mirror*, 1 December 1952, quoted in ibid., p.236.

46   Robert Kee, *The Green Flag: A History of Irish Nationalism* (London: Weidenfeld and Nicolson, 1972), p.686.

47   Ibid., p.684.

48   A similar conclusion can be drawn from reading the work of American journalists who covered the Vietnam War: '[they] are much better on how Americans endured despair than on how the Vietnamese inflicted it … [Their work] induces a sense that Vietnam was not a place but an evil state of mind in which all those names of real locations – Hue, Highway 1, Con Thien – were merely poisonous disorders of the American psyche, to be examined with horrid satisfaction.' See Maurice Walsh, 'Saigon Stories', a review of *Reporting Vietnam: American Journalism, 1959–75* (2 vols) (New York: Library of America, 1999) in *New Statesman*, 23 August 1999, p.42.

# BIBLIOGRAPHY

## PRIMARY SOURCES

### National Archives, Kew, London
Cabinet Minutes: CAB 16, CAB 23, CAB 24
Colonial Office Papers
(B Series – Sir John Anderson's private papers)
Press Censorship Records: CO 904

### National Archives, Dublin
Department of the Taoiseach Files
Press Censorship Records 1916–1919

### University College Dublin Archives
Desmond FitzGerald Papers
Ernest Blythe Papers

### National Library of Ireland
Art O' Brien Papers
Erskine Childers Papers
Frank Gallagher Papers
*Irish Bulletin* Summaries
*Irish Bulletin, The* [microfilm]
Kathleen Napoli McKenna Papers

### Trinity College Dublin Archives
Erskine Childers Papers
Frank Gallagher Papers

### John Rylands Library, Manchester
Manchester Guardian Archive

### British Library, London
Henry Wickham Steed Papers
Northcliffe Papers

### The Times *Archives*
A.B. Kay Correspondence
Arthur Brown Kay File
G.G. Dawson File
J.W. Flanagan File
Lews Alfred Northend File

### Library of Congress, Washington D.C.
Carl W. Ackerman Papers

### Bodleian Library, Oxford
Henry Wood Nevinson Papers
J.L. Hammond Papers

## CONTEMPORARY WORKS AND MEMOIRS

Ackerman, Carl W., *Trailing the Bolsheviki: Twelve Thousand Miles with the Allies in Siberia* (New York: Scribners, 1919).

—— *Mexico's Dilemma* (New York: George H. Doran, 1918).

—— *Germany, the Next Republic?* (London: Hodder and Stoughton, 1917).

American Commission on Conditions in Ireland, *Evidence on Conditions in Ireland: The American Commission on Conditions in Ireland* (Washington DC: Bliss Building, 1921).

Andrews, Todd, *Dublin Made Me: An Autobiography* (Cork: The Mercier Press, 1979).

Angell, Norman, *After All: The Autobiography of Norman Angell* (London: Hamish Hamilton, 1951).

—— *The Public Mind* (London: Noel Douglas, 1926).

—— *Human Nature and the Peace Problem* (London: W. Collins Sons, 1925).

—— *The Press and the Organisation of Society* (London: Labour Publishing Company, 1922).

Barry, Kevin (ed.), *James Joyce: Occasional, Critical and Political Writing* (Oxford: OUP, 2000.

Bell, Anne Olivier (ed.), *The Diary of Virginia Woolf,* vol. ii: 1920–1924 (London: Hogarth, 1978).

Belloc, Hilaire, *The Free Press* (London: George Allen and Unwin, 1918).

Brennan, Robert, *Allegiance* (Dublin: Browne and Nolan, 1950).

Brooks, Sydney, 'The press in war-time', *North American Review* 200 (December 1914), pp.858–69.

Callwell, Major-General Sir C.E., *Field-Marshall Sir Henry Wilson: His Life and Diaries*, vol. ii (London: Cassell, 1927).

Chesterton, G.K., *Irish Impressions* (London: W. Collins, 1919).

—— 'Introduction' to W.J. Lockington S.J., *The Soul Of Ireland* (London: Harding and Moore, 1919).

—— *What Are Reprisals?* (London: Peace with Ireland Council, 1918).

Childers, Erskine, *The Form and Purpose of Home Rule* (London: Simpkin, Marshall, Hamilton, Kent and Co., 1912).

Churchill, Winston, *The World Crisis: The Aftermath* (London: Thornton Butterworth, 1929).

Clarke, Tom, *My Northcliffe Diary* (London: Victor Gollancz, 1931).

Cockburn, Claud, *In Time of Trouble* (London: Rupert Hart-Davis, 1956).

Conrad, Joseph, *Notes on Life and Letters* (London: J.M. Dent, 1921).

Cook, Sir Edward, *The Press in War-Time,* (London: Macmillan, 1920).

Dell, Floyd, *Homecoming: An Autobiography* (New York: Farrar and Rinehart, 1933).

Ewart, Wilfred, *A Journey in Ireland 1921* (London: G.P. Putnam's Sons, 1922).

Figgis, Darell, *Recollections of the Irish War* (London: Ernest Benn, 1927).

Fyfe, Hamilton, *Sixty Years of Fleet Street* (London: W.H. Allen, 1949).

—— *My Seven Selves* (London: George Allen and Unwin, 1935).

Gibbs, Philip, *The Pageant of Years: An Autobiography* (London: William Heinemann, 1946).

—— *Realities of War* (London: Hutchinson, 1929).

—— *Adventures in Journalism* (London: William Heinemann, 1923).

—— *The Hope of Europe* (London: William Heinemann, 1921).

Goldring, Douglas, *The Nineteen Twenties: A General Survey and some Personal Memories* (London: Nicholson and Watson, 1945).

—— *Odd Man Out: The Autobiography of a 'Propaganda Novelist'* (London: Chapman and Hall, 1936).

Green, Alice Stopford, *Loyalty and Disloyalty: What it Means in Ireland* (Dublin: Maunsel and Co., 1919).

Greene, Graham, *Fragments of Autobiography* (London: Penguin, 1991).

Hackett, Francis, *American Rainbow: Early Reminiscences* (New York: Liveright, 1971).

Hackett, Francis, *The Invisible Censor* (New York: Books for Libraries Press, 1968).

Hall, J.B., *Random Records of a Reporter* (Dublin: Fodhla Printing Co., 1928).

Hammond, J.L., *The Terror in Action* (London: The Nation and The Athenaeum, 1921).

—— *C.P. Scott of The Manchester Guardian* (London: G. Bell and Sons, 1934).

Hayward, F.H. and B.N. Langdon-Davies, *Democracy and the Press* (Manchester: National Labour Press, 1919).

Heaton, John L. (ed.), *Cobb of 'The World', A Leader in Liberalism: Compiled from His Editorial Articles and Public Addresses* (New York: E.P. Dutton and Co., 1924).

Hirst, F.W., *The Six Panics and Other Essays* (London: Methuen, 1913).

Hobson, J.A., *Confessions of an Economic Heretic* (London: George Allen and Unwin, 1938).

—— *Imperialism: A Study* (London: James Nisbet, 1902).

Hogan, David (Frank Gallagher), *The Four Glorious Years* (Dublin: Irish Press, 1953).

Hopkinson, Michael (ed.), *The Last Days of Dublin Castle: The Diaries of Mark Sturgis*, (Dublin: Irish Academic Press, 1999).

Inglis, Brian, *West Briton* (London: Faber and Faber, 1962).

Jones, Thomas, *Whitehall Diary*, vol. i, 1916–1925 (Oxford: OUP, 1969).

Laurence, Dan H. (ed.), *Bernard Shaw Collected Letters*, vol. iii, 1911–1925 (London: Max Reinhardt, 1985).

Lauriston Bullard, F., *Famous War Correspondents* (London: Sir Isaac Pitman, 1914).

Lippmann, Walter, *Public Opinion*, (New York: Free Press Paperbacks, 1997, originally published 1922).

——*Liberty and the News* (New York: Harcourt, Brace and Howe, 1920).

Lowell, A.B., *Public Opinion in War and Peace* (Cambridge, MA: Harvard University Press, 1923).

MacKenzic, F.A., *The Irish Rebellion: What Happened and Why* (London: C. Arthur Pearson, 1916).

Macready, Sir Nevil, *Annals of an Active Life*, vols i and ii (London: Hutchinson and Co., 1924).

Martin, Hugh, *Ireland in Insurrection* (London: Daniel O' Connor, 1921).

Martin, Kingsley, *Truth and the Public* (London: Watts and Co., 1945).

Maxwell, William, 'The war correspondent in sunshine and eclipse', *The Nineteenth Century and After*, no. 433 (March 1913).

McKenna, Kathleen Napoli, 'The Irish Bulletin', in *The Capuchin Annual* (Dublin, 1970).

Montague, C.E., *Disenchantment* (London: Chatto and Windus, 1922).

Morison, Stanley, *The History of* The Times: *the 150th Anniversary and Beyond, 1912–1948*, vol. iv, part 2 (London: The Times, 1952).

Nevinson, Henry W., *Last Changes, Last Chances* (London: James Nisbet, 1928).

——*Changes and Chances* (London: James Nisbet, 1923).

——'The Anglo-Irish War', *The Contemporary Review* 120 (July 1921), pp.20–6.

——*A Modern Slavery* (London: Harper, 1906).

O'Malley, Ernie, *On Another Man's Wound* (Dublin: Anvil Books, 1994 edn).

Ostrogorski, Moisei, *Democracy and the Party System in the United States* (New York: Macmillan, 1910).

——*Democracy and the Organization of Political Parties*, vol. ii (London: Macmillan, 1902).

Phillips, W. Alison, *The Revolution in Ireland 1906–1923* (London: Longmans, Green and Co., 1923).

Pihl, Lis (ed.), *Signe Toksvig's Irish Diaries 1926–1937* (Dublin: The Lilliput Press, 1994).

Ponsonby, Arthur, *Falsehood in War-Time* (Torrance, CA: Institute for Historical Review, 1980, originally published 1928).

Pottle, Mark (ed.), *Champion Redoubtable: The Diaries and Letters of Violet Bonham Carter 1914–1945* (London: Phoenix, 1999).

Pritchett, V.S., *Midnight Oil* (London: Chatto and Windus, 1971).

——*Dublin: A Portrait* (London: The Bodley Head, 1967).

Raleigh, Walter, *The War and the Press* (Oxford: Clarendon Press, 1918).

Robertson, J.M., 'The Press Fetish', *Contemporary Review* 109 (January, 1916).

Ryan, Desmond, *Remembering Sion: A Chronicle of Storm and Quiet* (London: Arthur Barker, 1934).

Scott-James, R.A., *The Influence of the Press* (London: S.W. Partridge, 1913).

Scudamore, Frank, *A Sheaf of Memories* (London: T. Fisher Unwin, 1925).

Seldes, George, *Tell the Truth and Run* (New York: Greenberg, 1953).

—— *The Truth Behind the News 1918–1928* (London: Faber and Gwyer, 1929).

Self, Robert B. (ed.), *The Austen Chamberlain Diary Letters: The Correspondence of Sir Austen Chamberlain with His Sisters Hilda and Ida 1916–1937*, vol. v (Cambridge: CUP, 1995).

Steed, Henry Wickham, *Through Thirty Years 1892–1922: A Personal Narrative* (London: William Heinemann, 1924).

Stephens, James, *The Insurrection in Dublin* (Gerrards Cross: Colin Smythe, 1992 edn, originally published 1916).

Street, C.J.C., *The Administration of Ireland* (London: Philip Allan, 1921).

Wells, Warre B., *Irish Indiscretions* (London: George Allen and Unwin, 1923).

—— and N. Marlowe, *A History of the Irish Rebellion of 1916* (London: Maunsel, 1916).

Wilson, Edmund, *The Twenties: From Notebooks and Diaries of the Period* (New York: Farrar, Straus and Giroux, 1975).

Villard, Oswald Garrison, *Some Newspapers and Newspaper-men* (New York: Alfred A. Knopf, 1926).

## SECONDARY WORKS

Addison, Paul, *Churchill on the Home Front, 1900–1955* (London: Pimlico, 1993 edn).

Allason, Rupert, *The Branch: A History of the Metropolitan Police Special Branch 1883–1983* (London: Secker and Warburg, 1983).

Allen, Nicholas, *George Russell and the New Ireland 1905–30* (Dublin: Four Courts Press, 2003).

Anderson, Benedict, *Imagined Communities: Reflections on the Origins and Spread of Nationalism* (London: Verso, 1991).

Anderson, Mark Cronlund, *Pancho Villa's Revolution by Headlines* (Norman, OK: University of Oklahoma Press, 2000).

Anderson, Olive, *A Liberal State at War: English Politics and Economics During the Crimean War* (London: Macmillan, 1967).

Auden, W.H. (ed.), *G.K. Chesterton: A Selection from His Non-Fictional Prose* (London: Faber and Faber, 1970).

Augustejin, Joost, *From Public Defiance to Guerrilla Warfare: The Experience of Ordinary Volunteers in the Irish War of Independence 1916–1921* (Dublin: Irish Academic Press, 1996).

Ayerst, David, *The Guardian: Biography of a Newspaper* (London: Collins, 1971).

Bannister Jr, Robert C., *Ray Stannard Baker: The Mind and Thought of a Progressive* (New Haven: Yale University Press, 1966).

Barnett, Corelli, *The Collapse of British Power* (London: Eyre Methuen, 1972).

Bass, Gary, *Stay the Hand of Vengeance: The Politics of War Crimes Tribunal* (Princeton, NJ: Princeton University Press, 2000).

Bayly, C.A., *The Birth of the Modern World 1780–1914* (Oxford: Blackwell, 2004).

—— 'Representing copts and muhammadans: empire, nation and community in Egypt and India, 1880–1914', in Leila Tarazi Fawaz and C.A. Bayly (eds), *Modernity and Culture from the Mediterranean to the Indian Ocean* (New York: Columbia University Press, 2002).

Beaumont, Jacqueline, 'The making of a war correspondent: Lionel James of *The Times*', in David Omissi and Andrew S. Thompson (eds), *The Impact of the South African War* (Basingstoke: Palgrave, 2002).

—— '*The Times* at war, 1899–1902', in Donal Lowry (ed.), *The South African War Reappraised* (Manchester: MUP, 2000).

Bence-Jones, Mark, *Twilight of the Ascendancy* (London: Constable, 1993).

Bennett, Richard, *The Black and Tans* (New York: Barnes and Noble, 1995).

Benson, Rodney and Neveu, Erik, 'Introduction: field theory as a work in progress', in Rodney Benson and Erik Neveu (eds), *Bourdieu and the Journalistic Field* (London: Polity Press, 2005).

Bew, Paul, *John Redmond* (Dundalk: Dundalgan Press, 1996).

Bew, Paul, *Ideology and the Irish Question: Ulster Unionism and Irish Nationalism 1912–1916* (Oxford: Clarendon Press, 1994).

Blum, D. Steven, W*alter Lippmann: Cosmopolitanism in the Century of Total War* (Ithaca: Cornell University Press, 1984).

Boot, Max, *The Savage Wars of Peace: Small Wars and the Rise of American Power* (New York: Basic Books, 2002).

Bourdieu, Pierre, 'The political field, the social science field, and the journalistic field', in Rodney Benson and Erik Neveu (eds), *Bourdieu and the Journalistic Field* (London: Polity Press, 2005).

Bourke, Richard, *Peace in Ireland: The War of Ideas* (London: Pimlico, 2003).

Boyce, D.G., *The Irish Question and British Politics, 1868–1996* (London: Macmillan, 1996).

—— *Ireland 1828–1923: From Ascendancy to Democracy* (Oxford: Blackwell, 1992).

—— 'One last burial': culture, counter-revolution and revolution in Ireland, 1886–1916', in D.G. Boyce (ed.), *The Revolution in Ireland, 1879–1923* (London: Macmillan, 1988).

—— 'Crusaders without chains: power and the press barons 1896–1951', in James Curran, Anthony Smith and Pauline Wingate (eds), *Impacts and Influences: Essays on Media Power in the Twentieth Century* (London: Methuen, 1987).

—— 'Water for the fish: terrorism and public opinion', in Yonah Alexander and Alan O'Day (eds), *Terrorism in Ireland* (London: Croom Helm, 1984).

—— 'The Fourth Estate: the reappraisal of a concept', in George Boyce, James Curran and Pauline Wingate (eds), *Newspaper History from the Seventeenth Century to the Present Day* (London: Constable, 1978).

—— *Englishmen and Irish Troubles: British Public Opinion and the Making of Irish Policy* (London: Jonathan Cape, 1972).

—— 'How to settle the Irish Question: Lloyd George and Ireland 1916–1921', in A.J.P. Taylor (ed.), *Lloyd George: Twelve Essays* (London: Hamilton, 1971).

Boyle, Andrew, *The Riddle of Erskine Childers* (London: Hutchinson, 1977).

Brasted, H.V., 'Irish nationalism and the British Empire in the late nineteenth century', in Oliver MacDonagh, W.F. Mandle and Pauric Travers (eds), *Irish Culture and Nationalism 1750–1950* (London: Macmillan, 1983).

Brogan, Hugh, *The Life of Arthur Ransome* (London: Jonathan Cape, 1984).

Brown, Lucy, *Victorian News and Newspapers* (Oxford: Clarendon Press, 1985).

Brown, Terence, *Ireland: A Social and Cultural History 1922–79* (London: Fontana, 1981).

Burke, Peter, *Sociology and History* (London: George Allen and Unwin, 1980).

Cain, P.J., *Hobson and Imperialism: Radicalism, New Liberalism, and Finance 1887–1938* (New York: OUP, 2002).

Callanan, Frank, *T.M. Healy* (Togher: Cork University Press, 1996).

Campbell, John, *F.E. Smith, First Earl of Birkenhead* (London: Jonathan Cape, 1983).

Campbell, Kate, 'Journalistic discourses and construction of modern knowledge', in Laurel Brake, Bill Bell and David Finkelstein (eds), *Nineteenth Century Media and the Construction of Identities* (London: Palgrave, 2000).

—— 'On perceptions of journalism', in Kate Campbell (ed.), *Journalism, Literature and Modernity: From Hazlitt to Modernism* (Edinburgh: Edinburgh University Press, 2000).

Carroll, Francis M., *American Opinion and the Irish Question 1910–1923* (Dublin: Gill and Macmillan, 1978).

Cecil, Hugh, *The Flower of Battle: How Britain Wrote the Great War* (Hanover, NH: Steerforth Press, 1996).

Chalaby, Jean, *The Invention of Journalism* (London: Macmillan, 1998).

Chibnall, Steve, *Law and Order News: An Analysis of Crime Reporting in the British Press* (London: Tavistock Publications, 1977).

Clarke, Peter, *Hope and Glory: Britain 1900–1990* (London: Allen Lane, 1997).

Clarke, Peter, *Liberals and Social Democrats* (Cambridge: CUP, 1978).

Cockett, Richard, *Twilight of Truth: Chamberlain, Appeasement and the Manipulation of the Press* (London: Weidenfeld and Nicolson, 1989).

Cohen, Bernard C., *The Press and Foreign Policy* (Princeton, NJ: Princeton University Press, 1963).

Comerford, R.V., *Ireland* (London: Hodder Arnold, 2003).

Conboy, Martin, 'Communities and constructs: national identity in the British press', in Suzanne Stern-Gillet, Tadeusz Sławek, Tadeusz Rachwał and Roger Whitehouse (eds), *Culture and Identity: Selected Aspects and Approaches* (Katowice: University of Silesia, 1996).

Coogan, Tim Pat, *Michael Collins: A Biography* (London: Hutchinson, 1990).

Cox, Tom, *Damned Englishman: A Study of Erskine Childers, 1870–1922* (New York: Exposition Press, 1975).

Cullen, Fintan and R.F. Foster, *'Conquering England': Ireland in Victorian London* (London: National Portrait Gallery, 2005).

Curran, James, *Media and Power* (London: Routledge, 2002).

Curran, James and Jean Seaton, *Power Without Responsibility: The Press and Broadcasting in Britain* (London: Routledge, 1988).

Curtis, L.P. Jr, *Coercion and Conciliation in Ireland 1880–1892: A Study in Conservative Unionism* (Princeton, NJ: Princeton University Press, 1963).

Dalley, Jan, *Diana Mosley* (New York: Alfred A. Knopf, 2000).

Dangerfield, George, *The Strange Death of Liberal England* (London: Paladin, 1970).

Deane, Seamus, 'Irish national character 1790–1900', in Tom Dunne (ed.), *The Writer as Witness: Literature as Historical Evidence* (Cork: Cork University Press, 1987).

—— 'Wherever green is read', in Ciaran Brady (ed.), *Interpreting Irish History* (Dublin: Irish Academic Press, 1994).

Desmond, Robert W., *The Information Process: World News Reporting to the Twentieth Century* (University of Iowa Press, 1978).

Dodge, Toby, *Inventing Iraq: The Failure of Nation Building and a History Denied* (London: Hurst, 2003).

Dolan, Anne, *Commemorating the Irish Civil War: History and Memory 1923–2000*, (Cambridge: CUP, 2003).

Duffy, James, *A Question of Slavery* (Oxford: Clarendon Press, 1967).

Dunn, John, *Modern Revolutions: An Introduction to an Analysis of a Political Phenomenon* (Cambridge: CUP, 1972).

Eagleton, Terry, *Heathcliff and the Great Hunger* (London: Verso, 1995).

Edwards, Owen Dudley and Fergus Pyle, *1916: The Easter Rising* (London: MacGibbon and Kee, 1968).

Edwards, Ruth Dudley, *James Connolly* (Dublin: Gill and Macmillan, 1998).

Eksteins, Modris, *Rites of Spring: The Great War and the Birth of the Modern Age* (New York: Mariner Books, 2000).

Elliott, Philip, 'Press performance as a political ritual', in Harry Christian (ed.), *The Sociology of Journalism and the Press*, Sociological Revew Monograph 29, (Keele: University of Keele, 1980).

—— 'All the world's a stage or what's wrong with the national press', in James Curran (ed.), *The British Press: A Manifesto* (London: Macmillan, 1978).

English, Richard, *Irish Freedom: The History of Nationalism in Ireland* (London: Macmillan, 2006).

—— *Ernie O' Malley: IRA Intellectual* (Oxford: Clarendon Press, 1998).

Ensor, R.C.K., *England 1870–1914* (Oxford: Clarendon Press, 1985).

Ewing, K.D., and Conor Gearty (eds), *The Struggle for Civil Liberties, Political Freedom and the Rule of Law in Britain 1914–45* (Oxford: OUP, 2000).

Fanning, Ronan, Michael Kennedy, Dermot Keogh and Eunan O'Halpin (eds), *Documents on Irish Foreign Policy*, vol. i, 1919-1922 (Dublin: Royal Irish Academy, 1998).

Farnsworth, Beatrice, *William C. Bullitt and The Soviet Union* (Bloomington: Indiana University Press, 1967).

Farrell, J.G., *Troubles* (London: Phoenix, 1993).

Fegan, Melissa, *Literature and the Irish Famine: 1845–1919* (Oxford: Clarendon Press, 2002).

Ferguson, Naill, *Colossus: The Rise and Fall of the American Empire* (London: Penguin, 2005).

—— *Empire: The Rise and Demise of the British World Order and the Lessons for Global Power* (New York: Basic Books, 2003).

—— *The Pity of War* (New York: Basic Books, 1999).

—— 'Virtual history: towards a "chaotic" theory of the past' in Niall Ferguson (ed.) *Virtual History: Alternatives and Counterfactuals* (London: Picador, 1997).

Ferriter, Diarmaid, *The Transformation of Ireland* (London: Profile Books, 2004).

Fitzpatrick, David, *Harry Boland's Irish Revolution* (Togher: Cork University Press, 2003).

—— *Politics and Irish Life: Provincial Experience of War and Revolution* (Togher: Cork University Press, 1998).

—— 'Militarism in Ireland 1900–1922', in Thomas Bartlett and Keith Jeffery (eds), *A Military History of Ireland* (New York: CUP, 1996).

—— 'The overflow of the deluge: Anglo-Irish relationships, 1914-1922', in Oliver MacDonagh and W.F. Mandle (eds), *Ireland and Irish-Australia: Studies in Cultural and Political History* (London: Croom Helm, 1986).

Floto, Inga, *Colonel House in Paris: A Study of American Policy at the Paris Peace Conference 1919* (Princeton, NJ: Princeton University Press, 1980).

Forcey, Charles, *The Crossroads of Liberalism: Croly Weyl, Lippmann and the Progressive Era 1900–1925* (New York: OUP, 1961).

Foster, R.F., *W.B. Yeats: A Life*, vol. ii: The Arch-Poet 1915–1939 (Oxford: OUP, 2003).

—— *The Irish Story: Telling Tales and Making it Up in Ireland* (Londno: Allen Lane, 2001).

—— *Paddy and Mr Punch: Connections in Irish and English History* (London: Allen Lane, 1993).

—— *Modern Ireland 1600–1972* (London: Allen Lane, 1988).

Garvin, Tom, *1922: The Birth of Irish Democracy* (Dublin: Gill and Macmillan, 1996).

—— *The Evolution of Irish Nationalist Politics* (Dublin: Gill and Macmillan, 1981).

Geyelin, Philip, 'Vietnam and the press: limited war and an open society', in Anthony Lake (ed.) *The Vietnam Legacy: The War, American Society and the Future of American Foreign Policy* (New York: NYUP, 1976).

Glandon, Virginia, *Arthur Griffith and the Advanced Nationals Press: Ireland 1900–22* (New York: P. Lang, 1985).

Goldring, Maurice, *Pleasant the Scholar's Life: Irish Intellectuals and the Construction of the Nation State* (London: Serif, 1993).

Gott, Richard, *Cuba: A New History* (New Haven, CT: Yale University Press, 2004).

Gramling, Oliver, *AP: The Story of News* (New York: Farrar and Rinehart, 1940).

Grandin, Greg, *The Last Colonial Massacre: Latin America in the Cold War* (Chicago: University of Chicago Press, 2004).

Grigg, John, *Lloyd George: War Leader, 1916–1918* (London: Allen Lane, 2002).

Gross, John, *The Rise and Fall of the Man of Letters: Aspects of English Literary Life Since 1800* (London: Penguin, 1991).

Hale, Oron J., *Publicity and Diplomacy – with Special Reference to England and Germany 1890–1914* (Gloucester, MA: Peter Smith, 1964).

Hall, Stuart, 'Introduction', in A.C.H. Smith with Elizabeth Immirzi and Trevor Blackwell, *Paper Voices: The Popular Press and Social Change 1935–1965* (London: Chatto and Windus, 1975).

—— 'The Rediscovery of Ideology', in Michael Gurevitch, Tony Bennett, James Curran and Janet Woollacott (eds), *Culture, Society and the Media* (London: Methuen, 1982).

—— 'Encoding/Decoding', in Stuart Hall, Dorothy Hobson, Andrew Lowe and Paul Willis (eds), *Culture, Media, Language: Working Papers in Cultural Studies* (London: Hutchinson, 1980).

Hall, Stuart and Bill Schwarz, 'State and society, 1880–1930', in Mary Langan and Bill Schwarz (eds), *Crises in the British State 1880–1930* (London: Hutchinson, 1985).

Hallin, Daniel C., *We Keep America on Top of the World: Television Journalism and the Public Sphere* (London: Routeledge, 1994).

—— *The 'Uncensored War': The Media and Vietnam* (New York: OUP, 1986).

—— and Paolo Mancini, 'Field theory, differentiation theory, and comparative media research', in Rodney Benson and Erik Neveu (eds), *Bourdieu and the Journalistic Field*, (London: Polity Press, 2005).

—— and Paolo Mancini, *Comparing Media Systems: Three Models of Media and Politics* (Cambridge: CUP, 2004).

Hampton, Mark, *Visions of the Press in Britain, 1850–1950* (Urbana: University of Illinois Press, 2004).

Hancock, Sir W.K., *Survey of British Commonwealth Affairs vol. 1: Problems of Nationality 1918–1936* (London: OUP, 1937).

Harding, Jason, *The Criterion: Cultural Politics and Periodical Networks in Inter-War Britain* (Oxford: OUP, 2002).

Harris, Jose, *Private Lives, Public Spirit: A Social History of Britain 1870–1914* (Oxford: OUP, 1993).

Hart, Peter, *The IRA at War 1916–1923* (Oxford: OUP, 2003).

—— *British Intelligence in Ireland, 1920–21: The Final Reports* (Cork: Cork University Press, 2002).

—— *The IRA and its Enemies: Violence and Community in Cork 1916–1923* (Oxford: Clarendon Press, 1998).

Hawkins, Richard, 'Dublin Castle and the Royal Irish Constabulary', in T. Desmond Williams (ed.), *The Irish Struggle 1916–1926* (London: Routledge and Kegan Paul, 1966).

Heald, Morrell, *Transatlantic Vistas: American Journalists in Europe, 1900–1940* (Kent, OH: Kent State University Press, Ohio, 1988).

Helly, Dorothy O. and Callaway, Helen, 'Journalism as active politics: Flora Shaw, *The Times* and South Africa', in Jacqueline Beaumont, *The South African War Reappraised* (Manchester: MUP, 2000).

Hobsbawm, Eric, *The Age of Extremes: A History of the World 1914–1991* (New York: Pantheon Books, 1994).

Hohenberg, John, *Foreign Correspondence: The Great Reporters and Their Times* (New York: Columbia University Press, 1964).

Hooper, Glen (ed.), *The Tourist's Gaze: Travellers to Ireland 1800–2000* (Togher: Cork University Press, 2001).

Hopkinson, Michael, *The Irish War of Independence* (Dublin: Gill and Macmillan, 2002).

Hopkinson, Michael, *Green Against Green: The Irish Civil War* (Dublin: Gill and Macmillan, 1988).

Hoppen, Theodore K., *Ireland Since 1800: Conflict and Conformity* (London: Longman, 1989).

Howard, Michael, *War and the Liberal Conscience* (Oxford: OUP, 1981).

Howe, Stephen, *Ireland and Empire: Colonial Legacies in Irish History and Culture* (Oxford: OUP, 2000).

Hynes, Samuel, *A War Imagined: The First World War and English Culture* (London: Pimlico, 1992).

Inoue, Keiko, 'Propaganda II: Propaganda of Dail Eireann, 1919–21', in Joost Augusteijn (ed.), *The Irish Revolution, 1913–1923* (London: Palgrave, 2002).

Jeffery, Keith, *Ireland and the Great War* (Cambridge: CUP, 2000).

—— *The British Army and the Crisis of Empire 1918–1922* (Manchester: MUP, 1984).

John, Angela V., *War, Journalism and the Shaping of the Twentieth Century: The Life and Times of Henry W. Nevinson* (London: I.B.Tauris, 2006).

Jones, Maldyn A., *The Limits of Liberty: American History 1607–1992* (Oxford: OUP, 1995).

Kahler, Miles, *Decolonisation in Britain and France: The Domestic Consequences of International Relations* (Princeton, NJ: Princeton University Press, 1984).

Katz, Friedrich, *The Life and Times of Pancho Villa* (Palo Alto, CA: Stanford University Press, 1998).

Kaul, Chandrika, *Reporting the Raj: The British Press and India, c. 1880–1922* (Manchester: MUP, 2003).

—— 'Popular press and Empire: Northcliffe, India and the *Daily Mail*, 1896–1922', in Peter Catterall, Colin Seymour-Ure and Adrian Smith (eds) *Northcliffe's Legacy: Aspects of the British Popular Press 1896–1996* (London: Macmillan, 2000).

Kautt, William H., *The Anglo-Irish War, 1916–1921: A People's War* (Westport, CT: Praeger, 1999).

Kee, Robert, *The Green Flag: A History of Irish Nationalism* (London: Weidenfeld and Nicolson, 1972).

Kennedy, Dennis, *The Widening Gulf: Northern Attitudes to the Independent Irish State 1919–49* (Belfast: Blastaff Press, 1999).

Kennedy, Paul, *The Realities Behind Diplomacy: Background Influences on British External Policy 1865–1980* (London: Fontana, 1985).

Kiberd, Declan, *Irish Classics* (London: Granta Books, 2000).

—— *Inventing Ireland: The Literature of the Modern Nation* (London: Vintage, 1996).

——*Anglo-Irish Attitudes* (Derry: Field Day Theatre Co., 1984).

Kissane, Bill, *The Politics of the Irish Civil War* (Oxford: OUP, 2005).

Knightley, Phillip, *The First Casualty: The War Correspondent as Hero, Propagandist and Myth Maker* (London: Quartet, 1982).

Koss, Stephen, *The Rise and Fall of the Political Press in Britain* (London: Fontana, 1990).

——*Asquith* (London: Hamish Hamilton, 1985).

——*Fleet Street Radical: A.G. Gardiner and the Daily News* (London: Allen Lane, 1973).

LaFeber, Walter, *Inevitable Revolutions: The United States in Central America* (New York: Norton, 1993).

——*The American Age: United States Foreign Policy at Home and Abroad since 1750* (New York: Norton, 1989).

Laffan, Michael, *The Resurrection of Ireland: The Sinn Fein Party 1916-1923* (Cambridge: CUP, 1999).

Larsen, Egon, *First with the Truth: Newspapermen in Action* (London: Baker, 1968).

Lasch, Christopher, *The New Radicalism in America 1889-1963: The Intellectual as a Social Type* (New York: W.W. Norton, 1965).

——*The American Liberals and the Russian Revolution* (New York: Columbia University Press, 1962).

Lawlor, Sheila, *Britain and Ireland 1914-23* (Dublin: Gill and Macmillan, 1983).

Lee, J.J., *Ireland 1912-1985* (Cambridge: CUP, 1989).

Legg, Mary Louise, *Newspapers and Nationalism: The Irish Provincial Press, 1850-1892* (Dublin: Four Courts Press, 1999).

LeMahieu, D.L., *A Culture for Democracy: Mass Communication and the Cultivated Mind in Britain Between the Wars* (Oxford: Clarendon Press, 1988).

Levin Jr, N. Gordon, *Woodrow Wilson and World Politics: America's Response to War and Revolution* (Oxford: OUP, 1968).

Levitas, Ben, *The Theatre of Nation: Irish Drama and Cultural Nationalism 1890-1916* (Oxford: Clarendon Press, 2002).

Lewis, Joanna, '"Daddy wouldn't buy me a mau mau": the British popular press and the demoralization of empire', in E.S. Atieno Odhiambo and John Lonsdale (eds), *Mau Mau and Nationhood: Arms, Authority and Narration* (Oxford: James Currey, 2003).

Loughlin, James, 'Constructing the political spectacle: Parnell, the press and national leadership, 1879-86', in D. George Boyce and Alan O'Day (eds), *Parnell in Perspective* (London: Routledge, 1991).

Lowry, Donal, 'New Ireland, old empire and the outside world, 1922–49: the strange evolution of a "dictionary republic"', in Mike Cronin and John Regan (eds), *Ireland: The Politics of Independence, 1922–49* (London: Macmillan, 2000).

Lucas, John, *The Radical Twenties: Aspects of Writing, Politics and Culture* (Nottingham: Five Leaves, 1997).

Lyons, F.S.L., *Ireland Since the Famine* (London: Fontana, 1976).

——*John Dillon: A Biography* (London: Routledge and Keegan Paul, 1968).

Macardle, Dorothy, *The Irish Republic* (London: Corgi, 1968).

MacDonagh, Oliver, *The Emancipist: Daniel O'Connell 1830–47* (London: Weidenfeld and Nicolson, 1989).

——*States of Mind: A Study of Anglo-Irish Conflict 1780–1980* (London: Allen and Unwin, 1983).

MacMillan, Margaret, *Peacemakers: The Paris Conference of 1919 and Its Attempt to End War* (London: John Murray, 2002).

Maier, Charles, *Recasting Bourgeois Europe: Stabilization in France, Germany and Italy in the Decade After World War I* (Princeton, NJ: Princeton University Press, 1975).

Mancini, Paolo, 'Political complexity and alternative models of journalism: the Italian case', in Myung-Jin Park and James Curran (eds), *De-Westernizing Media Studies* (London: Routledge, 2000).

Marwick, Arthur, *The Explosion of British Society, 1914–62* (London: Pan Books, 1963).

Marzolf, Marion Tuttle, *Civilizing Voices: American Press Criticism 1880–1950* (New York: Longman, 1991).

Mathews, Joseph J., *Reporting the Wars* (Minneapolis, MN: University of Minnesota Press, 1957).

Mazower, Mark, *Dark Continent: Europe's Twentieth Century* (London: Allen Lane, 1998).

McColgan, John, *British Policy and the Irish Administration 1920–22* (London: Allen and Uynwin, 1983).

McDowell, R.B., *Crisis and Decline: The Fate of the Southern Unionists* (Dublin: Lilliput Press, 1997).

——*Alice Stopford Green: A Passionate Historian* (Dublin: Allen Figgis and Co., 1967).

McInerney, Michael, *The Riddle of Erskine Childers* (Dublin: E. and T. O'Brien, 1971).

McMahon, Deirdre, 'Ireland and the Empire–Commonwealth, 1900–1948', in Judith M. Brown and Wm. Roger Louis (eds), *The Oxford History of the British Empire, vol. iv: The Twentieth Century* (Oxford: OUP, 1999).

Menand, Louis, *The Metaphysical Club* (London: Flamingo, 2002).

Messinger, Gary S., *British Propaganda and the State in the First World War* (Manchester: MUP, 1992).

Middlemas, Keith (ed.), *Tom Jones: Whitehall Diary*, vols i and iii (New York: OUP, 1969 and 1971).

Mitchell, Arthur, *Revolutionary Government in Ireland: Dail Eireann 1919–22* (Dublin: Gill and Macmillan, 1995).

—— and Padraig O'Snodaigh (eds), *Irish Political Documents 1916–1949* (Dublin: Irish Academic Press, 1985).

Mockaitis, Thomas R., *British Counterinsurgency, 1919–1960* (London: Macmillan, 1990).

Moody, T.W., *Davitt and Irish Revolution 1846–82* (Oxford: Clarendon Press, 1981).

Morris, Jan, *Farewell the Trumpets* (London: Faber, 1978).

Morris, Joe Alex, *Deadline Every Minute: The Story of the United Press* (New York: Doubleday, 1957).

Murphy, John A., 'The influence of America on Irish nationalism', in David Noel Doyle and Owen Dudley Edwards (eds), *America and Ireland 1776–1976: The American Identity and the Irish Connection*, The Proceedings of the United States Bicentennial Conference of Cumann Merriman, Ennis, August 1976 (Westport, CT: Greenewood Press, 1980).

Myers, Kevin, 'The Irish and the Great War: a case of amnesia', in Richard English and Joseph Morrison Skelly (eds), *Ideas Matter: Essays in Honour of Conor Cruise O'Brien* (Dublin: Poolbeg Press, 1998).

Novick, Ben, *Conceiving Revolution: Irish Nationalist Propaganda during the First World War* (Dublin: Four Courts Press, 2001).

O'Brien, Conor Cruise, *Neighbours: The Ewart-Biggs Memorial Lectures* (London: Faber, 1980).

—— 'The embers of Easter', in Owen Dudley Edwards and Fergus Pyle (eds), *1916: The Easter Rising* (London: MacGibbon and Kee, 1968).

—— *Parnell and His Party 1880–90* (Oxford: Clarendon Press, 1957).

O Broin, Leon, *Protestant Nationalists in Revolutionary Ireland: The Stopford Connection* (Dublin: Gill and Macmillan, 1985).

O'Halpin, Eunan, *The Decline of the Union: British Government in Ireland 1892–1920* (Dublin: Gill and Macmillan, 1987).

Ousby, Ian, *The Road to Verdun: France, Nationalism and the First World War* (London: Pimlico, 2003).

Peatling, G.K., *British Opinion and Irish Self-Government 1865–1925: From Unionism to Liberal Commonwealth* (Dublin: Irish Academic Press, 2001).

Porter, Bernard, *The Origins of the Vigilant State: The London Metropolitan Police Special Branch Before the First World War* (Woodbridge: The Boydell Press, 1987).

Porter, Bernard, *Britain, Europe and the World 1850–1982: Delusions of Grandeur* (London: George Allen and Unwin, 1983).

Potter, Simon J., *News and the British World: The Emergence of an Imperial Press System 1876–1922* (Oxford: Clarendon Press, 2003).

Prochnau, William, *Once Upon a Distant War: Reporting from Vietnam* (Edinburgh: Mainstream Publishing, 1996).

Purcell, Edward A., *The Crisis of Democratic Theory: Scientific Naturalism and the Problem of Value* (Lexington: University Press of Kentucky, 1973).

Quagliariello, Gaetano, *Politics Without Parties: Moisei Ostrogorski and the Debate on Political Parties on the Eve of the Twentieth Century* (Aldershot: Avebury, 1996).

Ring, Jim, *Erskine Childers* (London: John Murray, 1996).

Robbins, K.G., 'Public opinion, the press and pressure groups', in F.H. Hinsley (ed.), *British Foreign Policy under Sir Edward Grey* (Cambridge: CUP, 1977).

Rosenstone, Robert A., *Romantic Revolutionary: A Biography of John Reed* (Cambridge, MA: Harvard University Press, 1990).

Ryan, Desmond, *Sean Treacy and the Third Tipperary Brigade IRA* (Tralee: Anvil Books, 1945).

Scannell, Paddy and David Cardiff, *A Social History of British Broadcasting: 1922–1939 – Serving the Nation*, vol. i (Oxford: Basil Blackwell, 1991).

Schama, Simon, *A History of Britain: The Fate of Empire 1776–2000* (London: BBC Books, 2002).

Schiller, Dan, *Objectivity and the News: The Public and the Rise of Commercial Journalism*, (Philadelphia: University of Pennsylvania Press, 1981).

Schlesinger, Philip, 'Rethinking the sociology of journalism: source strategies and the limites of media-centrism', in Marjorie Ferguson (ed.), *Public Communication: The New Imperatives* (London: Sage, 1990).

Schudson, Michael, *The Sociology of News* (New York: Norton, 2003).

—— *The Power of News* (Cambridge, MA: Harvard University Press, 1995).

—— *Origins of the Ideal of Objectivity in the Professions: Studies in the History of American Journalism and American Law 1830–1940* (New York: Garland, 1990).

Schwarz, Bill, 'Conservatism and "caesarism", 1903–22', in Mary Langan and Bill Schwarz (eds), *Crises in the British State 1880–1930* (London: Hutchinson, 1985).

Seaton, Jean, *Carnage and the Media: The Making and Breaking of News About Violence* (London: Allen Lane, 2006).

Semmel, Bernard, *The Governor Eyre Controversy* (London: MacGibbon and Kee, 1962).

Seymour-Ure, Colin, 'The press and the party system between the wars', in Gillian Peele and Chris Cook (eds), *The Politics of Reappraisal 1918–1939* (London: Macmillan, 1975).

Simpson, Brian A.W., *Human Rights and the End of Empire: Britain and the Genesis of the European Convention* (Oxford: OUP, 2001).

Skidelsky, Robert, *John Maynard Keynes vol. ii: The Economist as Saviour 1920–1937* (London: Macmillan, 1992).

——*John Maynard Keynes vol. i: Hopes Betrayed 1883–1920* (London: Macmillan, 1983).

——*Oswald Mosley* (London: Macmillan Papermac, 1981).

Somerville, C. John, *The News Revolution in England* (Oxford: OUP, 1996).

Starrt, James D., *Journalism's Unofficial Ambassador: A Biography of Edward Price Bell 1869–1943* (Athens, OH: Ohio University Press, 1979).

Stearn, Roger T., 'War correspondents and colonial war, c. 1870-1900', in John M. MacKenzie (ed.), *Popular Imperialism and the Military 1850-1950* (Manchester: MUP, 1992).

Steel, Ronald, *Walter Lippmann and the American Century* (London: The Bodley Head, 1980).

Steele, E.D., *Irish Land and British Politics: Tenant-Right and Nationality 1865–1870* (Cambridge: CUP, 1974).

Stein, M.L., *Under Fire: The Story of American War Correspondents* (New York: Julian Messner, 1968).

Stephens, Robert O., *Hemingway's Nonfiction: The Public Voice* (Chapel Hill: University of North Carolina Press, Chapel Hill, 1968).

Strout, Lawrence N., *Covering McCarthyism: How the Christian Science Monitor Handled Joseph R. McCarthy 1950–1954* (Westport, CT: Greenwood Press, 1999).

Taylor, A.J.P., *Beaverbrook* (London: Penguin, 1974).

——*English History 1914–1945* (Oxford: Clarendon Press, 1965).

Taylor, Philip, *Munitions of the Mind: A History of Propaganda from the Ancient World to the Present Era* (Manchester: MUP, 1995).

——'Publicity and diplomacy: the impact of the First World War upon Foreign Office attitudes towards the press', in David Dilks (ed.), *Retreat from Power: Studies in Britain's Foreign Policy of the Twentieth Century*, vol. i (London: Macmillan, 1981).

*The History of The Times Vol. 1: 'The Thunderer' in the Making 1785–1841* (London: The Times, 1950).

*The History of The Times Vol. 2: The Tradition Established 1841–1884* (London: The Times, 1939).

*The History of The Times Vol. 3: The Twentieth Century Test* (London: The Times, 1947).

Thompson, J. Lee, *Northcliffe: Press Baron in Politics, 1865–1922* (London: John Murray, 2000).

——*Politicians, the Press and Propaganda: Lord Northcliffe and the Great War 1914–1919* (Kent, OH: Kent State University Press, 1999).

Thornton, A.P., *The Imperial Idea and Its Enemies: A Study in British Power* (London: Macmillan, 1985).

——*Imperialism in the Twentieth Century* (London: Macmillan, 1978).

Tierney, Mark, Paul Bowen and David Fitzpatrick, 'Recruiting posters', in David Fitzpatrick (ed.), *Ireland and the First World War* (Dublin: Lilliput Press and Trinity History Workshop, 1988).

Tilly, Charles, *As Sociology Meets History* (New York: Academic Press, 1981).

Townshend, Charles, *Easter 1916: The Irish Rebellion* (London: Allen Lane, 2005).

——*Making the Peace: Public Order and Public Security in Modern Britain* (Oxford: OUP, 1993).

—— 'Policing insurgency in Ireland', in David M. Anderson and David Killingray (eds), *Policing and Decolonisation: Politics, Nationalism and the Police 1917–65* (Manchester University Press, 1992).

——*Britain's Civil Wars: Counterinsurgency in the Twentieth Century* (London: Faber and Faber, 1986).

——*Political Violence in Ireland: Government and Resistance since 1848* (Oxford: Clarendon Press, 1983).

——*The British Campaign in Ireland, 1919–1921* (Oxford: OUP, 1975).

Treglown, Jeremy, *V.S. Pritchett: A Working Life* (London: Chatto and Windus, 2004).

Tuchman, Gaye, *Making News* (New York: Free Press, 1978).

Tunstall, Jeremy, *Journalists at Work* (London: Constable, 1971).

Ward, Alan, *Ireland and Anglo-American Relations, 1899–1921* (London: Weidenfeld and Nicolson with the London School of Economics and Political Science, 1969).

Ward, Stephen J.A., *The Invention of Journalism Ethics: The Path to Objectivity and Beyond* (Montreal: McGill-Queen's University Press, 2004).

Weaver, Stewart A., *The Hammonds: A Marriage in History* (Palo Alto, CA: Stanford University Press, 1997).

Weber, Max, 'Politics as a vocation', in H.H. Gerth and C. Wright Mills (eds) *From Max Weber: Essays in Sociology* (London: Routledge, 1991).

Weiner, Joel, 'The Americanization of the British Press, 1830–1914', in Michael Harris and Tom O'Mally, *Studies in Newspaper and Periodical History Annual 1994* (London: Greenwood Press, 1994).

Welch, David, *Germany, Propaganda and Total War, 1914–1918: The Sins of Omission* (London: Athlone Press, 2000).

Wilkinson, Glenn R., *Depictions and Images of War in Edwardian Newspapers, 1899–1914* (London: Palgrave Macmillan, 2003).

Williams, Francis, *Dangerous Estate: The Anatomy of Newspapers* (Cambridge: Patrick Stephens, 1984).

Williams, T. Desmond (ed.), *The Irish Struggle 1916–1926* (London: Routledge and Kegan Paul, 1966).

Wilson, Bryan R., *Sects and Society: A Sociological Study of Three Religious Groups in Britain* (London: William Heinemann, 1961).

Woolf, Leonard, *An Autobiography, Volume 2: 1911–1969* (Oxford: OUP, 1980).

——*Downhill All the Way: An Autobiography of the Years 1919–1939* (London: The Hogarth Press, 1967).

Wrigley, Chris, *Lloyd George and the Challenge of Labour: 1918–1922* (London: Harvester Wheatsheaf, 1990).

Zuckerman, Larry, *The Rape of Belgium: The Untold Story of World War I* (New York: NYUP, 2004).

## ARTICLES

Brown, Lucy, 'The treatment of the news in mid-Victorian newspapers', in *Transactions of the Royal Historical Society*, 5th series, vol. xxvii (1977).

Bew, Paul, 'Moderate nationalism and the Irish revolution, 1916–1923', *The Historical Journal* 42/iii (1999), pp.729–49.

Bogacz, Ted, '"A tyranny of words": language, poetry and antimodernism in England in the First World War', *Journal of Modern History* 58/iii (September 1986), pp.643–68.

Brindley, Ronan, 'Woodrow Wilson, self determination and Ireland 1918–1919: a view from the Irish newspapers', *Eire-Ireland* 23/iv (winter 1988), pp.62–80.

Darnton, Robert, 'Writing news and telling stories', *Daedalus* 104 (spring 1975), pp.175–194.

De Nie, Michael, 'The famine, Irish identity, and the British press', *Irish Studies Review* 6/i (1998), pp.27–36.

Dooley, Brendan, 'From literary criticism to systems theory in early modern journalism history', *Journal of the History of Ideas* 51/iii (1990), pp.461–86.

Elliott, Philip, 'Press performance as a political ritual', in Harry Christian (ed.), *The Sociology of Journalism and the Press*, Sociological Review Monograph 29 (Keele: University of Keele, 1980), pp.86–94.

—— 'Reporting Northern Ireland: A study of news in Britain, Ulster and the Irish Republic', in *Ethnicity and the Media* (Paris: UNESCO, 1977).

Ellis, John S., '"The methods of barbarism" and the "rights of small nations": war propaganda and British pluralism', *Albion* 30/i (spring 1998), pp.49–75.

Flanagan, Kieran, 'The chief secretary's office 1853–1914: a bureaucratic enigma', *Irish Historical Studies* xxiv (1984–5), pp.197–225.

Foley, Michael, 'Colonialism and Journalism in Ireland', *Journalism Studies* 5/iii (2004), pp.373–85.

Gallagher, Frank, 'Literature of the Conflict', in *Irish Book Lover* 18/iii (May–June 1930), pp.69–71.

Gallagher, John, 'Nationalisms and the crisis of empire, 1919–1922', *Modern Asian Studies* 15/iii (1981), pp.355–68.

Glandon, Virginia E., 'The Irish press and revolutionary Irish nationalism', in *Eire-Ireland* 16/i (spring, 1981), pp.21–33.

Griffith, Paddy, 'Small wars and how they grow in the telling', *Small Wars and Insurgencies* 2/ii (August 1991), pp.216–31.

Hachey, Thomas E., 'British Foreign Office and new perspectives on the Irish issue in Anglo-American relations 1919–1921', *Eire-Ireland* 7/ii (1972), pp.3–13.

Hampton, Mark, 'The press, patriotism and public discussion: C.P. Scott, the *Manchester Guardian*, and the Boer War, 1899–1902', *Historical Journal* 44/i (2001), pp.107–34.

Hopkin, Deian, 'Domestic censorship in the First World War', *Journal of Contemporary History* 5/iv (1970), pp.151–69.

Hopkinson, Michael, 'President Woodrow Wilson and the Irish Question', *Studia Hibernica* 27 (1993), pp.89–111.

Jacobsen, Mark, '"Only by the sword": British counterinsurgency in Iraq, 1920', *Small Wars and Insurgencies* 2/ii (August 1991), pp.323–63.

Janowitz, Morris, 'Professional models in journalism: the gatekeeper and the advocate', *Journalism Quarterly* 52/iv (winter, 1975), pp.618–26.

Lawrence, Jon, 'Forging a peaceable kingdom: war, violence, and fear of brutalization in post-First World War Britain', *Journal of Modern History* 75 (September 2003), pp.557–89.

Lyons, F.S.L., 'Parnellism and Crime, 1887–90', in *Transactions of the Royal Historical Society*, 5th series, vol. xxiv, London (1974), pp.123–40.

Marquis, Alice Goldfarb, 'Words as weapons: propaganda in Britain and Germany during the First World War', *Journal of Contemporary History* 13/iii (July 1978), pp.467–98.

Mayer, Arno. J., 'Post-war nationalisms 1918–1919', *Past & Present* 34 (July 1966), pp.114–126.

McEwen, John M., 'The national press during the First World War: ownership and circulation', *Journal of Contemporary History* 17/iii (1982), p.466.

—— 'The press and the fall of Asquith', *The Historical Journal* 21/iv (1978), pp.863–83.

Molotch, Harvey and Marilyn Lester, 'News as purposive behaviour: on the strategic use of routine events, accidents and scandals', *American Sociological Review* 39 (1970), pp.101–12.

Moran, Sean Farrell, 'Patrick Pearse and the European revolt against reason', *Journal of the History of Ideas* 50/iv (October–December 1989), pp.625–43.

O'Brien, Conor Cruise, 'Liberty and terror: illusions of violence, delusions of liberation', *Encounter* 49/iv (October 1977), pp.34–41.

Peatling, G.K., 'The whiteness of Ireland under and after the union', *Journal of British Studies* 44/i (January 2005), pp.115–33.

—— 'New liberalism, J.L. Hammond and the Irish problem, 1897–1949', *Historical Research* 73/cxc (February 2000), pp.48–65.

Sayer, Derek, 'British reaction to the Amritsar massacre 1919–1920', *Past and Present* 131 (May 1991).

Schudson, Michael, 'The objectivity norm in American journalism', *Journalism* 2/ii (August 2001), pp.149–70.

Schwarz, Bill, 'Politics and rhetoric in the age of mass culture', *History Workshop Journal* 46 (1998), pp.129–59.

Seedorf, Martin F., 'Defending reprisals: Sir Hamar Greenwood and the "Troubles", 1920–21', *Eire-Ireland* 20/iv (winter 1990), pp.77–92.

Selth, Andrew, 'Ireland and insurgency: the lessons of history', *Small Wars and Insurgencies* 2/ii (August 1991), pp.299–322.

Smith, Anthony, 'War and ethnicity: the role of warfare in the formation, self-images and cohesion of ethnic communities', *Ethnic and Racial Studies* 4/iv (1981), pp.375–97.

Steigerwald, David, 'The synthetic politics of Woodrow Wilson', *Journal of the History of Ideas* 1/iii (July–September 1989), pp.465–84.

Streckfuss, Richard, 'Objectivity in journalism: a search and a reassessment', *Journalism Quaterly* 67/iv (winter 1990), pp.973–83.

Stubbs, John O., 'The unionists and Ireland, 1914–1918', *Historical Journal* 33/iv (December 1990), pp.867–93.

Townshend, Charles, 'The suppression of the Easter Rising', *Bullan* 1/i (spring 1994), pp.27–47.

Walker, Graham, '"The Irish Dr Goebbels": Frank Gallagher and Irish republican propaganda', *Journal of Contemporary History* 27/i (January 1992), pp.149–65.

Ward, Alan J., 'Lloyd George and the 1918 Irish conscription crisis', *The Historical Journal* 17/i (1974), pp.107–29.

Wilkinson, Glen R., 'At the coalface of history: personal reflections on using newspapers as a source', *Studies in Newspaper and Periodical History 1995 Annual,* London (1997), pp.211–221.

Zelizer, Barbie. 'Journalists as interpretive communities', *Critical Studies in Mass Communications* 10/ii (September 1993), pp.219–37.

## UNPUBLISHED THESES

Hamilton-Tweedale, Brian, 'The British press and Northern Ireland: a case study in reporting of violent political conflict' (unpublished PhD thesis, University of Sheffield, 1988).

Hayward, D.W., 'The British press and Anglo-American relations with particular reference to the Irish Question 1916–1922' (unpublished MA thesis, University of Manchester, 1960).

Kaul, Chandrika, 'Press and empire: the London press, government news management and India circa 1900–22' (unpublished PhD thesis, University of Oxford, 1999).

Leeson, David, 'The Black and Tans: British police in the first Irish War, 1920–1' (unpublished PhD thesis, McMaster University, Ontario, 2003).

Mander, Mary Sue, 'Pen and sword: a cultural history of the American war correspondent: 1895–1945' (unpublished PhD thesis, University of Illinois at Urbana-Champaign, 1979).

## NEWSPAPERS AND MAGAZINES

*Atlantic Monthly*

*Blackwood's Magazine*

*Christian Science Monitor*

*Daily Mail*

*Daily News*

*Guardian Review*

*Irish Times*

*Manchester Guardian*

*Morning Post, The*

*Nation, The*

*New Republic, The*

*New Statesman*

*New York Times*

*Philadelphia Public Ledger*

*The Times*

*World's Press News*

## INTERVIEWS

Dr Garret FitzGerald, Dublin, 20 January 2003.

# INDEX